THE UNITED STATES AND MEXICO

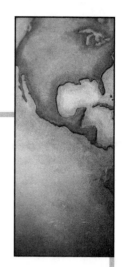

THE UNITED STATES AND MEXICO

BETWEEN PARTNERSHIP AND CONFLICT

JORGE I. DOMÍNGUEZ
AND
RAFAEL FERNÁNDEZ DE CASTRO

ROUTLEDGE
New York   London

Published in 2001 by
Routledge
29 West 35th Street
New York, NY 10001

Published in Great Britain by
Routledge
11 New Fetter Lane
London EC4P 4EE

Routledge is an imprint of the Taylor & Francis Group.

Printed in the United States of America on acid-free paper.

10   9   8   7   6   5   4   3   2   1

Library of Congress Cataloging-in-Publication Data

Domínguez, Jorge I., 1945–
    The United States and Mexico : between partnership and conflict / by Jorge I. Domínguez and Rafael Fernández de Castro.
        p. cm. — (Contemporary inter-american relations)
    Includes bibliographical references and index.
    ISBN 0-415-93060-X — ISBN 0-415-93061-8 (pbk)
    1. Unites States—Foreign relations–Mexico. 2. Mexico—Foreign relations—United States. I. Fernández de Castro, Rafael. II. Title. III. Series.

E183.8M6 D65 2001
327.73072—dc21   00-045785

TO MARY AND PATRICIA,

OUR PARTNERS IN BELLAGIO,

AND IN LIFE

CONTENTS

TABLES AND FIGURES

PREFACE

The transition from authoritarian rule to constitutional government.

The continent-wide economic depression of the 1980s and the subsequent shift toward more open market-conforming economies.

The end of the Cold War in Europe.

The transformation of relations with the United States.

Each of these major events and processes was an epochal change in the history of Latin America and the Caribbean. More striking is that all four changes took place within the same relatively short time, though all four did not affect each and every country in the same way. They became interconnected, with change on each dimension fostering convergent changes on other dimensions. Thus, at the beginning of the new millennium, we witnessed an important transformation and intensification in U.S.–Latin American relations.

This book is part of a series of ten books on U.S. relations with Latin American and Caribbean countries. Each of these books is focused on the fourth of these four transformations—namely, the change in U.S. relations with Latin America and the Caribbean. Our premise is that the first three transformations provide pieces of the explanation for the change in U.S. relations with its neighbors in the Americas and for the changes in the foreign policies of Latin American and Caribbean states. Each of the books in the series assesses the impact of the epoch-making changes upon each other.

The process of widest impact was the economic transformation. By the end of 1982, much of North America, Western Europe, and East Asia launched into an economic boom at the very instant when Latin America plunged into an economic depression of great severity that lasted approximately to the end of the decade. As a consequence of such economic collapse, nearly all Latin American governments readjusted their economic strategies. They departed from principal reliance on import-substitution industrialization, opened their economies to international trade and investment, and adopted policies to create more open market-conforming economies. (Even Cuba had changed its economic strategy by the 1990s, making its economy more open to foreign direct investment and trade.)

The region-wide economic changes had direct and immediate impact upon U.S.–Latin American relations. The share of U.S. trade accounted for by Latin America and the Caribbean had declined fairly steadily from the end of World War II to the end of the 1980s. In the 1990s, in contrast, U.S. trade with Latin America grew at a rate significantly faster than the growth of U.S. trade worldwide; Latin America had become the fastest-growing market for U.S. exports. The United States, at long last, did take notice of Latin America. Trade between some Latin American countries also boomed, especially within sub-regions such as the southern cone of South America, Venezuela and Colombia, the Central American countries, and, to a lesser extent, the Anglophone Caribbean countries. The establishment of formal freer-trade areas facilitated the growth of trade and other economic relations. These included the North American Free Trade Agreement (NAFTA), which grouped Mexico, the United States, and Canada; the MERCOSUR (southern common market), with Argentina, Brazil, Paraguay, and Uruguay; the Andean Community, whose members were Bolivia, Colombia, Ecuador, Peru, and Venezuela; the Central American Common Market (CACM); and the Caribbean Community (CARICOM). U.S. foreign direct and portfolio investment in large quantities flowed into Latin America and the Caribbean, financing the expansion of tradable economic activities; the speed of portfolio investment transactions, however, also exposed these and other countries to marked financial volatility and recurrent financial panics. The transformation in hemispheric international economic relations—and specifically in U.S. economic relations with the rest of the hemisphere—was already far-reaching as the twenty-first century began.

These structural economic changes had specific and common impacts on the conduct of international economic diplomacy. All governments in the Americas, large and small, had to develop a cadre of experts who could negotiate concrete, technical trade, investment, and other economic issues with the United States and with other countries in the region. All had to create teams of international trade lawyers and experts capable of defending national interests, and the interests of particular business firms, in international, inter-American, or sub-regional dispute-resolution panels or "court-like" proceedings. The discourse and practice of inter-American relations, broadly understood, became much more professional—less the province of eloquent poets, more the domain of number-crunching litigators and mediators.

The changes in Latin America's domestic political regimes began in the late 1970s. These, too, would contribute to change the texture of inter-American relations. By the end of 1990, democratization based on fair elections, competitive parties, constitutionalism, and respect for the rule of law and the liberties of citizens had advanced and was still advancing throughout the region, albeit unevenly and with persisting serious problems, Cuba being the principal exception.

Democratization also affected the international relations of Latin American and Caribbean countries, albeit in more subtle ways. The Anglophone Caribbean is a largely archipelagic region, long marked by the widespread practice of constitutional government. Since the 1970s, Anglophone Caribbean democratic governments rallied repeatedly to defend constitutional government on any of the islands where it came under threat and, in the specific cases of Grenada and Guyana, to assist the process of democratization in the 1980s and 1990s, respectively. In the 1990s, Latin American governments also began to act collectively to defend and promote democratic rule; with varying degrees of success and U.S. support, they did so in Guatemala, Haiti, Paraguay, and Peru. Democratization had a more complex relationship to the content of specific foreign policies. In the 1990s, democratization in Argentina, Brazil, Uruguay, and Chile contributed to improved international political, security, and economic relations among these southern cone countries. Yet, at times, democratic politics made it more difficult to manage international relations over boundary or territorial issues between given pairs of countries, including Chile and Peru, Colombia and Venezuela, and Costa Rica and Nicaragua. In general, democratization facilitated better relations between Latin American and Caribbean countries, on the one hand, and the United States, on the other. Across the Americas, democratic governments, including the United States and Canada, acted to defend and promote constitutional government. Much cooperation over security, including the attempt to foster cooperative security and civilian supremacy over the military, would have been unthinkable except in the new, deeper democratic context in the hemisphere.

At its best, in the 1990s, democratic politics made it possible to transform the foreign policies of particular presidential administrations into the foreign policies of states. For example, Argentina's principal political parties endorsed the broad outlines of their nation's foreign policy, including the framework to govern much friendlier Argentinian relations with the United States. All Chilean political parties were strongly committed to their country's transformation into an international trading state. The principal political parties of the Anglophone Caribbean sustained consistent long-lasting foreign policies across different partisan administrations. Mexico's three leading political parties agreed, even if they differed on specifics, that NAFTA should be implemented, binding Mexico to the United States and Canada. And the Bush and Clinton administrations in the United States followed remarkably compatible policies toward Latin America and the Caribbean with regard to the promotion of free trade, pacification in Central America, support for international financial institutions, and the defense of constitutional government in Latin America and the Caribbean. Both administrations acted in concert with other states in the region and often through the Organization of American States. Democratic procedures, in these and other cases, served to establish the credibility of a state's foreign policy, because all actors would have reason to expect that the framework of today's foreign policy would endure tomorrow.

The end of the Cold War in Europe began following the accession in 1985 of Mikhail Gorbachev to the post of general-secretary of the communist party of the Soviet Union. The end accelerated during the second half of the 1980s, culminating with the collapse of communist regimes in Europe between 1989 and 1991 and the breakup of the Soviet Union itself in late 1991. The impact of the end of the

U.S.–Soviet conflict on the hemisphere was subtle but important: the United States was no longer obsessed with the threat of communism. Freed to focus on other international interests, the United States discovered that it shared many practical interests with Latin American and Caribbean countries; the latter, in turn, found it easier to cooperate with the United States. There was one exception to this "benign" international process. The United States was also freed to forget its long-lasting fear of communist guerrillas in Colombia (who remained powerful and continued to operate nonetheless) in order to concentrate on a "war" against drug trafficking, even if it undermined Colombia's constitutional regime.

This process of the end of the Cold War also had a specific component in the Western Hemisphere, namely, the termination of the civil and international wars that had swirled in Central America since the late 1970s. The causes of those wars had been internal and international. In the early 1990s, the collapse of the Soviet Union and the marked weakening of Cuban influence enabled the U.S. government to support negotiations with governments or insurgent movements it had long opposed. All of these international changes made it easier to arrange for domestic political, military, and social settlements of the wars in and around Nicaragua, El Salvador, and Guatemala. The end of the Cold War in Europe had an extraordinary impact on Cuba as well. The Cold War did not end the sharp conflict between the U.S. and Cuban governments, but the latter was deprived of Soviet support, forcing it thereby to recall its troops overseas, open its economy to the world, and lower its foreign policy profile. The United States felt freer to conduct a "Colder War" against Cuba, seeking to overthrow its government.

Two other large-scale processes, connected to the previous three, had a significant impact in the international relations of the Western Hemisphere. They were the booms in international migration and cocaine-related international organized crime. To be sure, emigration and organized crime on an international scale in the Americas are as old as the European settlement begun in the late fifteenth century and the growth of state-sponsored piracy in the sixteenth century. Yet the volume and acceleration of these two processes in the 1980s and 1990s were truly extraordinary.

One effect of widespread violence in Central America and Colombia, and of economic depression everywhere, was to accelerate the rate of emigration to the United States. Once begun, the process of migration to the United States was sustained through networks of relatives and friends, the family-unification provisions of U.S. legislation, and the relatively lower costs of international transportation and communication. By the mid-1990s, over 12 million people born in Latin America resided in the United States; two-thirds of them had arrived since 1980. The number of people of Latin American ancestry in the United States was even larger, of course. In the 1980s, migrants came to the United States not just from countries, such as Mexico, of traditional emigration, but also from countries, such as Brazil, that in the past had generated few emigrants. As the twentieth century ended, more persons born in Latin America lived in the United States than lived in the majority of the Latin American states. The United States had also come to play a major role in the production and consumption of the culture, including music, book publishing, and television programming, of the Spanish-speaking peoples. All of these trends are likely to intensify in the twenty-first century.

Had this series of books been published in the mid-1970s, coca and cocaine would have merited brief mention in one or two of the books, and no mention in most of them. The boom in U.S. cocaine consumption in the late 1970s and 1980s changed this. The region-wide economic collapse of the 1980s made it easier to bribe public officials, judges, police, and military officers. U.S. cocaine supply interdiction policies in the 1980s raised the price of cocaine, making the coca and cocaine businesses the most lucrative in depression-ravaged economies. The generally unregulated sale of weapons in the United States equipped gangsters throughout the Americas. Bolivia and Peru produced the coca. Colombians grew it, refined it, and financed it. Criminal gangs in the Caribbean, Central America, and Mexico transported and distributed it. Everywhere, drug traffic-related violence and corruption escalated.

The impact of economic policy change, democratization, and the end of the Cold War in Europe on U.S.–Latin American relations, therefore, provides important explanations common to the countries of the Americas in their relations with the United States. The acceleration of emigration, and the construction and development of international organized crime around the cocaine business, were also key common themes in the continent's international relations during the closing fifth of the twentieth century. To the extent pertinent, these topics appear in each of the books in this series. Nonetheless, each country's own history, geographic location, set of neighbors, resource endowment, institutional features, and leadership characteristics bear as well on the construction, design, and implementation of its foreign policy. These more particular factors enrich and guide the books in this series in their interplay with the more general arguments.

As the 1990s ended, dark clouds reappeared on the firmament of inter-American relations, raising doubts about the "optimistic" trajectory that seemed set at the beginning of that decade. The role of the military in the running of state agencies and activities that normally belong to civilians rose significantly in Colombia, Venezuela, and Peru, and in January 2000, a military coup overthrew the constitutionally elected president of Ecuador; serious concerns resurfaced concerning the depth and durability of democratic institutions and practices in these countries. Venezuela seemed ready to try once again much heavier government involvement in economic affairs. And the United States had held back from implementing the commitment to hemispheric free trade that both Presidents George H. Bush and Bill Clinton had pledged. Only the last of these trends had instant international repercussions, but all of them could affect adversely the future of a Western Hemisphere based on free politics, free markets, and peace.

THIS PROJECT

Each of the books in the series has two authors, typically one from a Latin American or Caribbean country and another from the United States (and, in one case, the United Kingdom). We chose this approach to facilitate the writing of the books and ensure that the books would represent the international perspectives from both parts of the U.S.–Latin American relationship. In addition, we sought to embed each book within international networks of scholarly work in more than one country.

We have attempted to write short books that ask common questions to enable various readers—scholars, students, public officials, international entrepreneurs, and the educated public—to make their own comparisons and judgments as they read two or more volumes in the series. The project sought to foster comparability across the books through two conferences held at the Instituto Tecnológico Autónomo de México (ITAM) in Mexico City. The first, held in June 1998, compared ideas and questions; the second, held in August 1999, discussed preliminary drafts of the books. Both of us read and commented on all the manuscripts; the manuscripts also received commentary from other authors in the project. We also hope that the network of scholars created for this project will continue to function, even if informally, and that the Web page created for this project will provide access for a wider audience to the ideas, research, and writing associated with it.

We are grateful to the Ford Foundation for its principal support of this project, and to Cristina Eguizábal for her advice and assistance throughout this endeavor. We are also grateful to the MacArthur Foundation for the support that made it possible to hold a second successful project conference in Mexico City. The Rockefeller Foundation provided the two of us with an opportunity to spend four splendid weeks in Bellagio, Italy, working on our various general responsibilities in this project. The Academic Department of International Studies at ITAM hosted the project throughout its duration and the two international conferences. We appreciate the support of the Asociación Mexicana de Cultura, ITAM's principal supporter in this work. Harvard University's Weatherhead Center for International Affairs also supported aspects of this project, as did Harvard University's David Rockefeller Center for Latin American Studies. We are particularly grateful to Hazel Blackmore and Juana Gómez at ITAM, and Amanda Pearson and Kathleen Hoover at the Weatherhead Center, for their work on many aspects of the project. At Routledge, Melissa Rosati encouraged us from the start; Eric Nelson supported the project through its conclusion.

    Jorge I. Domínguez   *Rafael Fernández de Castro*
    HARVARD UNIVERSITY   ITAM

INTRODUCTION

FOR BETTER OR FOR WORSE, MEXICO AND THE UNITED STATES ARE wedded to each other. They share one of the planet's longest land boundaries. This border separates the world's most developed economy from one still marked by inefficiencies, underdevelopment, and millions of very poor people. The two governments went to war in the mid-nineteenth century; the United States seized the northern half of Mexico. The United States intervened militarily in Mexico at various times in the nineteenth and twentieth centuries, most recently in the midst of the Mexican revolution during the second decade of the twentieth century. These legacies are not forgotten. The Mexican revolution, in turn, mobilized the Mexican nation. The post-revolutionary governments heightened the Mexican sense of patriotism and affirmed sovereignty in various ways, including the expropriation of the property of U.S. citizens and firms.

As the twentieth century closed, however, Mexico—not Japan, not Germany— had become the second most important trade partner of the United States. The United States was Mexico's principal economic partner on many dimensions. In the 1990s, the rate of growth of U.S. exports to Mexico well exceeded the rate of growth of U.S. exports to the rest of the world. Mexico's financial markets had become linked with those of the United States; investment in Mexico had become a routine instrument in the decisional repertoire of U.S.-based multinational enterprises. U.S. firms owned some of the most important and fastest-growing firms in the Mexican economy; some voices in Mexico expressed worry about excessive dependence on a country with which both the past and the present were so problematic. There were also serious concerns in Mexico that poverty and many forms of inequality persisted, which some blamed on the acceleration of economic integration with the United States. Yet, as the new millennium began, the new U.S.–Mexican economic partnership had put an end to the long-standing Mexican tradition of keeping relations at arm's-length from the dangerous northern neighbor. U.S.–Mexican economic relations had become an important and dynamic engine of growth throughout North America.

Mexicans were doing the most, too, to modify the demographic composition of the United States. In the late 1990s, some seven million people born in Mexico lived in the United States; at that time, the population of Mexican origin in the United States exceeded 18 million, seven percent of the total U.S. population. Mexicans and Mexican-origin people in the United States had a particularly important impact on life and work in California, Texas, and Illinois, but they were also significant throughout much of the country.

U.S. citizens of Mexican origin had come to play significant roles in the United States. Many were elected to public office or served with distinction in the armed forces of the United States. Others were eminent U.S. performers, artists, musicians, scholars, professionals, diplomats, business entrepreneurs, or labor union leaders. Many others were hardworking factory, agricultural, and service workers who contributed much to the betterment of life in the United States through the sweat of their brow. They held strong feelings of loyalty and patriotism as citizens of the United States. They were proud of their membership in a nation constructed from immigrants like themselves, drawn from every corner of the world by the promises and beliefs engraved on the Statue of Liberty and spelled out in the American Declaration of Independence.

In the 1990s, however, no fewer than two hundred thousand Mexicans per year entered the United States without proper documents. During this decade, Mexicans accounted for more than half of the undocumented migrants entering the United States every year. In addition, organized gangs trafficked in drugs, weapons, and other forms of contraband.

The United States responded with growing alarm and determination to the transborder spread of illegal migrants, drug trafficking, and other forms of crime. In the 1990s, the U.S. government built electronic and other fences to impede easy access to the United States across the southwestern border, to detect those seeking to breach the border without authorization, and to arrest, imprison, and deport those who broke the law. The United States deployed thousands of security officials from various agencies and jurisdictions to staff the barricades at the nation's southwestern gates.

LEARNING TO COOPERATE

There is no one single explanation for the manifold changes in U.S.–Mexican relations. We argue, however, that the shift from a broad and persistent pattern of either conflict or neglect that prevailed for most of the independent existence of both states to a new partnership in their bilateral relations can be best understood as a process of learning, accelerated by cumulative crises. The crises in the 1980s over trade, drug trafficking, migration, or policies toward Central America forced both national governments to seek to find alternative ways to deal with each other. Profound changes in the international system and within Mexico provided constraints as well as opportunities. The first trade agreements created conditions of greater trust, and shared commitment, that permitted the design and implementation of subsequent agreements. The two governments moved from agreements that made them vulnerable to sanctions, if either were to violate the agreed-upon terms, to commitments that sought to improve joint gains from collaboration. The scope of agreements widened beyond trade matters to encompass other issue areas. Many areas of conflict remain in the bilateral relationship, but this mixture in the 1990s of partnership and conflict was a departure from a shared past.

After a century of deep hostility and conflict, in the 1940s, during World War II, the governments of the United States and Mexico became allies to fight against Germany, Italy, and Japan. They built effective means of wartime collaboration. After World War II, however, U.S.–Mexican relations, though proper and, in some respects, cordial, were remarkably uninstitutionalized. This resulted from the Mexican government's decision not to join key international institutions, such as the General Agreement on Tariffs and Trade (GATT), or to negotiate comprehensive bilateral trade treaties with the United States. From the 1940s to the 1980s, neither the United States nor Mexico invested much effort in dealing with each other in an institutionalized fashion.

In the years after World War II, the Mexican government's economic policies sought economic autarchy and no more than a limited engagement in the world economy or with the economy of its northern neighbor. Mexico collaborated as little as possible with U.S. foreign policy, although it also typically sought to avoid open political confrontations with the United States. Unlike other Latin American countries, during the Cold War, Mexico did not construct a panoply of military relations with the U.S. armed forces. Mexico did not support most U.S. military policies in the multilateral institutions of the Western Hemisphere from the 1950s through the 1980s, nor did it construct bilateral institutions for security collaboration with the United States to combat crime, guerrillas, or communist threats. Mexico rejected bilateral assistance from the United States under the Alliance for Progress. Mexico's collaboration with the United States during World War II included the first of a series of bilateral migration agreements; the last of these expired in 1964, never to be renewed.

In the 1980s, the Mexican economy collapsed. Hardships heightened; poverty spread. The Mexican political system was shaken to its foundations for the first time since the 1930s. The central government and the official political party, the Institutional Revolutionary Party (PRI), began to lose their grip on the society, the economy, and the polity. Organized crime, particularly drug trafficking, gained a foothold during the 1980s. Emigration to the United States accelerated. The Mexican government needed the assistance of the U.S. government to cope with these myriad plagues. The United States helped to rescue the Mexican economy from the financial crash in 1982 to 1983. The United States also confronted, however, what it deemed unacceptable Mexican policies in the areas of trade, finance, investment, transnational organized crime (especially drug trafficking), and migration, as well as Mexican policies toward the wars in Central America and the

Cuban government's international role. For much of the 1980s, U.S. and Mexican officials in charge of bilateral relations rose every morning to face their inter-governmental conflicts at breakfast.

Slowly and painfully, in the second half of the 1980s, the two governments began to reach agreements and construct new institutions to address their multiple disputes in economic arenas. One accelerating factor was the end of the Cold War in Europe. It removed some obstacles to U.S.–Mexican collaboration, among others their differences over policies toward Central America and their assessments of the Soviet Union. The collapse of the communist governments of Europe between 1989 and 1991 also focused Western European countries on the multiple transformations under way in Eastern Europe, distracting Europe, therefore, from events elsewhere in the world. Moreover, Japan's economy stalled in the 1990s, entering a prolonged slowdown. From Mexico's perspective, consequently, the international system had changed dramatically. Mexico was constrained into cooperating with the United States by the disappearance of economic and political alternatives elsewhere in the world. Mexico also uncovered new opportunities for economic collaboration with the United States and, at long last, made use of them.

Trade issues led the way in the construction of institutionalized relations between the United States and Mexico, culminating in the first half of the 1990s with the enactment of the North American Free Trade Agreement (NAFTA), which includes Canada, Mexico, and the United States. NAFTA created rules and procedures for free trade across North America on a schedule to be completed mostly in 2010, facilitated capital flows and especially direct investment, and created dispute settlement forums and institutions to address the normal conflicts expected to arise from such intense high-volume economic relations. In NAFTA's first five years, bilateral trade boomed; U.S. direct investment in Mexico accelerated. The dispute-settlement procedures were used effectively to resolve disputes without rancor. This institutionalization of trade relations was a trilateral response to resolve practical problems.

Flush from this success, the U.S. and Mexican governments designed and launched new institutions in other areas that were also bedeviled by thorny problems. By the end of the twentieth century, the disposition to cooperate, and the institutionalized means for doing so, had spread, to varying degrees, to other arenas. Among them were environmental degradation at the border, military training, counter-narcotics traffic operations, central bank cooperation, the exchange of information about domestic labor law enforcement, joint efforts to bring to an end wars in El Salvador and Nicaragua, relations between local governments at the border, and so forth.

There was also a good deal of quiet cooperation over the delicate process of democratization in Mexico and the attempts to improve respect for human rights and the rule of law in Mexico. The Mexican government acknowledged that, under international law, international human rights entities had the right to comment on Mexico's observance of its own and international law with regard to human rights and democracy. By the late 1990s, the Mexican government also permitted international election observers. The U.S. government, for its part, encouraged Mexico's political opening while eschewing coercive tactics.

These efforts culminated in the national elections held on July 2, 2000. The leading opposition candidate, Vicente Fox, was elected president of Mexico, heading a coalition led by the National Action Party (PAN). No party won an outright majority of either chamber in the federal congress; the long-ruling PRI won the largest number of seats in both chambers. The left-wing Party of the Democratic Revolution (PRD) elected the head of the government of Mexico City while the PRI still retained approximately two-thirds of the governorships. The days of virtual single-party rule were over indeed.

As the stakes of the bilateral relationship rose, the number of actors multiplied. The U.S. and Mexican central governments remained decisive actors, but their modes of operation became much more decentralized. Specialized bureaucratic agencies established their own bilateral channels for contact. State governors, border patrol chiefs, and drug enforcement officials at times pursued their own rogue foreign policies. Non-governmental actors also assumed greater salience. Business entrepreneurs, mass media organizations, and human rights and democracy activists, among others, became protagonists in aspects of U.S.–Mexican relations.

New means to cope with this increasingly complex relationship arose as well. In the 1990s, the presidents of the two countries took a more hands-on approach to foster bilateral cooperation and manage the increasing communicative diversity. The public in both countries, to the occasional surprise of politicians and academics, held a good opinion of the other country and provided political support for cooperative strategies. Mexican political parties, albeit much more evenly competitive than in decades past, agreed on the broad outlines of framework of cooperative relations with the United States. Finally, the diplomatic practices and approaches of both countries converged, becoming both more professional and comparably active in representing the interests of the respective governments in the capital cities of the other.

The importance of the new and growing U.S.–Mexican economic partnership was deeply felt, above all, in the two capital cities. The voices of U.S. critics of Mexico were attenuated as a consequence, and the Mexican left was induced to recognize the significance to Mexico of economic integration with the United States. On the other hand, unlike the relationship between the United States and Canada, U.S.–Mexican relations cannot yet manage effectively certain controversial issues such as drug trafficking and migration; every time a bilateral dispute resurfaces on these topics, the entire post-NAFTA partnership seems to be placed at risk.

Mexico's new and deeper relations with the United States and Canada raised new questions about Mexico's relations with Latin American countries. Mexican trade and investment relations with other Latin American countries had never been as important for Mexico as relations over these issues with the United States. But there had never been any doubt that Mexico's political and cultural identity was firmly anchored in Latin America. The expression "North American" had always referred to the United States and Canada, not to Mexico. As the 1990s closed, most Mexicans felt decisively Latin American, but they had just barely begun to grapple with the more profound meanings of the new relationship to the northern neighbors. Mexico was both Latin American and North American. One task for Mexico in the twenty-first century is to sort out these multiple layers of identity.

As the new millennium began, one theme remained crystal clear: the United States and Mexico were becoming relentlessly more important for each other. The states of North America were at peace with each other; war between them had long ago become unthinkable. One consequence of this achievement was that intersocietal cross-penetration was taking place by consent. It had become the norm in economic, demographic, criminal, environmental, musical, gastronomic, literary, and other issue areas. There was only one North America. It was up to its peoples, and the states that claimed to act in their name, whether their new closeness would generate discomfort and dysfunction or, instead, harness the cooperative energies of the world's most dynamic subcontinent.

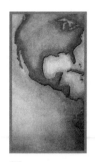

HISTORY I

MEXICO AND THE UNITED STATES EXHIBIT A SURPRISING AND unprecedented level of inter-governmental and even inter-societal cooperation as they enter the twenty-first century. In the 1970s and the early 1980s, few would have forecast that these two countries would have signed and ratified a document as comprehensive as the North American Free Trade Agreement (NAFTA), or that official Mexico would have chosen to portray itself as "North American." In this book, we seek to explain and describe the transformation of U.S.–Mexican relations that began in the late 1980s and continued through the end of the twentieth century. We argue that this was a multifaceted process whose origins encompass the consequences of the end of the Cold War in Europe as well as the individual decisions made by U.S. and Mexican presidents, business executives, and ordinary citizens. We will explore these explanations with greater precision in the chapters that follow.

In this chapter, we sketch three broad pictures characterizing the prospects for U.S.–Mexican bilateral relations. Decision-makers in both countries, especially Mexico, could have considered these images as they approached the momentous decisions taken in the late 1980s and early 1990s that led to the dramatic shift from confrontation to collaboration in many though not all areas in their bilateral relations. Each image is drawn from the history of U.S.–Mexican bilateral relations. In our discussion of each, we comment on the past to enable the reader to understand the magnitude of the eventual change in this relationship in the 1980s and 1990s. We also identify the style of the relationship that might have been remembered by decision-makers just prior to the historic changes launched in the second half of the 1980s.

George H. Bush (1989–93) and Carlos Salinas de Gortari (1988–94) were elected presidents of the United States and Mexico, respectively, in 1988. At the time, there were three possible scenarios for the future of U.S.–Mexican relations: conflict, bargained negligence, or cooperation. These options represented the types of relationships that had existed between the two countries since Mexican independence, and they were the images to which they, their officials, and their peoples referred in order to understand how the two countries had related to each other.

Conflict: Most of the Nineteenth Century and the Mexican Revolution

Conflict dominated the U.S.–Mexcian relationship for most of the nineteenth century and during the Mexican Revolution that began in 1910. When conflict permeated relations, Washington behaved as the dominant power and generally imposed its will. Conflict was the predominant pattern in U.S.–Mexican relations until about 1940. This image of bilateral conflict long held sway, consequently, as the most likely style for their relations. During the nineteenth century, moreover, the United States often pursued its ends through military means.

From Mexican independence from Spain in 1821 to the end of the French military intervention in Mexico in 1867, U.S.–Mexican relations were turbulent and unstable. Mexico's domestic instability was the primary cause of this shaky relationship. Regional interests and factions prevailed over the Mexican national government, creating an atmosphere of political and social unrest until 1880. The continued struggles between the centralists and federalists, who eventually evolved into conservatives and liberals, prevented all but two presidents from serving a full term, severely hindering the construction of a central state.

Two other elements further complicated bilateral affairs: U.S. expansionism and the European quest for political and economic influence in the former Spanish colony. U.S. expansionism was a complex phenomenon. It involved territorial and national security considerations, sociocultural forces and traditions, and regional interests of the time. The United States participated in Mexico's political struggles directly and indirectly. Mexican liberal politicians, both radical and moderate, admired U.S. institutions as examples of a modernity that fostered economic growth. The United States was their natural ally, and they proposed the adoption of a similar governmental system for Mexico. Mexican conservatives wanted to preserve the political institutions inherited from Spain. They actively sought closer ties with the European powers and even supported and encouraged their direct involvement in Mexico. This finally was accomplished in 1864 with the establishment of Maximilian of Habsburg as emperor of Mexico with the support of the French army.[1] (The French withdrew from Mexico in 1867, however, and Maximilian himself was overthrown and shot.)

No other Latin American country suffered more from nineteenth-century U.S. expansionist appetites than Mexico. The violent rebellion and subsequent secession of Texas from Mexico in 1836, and its eventual annexation by the United States in 1845, can be explained by the convergence of Washington's expansionism and Mexico's inability to establish coherent colonization and control policies. As noted by the historians Josefina Vázquez and Lorenzo Meyer, "with the arrival of a declared expansionist to the United States presidency, James K. Polk [in 1845], it was easy to predict what would follow."[2] In 1846, stating that it was "defending the national territory," the United States declared war on Mexico and immediately invaded Mexican soil. Within a few months, the U.S. army reached and conquered Mexico City. Two years later, in 1848, the Treaty of Guadalupe-Hidalgo formally ended the war. The United States compelled Mexico to yield a vast amount of territory, that is, present-day California, Arizona, New Mexico, and parts of Colorado and Nevada. The heavy human, territorial, and economic toll of the war alarmed the nation, then on the brink of disintegration. Mexico's attitude henceforth would be marked with distrust toward its northern neighbor. The United States became a catalyst for Mexican nationalism.

Virulent U.S.–Mexican conflict reappeared during the years of the Mexican revolution. The revolution was a complex civil war. It began as a quest for a new president and clean elections, but suddenly it became a social vindication for those groups ignored by President Porfirio Díaz's modernization project. Porfirio Díaz was Mexico's longest-ruling dictator who governed from 1876 to 1880 and again from 1884 to 1911. One Mexican scholar has characterized the Mexican revolution, which lasted for most of the 1910s, as an intervened civil war.[3] The U.S. government intervened in Mexico repeatedly during these years. For example, President Woodrow Wilson (1913–21) ordered U.S. troops to invade Mexico's principal port of Veracruz in 1914 to prevent a large arms convoy from reaching the army of General Victoriano Huerta, who had come to power after the assassination of constitutional president Francisco I. Madero in 1912. Eventually, this U.S. invasion allowed the troops of Venustiano Carranza, the head of the constitutionalist faction, to seize Veracruz. Carranza benefited from U.S. help and eventually became the most powerful leader during the revolutionary wars. In 1916, he was elected president and convoked the constitutional assembly that adopted a new national constitution in 1917; this constitution remains in effect. The Mexican Constitution of 1917 was designed to assert greater national sovereignty in the creation of economic and social programs and curtail the clout that had hitherto been exercised by foreign interests. But because U.S. economic interests had made important gains during the long Díaz regime, the United States soon reacted adversely to these nationalistic policies.

During the 1930s, the United States struggled to overcome the Great Depression, which began in 1929. In due course, the United States would consolidate its industrial base, emerging after World War II as the world's premier economic and military power. Mexico consolidated the political institutions of the presidency and the official party that would provide political stability for the rest of the century. At the same time, U.S.–Mexican relations remained turbulent. The treatment in Mexico of U.S. citizens and their property during the Mexican revolution had become a particularly thorny issue. The U.S. government also pressured Mexico on other matters, such as its foreign debt and the migration of Mexicans to the United States. On the other hand, the U.S. government chose not to retaliate against President Lázaro Cárdenas's (1934–40) decision in 1938 to expropriate the foreign-owned oil companies, because it did not want to risk the possibility that Mexico might align with Japan, Germany, and Italy during World

War II. (Cardenas's nationalistic economic policy had taken advantage of the rigidity shown by the foreign oil companies during a labor strike in 1938. After foreign oil companies rejected the decision of Mexico's Supreme Court that they must increase wages, President Cárdenas expropriated all 16 foreign oil companies.) In 1940, few U.S. or Mexican citizens had reason to expect that anything other than conflict would mark their bilateral relations, despite the occasional elements of collaboration that, as we will soon see, had appeared in their relations from time to time.

BARGAINED NEGLIGENCE, 1940–88

A new style became dominant in U.S.–Mexican bilateral relations during the second half of the 1940s; it would endure as the predominant characteristic until the late 1980s. It had two features. Bilateral bargaining (rather than sheer U.S. imposition or Mexican defiance) became the operating procedure for bilateral relations, on the one hand; on the other hand, each of the two governments, deliberately or inadvertently, invested little effort in improving the quality of bilateral relations or deepening the opportunities for institutionalized collaboration. We call this style "bargained negligence."

At the beginning of the Cold War in the late 1940s, Mexico and the United States formed a tacit bargain: so long as Mexico refrained from supporting the Soviet Union or adopting communist practices in its political system, the United States would refrain from directly intervening in Mexican affairs. With the assurance of stable neighbors on its southern (Mexico) and northern (Canada) frontiers, the United States turned its attention to the Cold War struggle in Europe and Asia. No political order in Mexico was able to survive without U.S. self-restraint.[4] While Mexico benefited from the non-interventionist policy of the United States, it can be argued that the United States took this bargain to the extreme. Instead of simply respecting the sovereignty of Mexico, the U.S. government almost completely ignored Mexico.

Negligence thus became the most recurrent theme in everyday U.S. policy and diplomacy toward Mexico during the Cold War era. The polarization of world affairs into eastern and western blocs led by the Soviet Union and the United States, respectively, clearly defined the years from the late 1940s to the late 1980s and determined U.S. foreign policy priorities: containment of the Soviet threat and the support of capitalism over communism. Mexico was not a U.S. foreign policy priority; neglect prevailed in U.S. policy toward its southern neighbor. Mexico became a priority in Washington only at critical moments, such as in 1968, during a large-scale demonstration by university students in Mexico City against the national government's authoritarian practices; the worldwide oil shock of 1979, when the price of oil skyrocketed coincidentally right after the Mexican discovery of huge petroleum reserves; the debt crisis of 1982, when Mexico de facto defaulted on its external debts of nearly $80 billion (at current prices of the time), placing many U.S. banks at risk; and the murder in 1985 in Mexico of Enrique Camarena, an agent of the U.S. Drug Enforcement Administration (DEA), with the alleged complicity of Mexican officials.[5]

The phrase attributed to the dictator Díaz, "poor Mexico so far from God and so close to the United States," foreshadowed the Mexican attitude toward Washington for much of the twentieth century. Mexico's response to U.S. negligence began in the 1940s with its own form of negligence. During the Cold War, an isolationist and nationalistic attitude prevailed in Mexican official circles. During these years, Mexico developed rapidly using the import substitution industrialization model, an inward-oriented industrial development strategy based primarily on barriers against imports. This economic model enabled Mexico to alter the composition of its international trade to a considerable degree, thus avoiding "dependence" on the United States.

Few things have been more divergent in U.S.–Mexican relations during the post–World War II period, argues Sidney Weintraub, than trade policy.[6] The United States was the principal force promoting trade liberalization in the Western Hemisphere and the strongest supporter of the General Agreement on Tariffs and Trade (GATT). In contrast, Mexico developed a highly protectionist trade regime and did not join GATT until four decades after its creation. These divergent trade policies would eventually become a source of mutual recrimination and misunderstanding. So long as both countries prospered, as they did until the 1970s, conflict was muted. Conflict deepened during the 1970s, in part because the U.S. economy entered a decade-long stagnation with relatively high inflation, while Mexico experienced what proved to be a short-lived boom thanks to its discovery of vast petroleum reserves. Conflict deepened in the early 1980s, in part because the Mexican economy crashed in 1982–83. But the conflict became severe, in part because the United States started to shift away from near sole reliance on a multilateral approach to free trade policies to preferential bilateralism (a free trade agreement with Canada) and selective protectionist policies in some economic sectors.

For almost five decades, Mexican policy-makers emphasized the problems of having a superpower as a neighbor, failing to recognize the potential advantages of having access to the world's largest market. In general terms, they were unwilling to risk the establishment of a closer relationship with the United States. A well-known Mexican diplomat, the late Jorge Castañeda, exemplified the Mexican distrust toward the United States when he said, "I cannot believe any signs of good intentions, sympathy, or moral considerations on the part of the United States that could make them change their basic attitude towards Mexico."[7]

Even as late as 1988, it would have been difficult to imagine that U.S.–Mexican relations would be characterized by anything more positive than indifference. Furthermore, during the last three years of the administrations of Ronald Reagan (1981–89) and Miguel de la Madrid (1982–88), the general tone of the bilateral relationship changed briefly from bargained negligence to conflict. The relationship became tense as a result of the murder of U.S. DEA agent Camarena, which a number of U.S. officials blamed on some Mexican government officials. This highly publicized incident produced recriminations from Washington concerning Mexico's inability to cope with the flow of narcotics entering the United States. In addition, a deteriorating Mexican economy in the final years of de la Madrid's administration increased the likelihood that conflict would dominate future U.S.–Mexican relations. From this perspective, bargained negligence certainly seemed the most hopeful outcome that could reasonably be expected in U.S.–Mexican relations.

BILATERAL COOPERATION

The themes that we have sketched in the two previous sections characterize the bulk of the history between the two countries. Nevertheless, there have been a few brief periods of bilateral cooperation at certain crucial moments in the history shared by the United States and Mexico.[8] For the most part, the most cooperative moments in this history have been the result of economic interests or foreign threats. We will describe the most salient examples.

In the late 1860s, President Benito Juárez organized the liberal triumph over Mexican conservatives in the Mexican civil war. Upon the end of the nearly simultaneous civil war in the United States, the U.S. government also made it clear to the French government that it did not favor the French occupation of Mexico, backed by Mexican conservatives, that had resulted in the installation of Maximilian of Habsburg as emperor of Mexico in 1864. Maximilian's execution and the withdrawal of French troops in 1867 created better circumstances for U.S.–Mexican relations. General Díaz soon became the key political figure in Mexico. Anxious to become president, Díaz led a successful coup in 1876; because "no reelection" had been a slogan of his rebellion, he left power in 1880. But in 1884, Díaz was again elected president, and he stayed in office until 1910. Díaz's long tenure enabled him to overcome the initial refusal of U.S. president Rutherford Hayes to recognize his government. As Díaz consolidated his power, U.S.–Mexican relations gradually became more cordial. The cornerstone of this new relationship was the Mexican government's interest in fostering U.S. investments in key economic sectors. U.S. companies invested heavily in Mexican railroads and mining. In 1883, a trade reciprocity treaty was signed, which would lower tariffs and legal barriers. Ironically, the treaty never went into effect because the U.S. House of Representatives never approved the tax laws needed to implement the agreement. Nevertheless, total trade between Mexico and the United States grew from nine million pesos in 1870 to 117 million pesos in 1910. In addition, U.S. investments in Mexico increased during the Díaz regime. By 1911, the worth of U.S. foreign investment in Mexico had surpassed that of Great Britain, which made Mexico, at the end of the nineteenth century, the only country in mainland Latin America where U.S. investment was greater than British investment.[9]

Some have argued that present-day Mexican diplomacy should learn some lessons from the Díaz regime's policies toward the United States. Mexican diplomacy during this period had actively sought to shape decision-making in Washington, and it attentively managed border issues.[10] The Mexican envoy to Washington in the 1880s, Matías Romero, negotiated the reciprocity agreement with Washington and also engaged in what today would be known as a public relations campaign to improve Mexico's image in Washington. Border issues were dealt with on a case-by-case approach, preventing an unattended dispute from creating friction between the two nations.[11] The cooperative nature of bilateral relations, however, was not significant enough to change the latent Mexican distrust of the United States. Díaz was always conscious of the enormous pressures that the U.S. government exerted upon him and his government prior to extending U.S. recognition to his government; consequently, Díaz continued to promote an aggressive diplomacy to attract European investment.[12]

Another important instance of cooperation began with a foreign threat. On June 2, 1942, Mexico declared war on the axis countries, becoming a U.S. ally. During World War II, bilateral cooperation emerged in both military and economic fields. In 1942, an agreement was signed to lower trade barriers, which also reopened the U.S. market for Mexican oil. Soon Mexican oil exports to the United States boomed. Other agreements facilitated U.S. loans to develop communications and stabilize Mexican public finances. In addition, the United States and Mexico signed an immigration agreement in 1942. Under a series of temporary guest worker agreements from 1942 to 1964, known as the Bracero Agreements, a U.S. agency—the Administration of the Agricultural Insurance—hired Mexicans to work in agricultural and rail industries in the United States. Approximately 300,000 Mexicans came to work in the United States during the war in response to the labor shortages produced by the war effort. When the agreement was finally terminated in 1964, almost 4.5 million Mexicans had entered the United States under the auspices of the Bracero Agreements.[13]

Another important episode of U.S.–Mexican collaboration occurred in the late 1970s, in part as a result of Mexico's increased oil export capacity during the worldwide oil crisis of 1979. In what was arguably the most important effort by the U.S. government to better coordinate policy-making toward Mexico, the Carter administration established a coordinator for Mexican affairs and created a binational commission.[14] In 1978, the U.S. National Security Council initiated a significant review of U.S. policy toward Mexico. The study involved 14 agencies; it concluded that more coordination was necessary. However, in the end these efforts to improve the coordination of U.S. policy toward Mexico were not successful. The tension between this administration and that of President José López Portillo (1976–82) continued to increase until the end of the Carter administration in 1980.

These instances of bilateral cooperation were too brief or too narrow to have left a lasting impact on the public consciousness of both countries. Cooperation during the Díaz dictatorship carried too much adverse ideological remembrance to serve as an effective model for the late twentieth century. Cooperation during World War II seemed far too confined to a specific and unusual moment. And the Carter administration's attempt to improve bilateral cooperation failed, reaffirming thereby the preconception in both countries that either conflict or bargained negligence was the more typical pattern for bilateral relations.

THE TURNING POINT

During the Salinas and Bush presidencies, therefore, the change in the U.S.–Mexican relationship had to be constructed despite a history of non-cooperation and the expectation that collaboration would fail in the end. The relationship evolved from a distant handshake to a hands-on, problem-solving approach. A year after taking office, President Salinas decided to seek a free trade agreement with the United States. The NAFTA negotiation launched an extraordinary period of cooperation between the two governments. NAFTA broke with Mexico's continued struggle to escape the overwhelming presence of its northern neighbor. For the first time in the history of bilateral affairs, the Mexican government sought to foster economic integration with the United States instead of resisting it. NAFTA represents the most important effort in the history of U.S.–Mexican relations to establish a partnership based on shared economic interests. NAFTA can be seen as the most important agreement in the history of U.S.–Mexico relations since the Guadalupe-Hidalgo Treaty of 1848. Contrary to the 1848 accord when Mexico ceded a vast amount of territory to the United States, NAFTA is a cooperative pact that facilitates and encourages economic integration.

Presidents Bill Clinton (1993–2001) and Ernesto Zedillo (1994–2000) continued their predecessors' efforts to develop a cooperative bilateral relationship. They met at least once a year and continued the endeavor to institutionalize bilateral affairs. During NAFTA's first five years, Mexico became the second-largest trade partner of the United States. In 1999, two-way bilateral trade neared $180 billion. NAFTA's mechanism for dispute resolution allowed it to overcome numerous trade disputes without rancor. As a consequence, U.S.–Mexican economic relations became businesslike.

At the outset of the twenty-first century, however, the budding economic partnership between Mexico and the United States faced three broad challenges. First, there was a growing conflict and occasional mismanagement in the difficult and sensitive areas of drug trafficking and migration. Second, the positive attitude in both nations' executive branches did not extend to their legislative branches. The U.S. Congress continued to behave in a paternalistic, unilateral, and often antagonistic manner in certain issue areas of U.S.–Mexican relations, such as drug trafficking and migration. It remained suspicious of the new North American partnership based on economic interests. For its part, the Mexican Congress continued to show the nationalism that had permeated the country's diplomacy during the Cold War—an approach that acquired significance especially by the late 1990s, because the Mexican Congress acquired greater authority over foreign policy decisions. Third, some state and local governments, particularly on the U.S. side of the border, became active and at times contentious in bilateral affairs. In particular, relations between the state of California and Mexico were very difficult during most of the 1990s.

The images and actual experiences that characterized U.S.–Mexican relations for most of two centuries had given scant hope to those who hoped for sustained bilateral collaboration. This made the construction of collaboration since the late 1980s all the more remarkable. Yet, as we have noted, the older images of conflict and suspicion lingered on, especially in the national legislatures and specific regional settings, shaping and constraining the construction of collaboration. Above all, this chapter has shown that bilateral cooperation did not evolve "naturally" from a long and blissful history of bilateral relations. "Something" had to change to open new paths in U.S.–Mexican relations. To explain the reasons for that grand change is the task of the next chapter.

THE CHANGES IN THE
INTERNATIONAL SYSTEM:
EFFECTS ON THE BILATERAL
RELATIONSHIP II

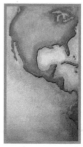

THE INTERNATIONAL SYSTEM CHANGED DRAMATICALLY BETWEEN 1989 and 1991. The Cold War ended in Europe. The communist regimes of Eastern and Central Europe tumbled; most of their replacements sought to enact a transition to democracy, a market economy, and international alignment with the United States and its allies. After four-and-a-half decades of intense worldwide struggle with the Soviet Union, the United States triumphed; it was the world's sole superpower. The Soviet Union decomposed in 1991 to 1992 into many newly independent republics, and Russia itself was gravely weakened militarily, politically, and economically. The impact of the end of the Cold War in Europe upon U.S. foreign policy was enormous. The United States became free to pursue other foreign policy interests and goals.

The direct and indirect impact of these changes also decisively altered U.S.–Mexican relations, both because the United States could pursue other objectives and also because the conduct and content of Mexican foreign policy changed. In the 1990s, Mexico ordinarily sought to "bandwagon" with the United States on most international issues and resist the United States over very few matters. Never before in the history of U.S.–Mexican relations could the previous sentence have been written. The centerpiece of the new bilateral relationship was the North American Free Trade Agreement (NAFTA), which went into effect on January 1, 1994. However, the U.S.–Mexican relationship had turned already in June 1990, when Presidents George Bush (1989–93) and Carlos Salinas de Gortari (1988–94) publicly announced their intentions to negotiate a free trade agreement.

These changes represented significant departures for both countries. Mexican international behavior, especially in the twentieth century, had followed a maxim first described by Thucydides to characterize the international system of antiquity: "The strong do what they can and the weak suffer what they must."[1] That concept is evoked in the opening line of Mario Ojeda's classic study of Mexican foreign policy after World War II. Ojeda proposes to explain Mexican foreign policy not as a peculiar expression of the nation's history but, instead, as a foreign policy similar to "that of any weak country." Ojeda notes that "Mexico did not escape from the phenomenon of the construction of U.S. hegemony as a result" of the end of World War II in 1945. Instead, "as a weak country, Mexico must juggle pragmatically its national interests with the reality of international politics and its propinquity to the United States."[2]

Unsaid by Ojeda (because it would have been obvious to his readers when the book was first published in 1976), the "reality of international politics" included a second superpower, armed with nuclear weapons, and also powerful politically, economically, and in conventional military terms: the Soviet Union. The task for U.S. and Mexican internationalists, therefore, was to work within a competitive international system while recognizing the specific opportunities and burdens posed by U.S.–Mexican propinquity. In the years after World War II, Mexico's foreign policy sought to retain substantial independence from the United States in various issue areas, even if Mexico aligned firmly with the United States on many other issues. In the construction of their relationship, the United States and Mexico seemed to operate as if they were following a key rule, also first formulated by Ojeda:

> The United States recognizes and accepts Mexico's need to dissent from U.S. policy in everything that is fundamental for Mexico, even if it is important but not fundamental for the United States. In exchange, Mexico cooperates in everything that is fundamental or merely important for the United States, though not for Mexico.[3]

Mexico did not, therefore, seek to balance U.S. power across all issue areas from the 1940s to the 1980s. Instead, its foreign policy combined balancing against, and bandwagoning with, the United States from the 1940s through the 1980s. Mexico was too weak to attempt to balance the United States comprehensively, but it would try to do it over particular issues. Examples of Mexican policies balancing U.S. policies include attempts in the 1970s to create a "new international economic order" and efforts in the 1980s to contain U.S. policies in Central America.

At the end of the Cold War in Europe, Mexico's weak position in the international system could still be described as Ojeda did in 1945 except that, in the 1990s, the Soviet Union and European communist regimes had collapsed. Mexico responded to heightened U.S. hegemony by bandwagoning with the United States on virtually all issues. "The year 1990 shall be considered an historic date in the evolution of U.S.–Mexican relations," wrote Lorenzo Meyer, because Mexican elites brought about "an historic shift in the definition of the national interest facing the powerful northern neighbor."[4]

Mexico's response to the changing international system in the 1990s was at odds with the predictions of a dominant scholarly literature in international relations known as "neorealism" whose leading exponent was Kenneth Waltz. Writing about the international system *after* the end of the Cold War, Waltz argued (as he had argued about the international system before 1990) that "the response of other countries to one among them seeking or gaining preponderant power is to try to balance against it. Hegemony leads to balance, which is easy to see historically and to understand theoretically."[5] This school of thought had no difficulty explaining why Mexico in the nineteenth and early twentieth centuries sought to balance the power of the United States. Mexico's hybrid foreign policy from the 1940s through the 1980s, however, posed some difficulties for neorealist understandings, but Mexico's general abandonment of a "balancing" strategy in the 1990s is inexplicable from this scholarly perspective. In order to understand why Mexican elites behaved as they did, we must, therefore, think through the specifics of the context for their decisions and those of the U.S. government in the 1990s.

The Impact of the End of the Cold War in Europe on U.S.–Mexican Relations

The end of the U.S.–Soviet confrontation and the collapse of communist governments in Europe had no significant direct effect on Mexico, but, slowly and subtly, the repercussions from those epochal global transformations profoundly affected Mexico's own international environment and its relations with the United States. In particular, the collapse of the Soviet Union and of communist governments in Eastern Europe, the termination of the civil and international wars swirling in and about Nicaragua, and the weakening and eventual end of Soviet backing for the Cuban government left indelible imprints on Mexican foreign relations.

During the presidencies of Luis Echeverría (1970–76) and José López Portillo (1976–82), Mexico sought to diversify its international political and economic relations. The search for a more independent Mexican foreign policy stemmed from a broadly shared consensus among Mexican foreign policy elites within and outside the government.[6] Mexico played a leading worldwide role in formulating a proposal for a "new international economic order," endorsed by the United Nations General Assembly over U.S. opposition. Mexico became a significant international actor among Latin American governments, disagreeing often with the United States over a wide array of policies in the region and beyond. The highpoint of such efforts was reached in the late 1970s when, emboldened by new discoveries of vast petroleum reserves, President López Portillo sought to wield Mexico's new international clout.[7] One key to such possible diversification was to expand political relations with Western European countries that would, as one consequence, also help to diversify economic relations. This attempt failed.[8]

By the mid-1950s, Western European economies had recovered from World War II. From that time through the end of the 1980s, the Western European share of Mexican trade oscillated between 15 and 20 percent; variations in those shares were relatively minor and did not depart from the trend. The U.S. share remained similarly constant, ranging between 60 and 65 percent of Mexican trade for the same years.

Mexico sought also to obtain European support to balance U.S. policies in Central America in the late 1970s and early 1980s. At first, European social democratic parties and governments seemed receptive. This Mexican-European entente proved ephemeral, however. European governments soon accorded greater priority to their overall relations with the United States than to pressing their objections to U.S. policies toward Central America. By the late 1980s, Mexican officials understood that they should expect little Western European support to contain U.S. policies in Central America.[9]

The end of the Cold War in Europe proved devastating to Mexico's attempt to diversify its relations by drawing closer to Western Europe. In response to the collapse of communist governments in Eastern Europe, the European Community—soon to be renamed the European Union (EU)—and its principal member governments focused their attention and resources on assisting the former communist countries to undergo the multiple transitions to democratic politics, market economies, and a new foreign policy aligned more with Western Europe and the United States than with Russia. Western European governments focused on connecting their eastern neighbors to both the European Union and the North Atlantic Treaty Organization (NATO). The "enlargement" of these two organizations and the complexities and costs associated with the process of making Eastern and Central Europe part of a democratic, market-oriented Europe allied with the Western powers left little time, energy, or resources to improve and deepen European-Mexican relations.

The end of the Cold War in Europe helps to explain why Mexican–Western European relations did not deepen, but events in Europe prior to the end of the Cold War contributed as well to this outcome. Western Europe's self-absorption was a long-term obstacle for Mexican policies of diversification. The deepening of European integration, propelled by the agreements in the mid-1980s and the early 1990s to create a single market in 1992 and a single currency in 1999, might have sufficed to prevent closer European-Mexican relations, even if the Cold War had not ended and the prospects of enlargement to the east had not materialized.[10]

The combined processes of EU enlargement and deepening monopolized the attention and resources of European governments and focused the energies of European business firms. These European processes and NAFTA diverted EU and Mexican trade away from each other. From 1990 to 1995, the EU share of Mexico's trade fell from 11.4 to 7.1 percent. Alarmed about the perceived excessive concentration of its international trade, in May 1995 Mexico asked the EU to open negotiations to reach new economic accords. A framework agreement on political and economic relations was signed on December 8, 1997.[11] In November 1998, negotiations began toward a free trade agreement between Mexico and the EU; by the end of 1998, the EU share of Mexican trade had fallen further to 6.4 percent. On November 24, 1999, a Mexican–EU free trade agreement was reached.[12] No doubt this free trade agreement will intensify Mexican–EU trade, but Mexican exports to the EU actually fell in the six months between the treaty signature and its going into effect on July 1, 2000.[13] In any event, the outcome is unlikely to exceed the proportionate level of Mexican–EU trade reached in 1990. This Mexican–EU free trade agreement should be understood as a defensive reaction to declining trade relations in contrast to NAFTA—a creative response to dynamic and rapidly increasing U.S.–Mexican economic interactions.

In any event, in the late 1980s and early 1990s, this pattern of relations with Europe dissuaded Mexican officials from betting that the future of Mexican prosperity was to be found in London, Paris, Madrid, or Berlin. It would be found, instead, in Washington, Dallas, Chicago, and New York. This realization came forcefully to Mexican president Salinas during his trip to Europe in February 1990. In previous weeks, one after another of Europe's former communist governments had tumbled. At the international conference in Davos, Switzerland, the president of Mexico expected much attention to the reforms that his government had undertaken during the previous year. Instead, the focus of attention was Poland, Czechoslovakia, Hungary, and East Germany. European elites signaled their disinterest in Mexico.[14]

The end of the Cold War in Europe also had an indirect effect on Central America: it helped to end the Cold War in Central America. This was the second important impact of the end of the Cold War in Europe on U.S.–Mexican relations. As already noted, Mexican foreign policy had sought to counter U.S. policies toward Nicaragua and El Salvador in the late 1970s and throughout much of the 1980s. Mexico had sought cooperation from Western European and Latin American governments, and, especially during the López Portillo presidency, it acted on its own. The López Portillo administration contributed materially in 1979 to the overthrow of Anastasio Somoza's government and provided substantial economic assistance to the Sandinista government (1979–90) in Nicaragua; it also became the non-communist government closest to the Salvadoran insurgents, the Frente Farabundo Martí de Liberación Nacional (FMLN). President Miguel de la Madrid (1982–88) sought closer economic relations with the United States but continued to seek international support to counter U.S. policies in Central America. U.S.–Mexican disputes over Central America often embittered even the personal relations between key decision-makers in both countries.[15]

Many factors contributed to the end of Central America's wars. One of them was the declining willingness and capacity of the Soviet government to support the Sandinista government in Nicaragua militarily and economically. Between 1987 and 1989, just as importantly, intense negotiations among the Central American governments and within Nicaragua led to a series of agreements, one of which was the Nicaraguan government's call for free, competitive elections to be held under a United Nations supervision on February 25, 1990. That Nicaraguan decision was facilitated by a concurrent U.S. government decision: the Bush administration set aside the policies of its predecessor and indicated its willingness to accept a Sandinista government in Nicaragua provided it were freely chosen in truly fair elections. This decision, in turn, was possible only in the context of rapidly improving U.S.–Soviet relations that were ending the Cold War in Europe. To general surprise, the Sandinistas lost those elections; domestic pacification soon followed. All of a sudden, a dispute that had pitted Mexico against the United States disappeared.

By the end of February 1990, the international context for the Salinas administration had changed substantially. President Salinas himself would summarize his conclusions for the public in his state of the nation address in September 1990. The United States, he argued, had come to exercise military primacy; and in the economic realm, the world was being reconstituted into three major blocs, one each in Europe, the Asia-Pacific region, and North America.[16] Trade integration with the United States had become a necessity, in his view, given the paucity of other options, and it had become possible thanks to the elimination of sources of tension with the United States, one of which was the solution to the Nicaraguan crisis. The end of the Cold War in Europe, indeed, contributed to U.S.–Mexican rapprochement.

The third impact of the end of the Cold War in Europe upon U.S.–Mexican relations was the weakening of Cuba's capacity to project international power. By January 1991, the Soviet Union had ended nearly all subsidies to the Cuban economy. The Cuban economy plunged in the years that followed. The collapse of the Soviet Union later in 1991 led directly to the termination of the Soviet-Cuban military alliance; Russia established no military alliance with Cuba. From 1988 through 1991, Cuban troops were repatriated from Angola, Ethiopia, Nicaragua, and other countries. During 1991, Cuba suspended its material assistance to the insurgency in El Salvador, and it eventually supported the peace agreement reached at the end of that year between the government of El Salvador and the insurgency. Later on, Cuba would suspend its support for insurgency in Guatemala, contributing thereby to the 1996 peace agreement in that country.

In a relatively short time, therefore, the end of the Central American wars, the threats of Soviet or Cuban military intervention, Cuba's interventionist policies, and communist insurgencies removed obstacles to closer U.S.–Mexican collaboration. Mexico had had a long and complex relationship with Cuba; it would remain complex in the 1990s, but the United States no longer saw it as a security threat.[17] Mexico no longer sought to balance U.S. policy in Central America, as it did during the preceding decade. A realistic assessment of the new international situation, Mexican government leaders believed, called for bandwagoning with the United States. In turn, the United States no longer feared communist military victories in Central America, nor did it fear that Mexico might be infected by communism. The United States stopped pressuring Mexico concerning these security matters. Moreover, the European preoccupation with the former communist countries in Europe at long last persuaded Mexican leaders that little diversification of relations could be expected from Europe. This new context made much more feasible U.S.–Mexican collaboration over a wide array of issues, eventually even including security.

THE WEDDING THAT NEVER HAPPENED: JAPANESE–MEXICAN RELATIONS

In the 1970s and 1980s, many Mexicans believed that Japan could be Mexico's ideal partner for rapid economic growth as a source of both investment and trade. The basis for these expectations was very limited, however. These hopes about Japan's role were often juxtaposed to the perception that the United States was a less desirable partner, if a partner at all.[18] In the 1988 Mexican presidential election, public opinion polls showed that the Japanese were esteemed more highly than U.S. citizens.[19]

Japanese share of foreign direct investment in Mexico rose from about one percent in the 1960s to about four percent in 1980, while Japan's share of Mexican exports and imports ranged between four and five percent. By 1990, at the peak of the Japanese economic boom, Japan's share of Mexican imports and exports had risen to about six percent (mainly at the expense of the European share).

In the 1990s, Japan entered into a decade-long economic stagnation, with serious difficulties in its financial system and stock market. Japanese banks retrenched, as did their customers. Already by 1992 Mexican exports to Japan as a share of all Mexican exports fell to below three percent. The growth of Japanese foreign direct investment in Mexico slowed to a crawl.[20] The Japanese political system also underwent major transformations in the 1990s, making it more difficult for Japan to play an active role in international affairs.

Even before it became evident that Japan's economic performance in the 1990s would be poor, Mexican leaders decided that it was unlikely that Japan would rescue Mexico from underdevelopment. Highly sophisticated Mexican officials and intellectuals believed that Japan would be heading an integrated East Asian economy not unlike Europe's, though with a much lower level of institutionalization. Mexican elites believed that the world was dividing into three blocs, Europe, Japan-led East Asia, and North America, and that they better join the third bloc quickly.[21] This strong belief deepened the consequences for Mexico of the changes that had taken place in Europe; that is, the United States became Mexico's preferred alternative for partnership in the 1990s.

There is no evidence that Mexican officials understood well that Japan's relations with China, Taiwan, and South Korea were extremely complicated, and that none of these three governments was ready to play second fiddle to Japanese leadership, even if it had been forthcoming. Mexican policy toward Japan, therefore, was motivated by quite different images of Japan from the 1960s to the 1990s. The one common thread among these images is that they were all inaccurate representations of Japan's role in the world.

Mexico's Latin American Non-Option

Mexico played a leading role among Latin American countries in the 1970s, and it spearheaded the Latin American resistance to U.S. policies in Central America in the 1980s. In August 1980, Mexico and Venezuela set up the San José Accord to sell petroleum at a discount to Central American and Caribbean countries in order to cushion the impact of the rise of the world price of petroleum in 1979. Mexico played a prominent role in the so-called Contadora group (also including Colombia, Panama, and Venezuela) that sought to find a solution to the U.S.–Nicaraguan confrontation in the 1980s without promoting the overthrow of Nicaragua's government, which had been the U.S. government's principal objective. Mexico had been a leader of the "Third World" and the Non-Aligned Movement in navigating the shoals between the United States and the Soviet Union. The end of the U.S.–Soviet rivalry deprived the Non-Aligned Movement of its central reason for being, and it rendered moot a number of Mexican policies. The end of the wars in and around Nicaragua did away not just with that conflict but also with Mexico's leading role in bringing together Latin American countries to resist U.S. policies.

More importantly, Latin America did not provide practical solutions for the concrete problems that Mexico confronted at the end of the 1980s. The key priority for the Mexican government was to reactivate the nation's economy in order to restore political, economic, and social stability and improve the chances for prosperity. Mexican trade with Latin American countries had always accounted for an insignificant share of Mexican exports and imports. Most Latin American countries were mired in a decade-long economic recession in the 1980s. Latin America was also a capital-importing region, while Mexico needed new sources of international financing. The Salinas administration, therefore, continued to offer warm hugs and rhetorical solidarity to other Latin Americans, but it decisively abandoned the "Third World"-type foreign policies of its predecessors and reached out to the U.S. government.

This Mexican government decision took hold perhaps more deeply than its leaders had intended. Three additional changes would contribute to placing significant distance between Mexico and other Latin American countries. First, NAFTA benefited Mexico the most, provided it did not share the U.S. market with other Latin American countries. Mexico's official position would welcome generalized free trade in the Americas, but Mexico's practical interests were well served by NAFTA alone. Therefore, Mexico's principal national interests privileged its economic relations with the United States over charitable feelings toward Latin America. Second, Mexico's trade (SECOFI) and finance (Hacienda) ministries typically managed trade and financial relations with the United States. The relative importance of the foreign ministry—the flag-bearer of Third Worldism in the Mexican government—declined. Therefore, the redeployment of bureaucratic power within the Mexican government strengthened those who advocated closer relations with the United States and weakened those who advocated closer relations with Latin America. Finally, there was an intellectual shift at the peak of the Mexican government. President de la Madrid obtained a Master of Public Administration degree at Harvard. Salinas was invariably identified in the mass media as "Harvard-educated," because he got a Master's degree and a Ph.D. there. President Zedillo got his Ph.D. in economics from Yale. Many of their ministers and deputy ministers were similarly trained in U.S. universities. Therefore, Mexico's most important decision-makers had spent important parts of their personal and professional lives in the United States, not in Latin America, and they had become accustomed to think as their U.S. teachers had taught them.

The cost to Mexico of this distancing from Latin America is probably significant but difficult to document. We suspect that many Mexicans would prefer to strengthen their bonds of affection and identity with other Latin Americans but have difficulty finding practical ways of doing so. There are occasional lamentations in Mexican discourse about the paths not taken in Mexican foreign policy toward Latin America; for example, the foreign policy platforms of all presidential candidates, including that of the eventual winner, Vicente Fox, during the 2000 election campaign yearned for closer relations with other Latin American countries. President-elect Fox's first international trip was a visit to southern South American countries to call attention to Mexico's Latin-Americanist vocation; only later did Fox visit the United States and Canada. We expect that debates about Mexican "identity" in the Western Hemisphere will be a significant focus of public concern early in the twenty-first century. But we doubt that Mexico's practical interests would be trumped by the romance of Latin American solidarity.

CHANGES IN THE UNITED STATES

Several of the changes already discussed help to explain the change in U.S. policy toward Mexico. The disappearance of U.S.–Mexican conflict over Central America, especially over Nicaragua, and the loss of U.S. fear of Cuban or Soviet influence in Mexico, facilitated a change in U.S. policy. The United States did not have the European and Japanese options that Mexico once wistfully explored. But several additional considerations bore on the change in U.S. policy.

The first reason was the most important. As we explain in detail in chapter four, the U.S. government—and specifically U.S. Special Trade Representative Carla Hills—became frustrated with the slow progress of GATT's Uruguay Round trade negotiations. The Bush administration reached the judgment that NAFTA could serve to jump-start a wider multilateral process of trade liberalization; it also complemented and broadened the recent U.S. free trade agreement with Canada. NAFTA thus became a worthwhile objective in itself as well as an instrument to achieve other U.S. trade negotiation objectives.

A second reason was the Mexican initiative. It was bold, it was innovative, and the Mexican government was persistent. The initiative could be defended well beyond the scope of U.S. trade interests. The NAFTA idea could assist the United States in redefining its long-troubled relationship with Mexico. And it came at just the right moment as President Bush was looking for a way to describe and shape a new world order; the United States would set an example in breaking new ground in relations between rich and poor countries. This was policy "vision" in its most dramatic state.

There were several coincidental reasons. Bush and Salinas were both elected presidents of their respective countries in 1988. As such, they were facing the normal problems of new administrations: how to define their policy agendas, how to identify goals and strategies, how to look for allies to assist them to accomplish their purposes. Their administrations went through this policy analysis process at the same time and under the same world-historical conditions. Another coincidental reason was the role of Texans. Not all Texans would favor free trade between the United States and Mexico. One Texan who opposed NAFTA vigorously was the millionaire presidential candidate H. Ross Perot. But, as we show in chapter seven, Texas is the U.S. state with the highest stakes in its relations with Mexico. Bush believed in the worth of U.S.–Mexican free trade even before Salinas proposed it; he had made Texas his adopted home. His secretary of state, James Baker, and his secretary of commerce, Robert Mossbacher, were also Texans. And Senator Lloyd Bentsen (D-TX) provided the continuity from the Bush to the Clinton administration on this issue, when he became Bill Clinton's first treasury secretary.

NAFTA ratification by the U.S. Congress succeeded on the basis of an ad hoc coalition between the Republicans who wished to honor President Bush's accomplishment and a minority of congressional Democrats who followed President Clinton's lead to sketch a more "centrist" approach to Democratic party trade policy. Support for NAFTA served to mark out Clinton's pro-business credentials during his presidential campaign; NAFTA ratification was the first major legislative accomplishment of the Clinton presidency. Just as important, support for NAFTA became a unifying nonpartisan theme of the U.S. foreign policy establishment in the early 1990s. Ratification was supported by past presidents and secretaries of state and treasury. Wars began to break out in the Balkans, the Caucasus, and the central lakes region in Africa; the post–Cold War security order was coming apart. In contrast, NAFTA and, more generally, international free trade stood as a symbol and a reality of a new world economic order ushered by the United States as part of its victory in the Cold War.

Toward Institutionalist Problem Solving in U.S.–Mexican Relations

The changes evident in U.S.–Mexican relations in the 1990s have other roots that predate, and are unrelated to, the end of the Cold War in Europe or relations with

Japan. One striking feature of U.S.–Mexican relations before 1990 was their weak institutionalization. These two countries had a great many interactions but were, nevertheless, bereft of significant agreements to cope with routine disputes over trade, investment, migration, or security issues. This was not the result of a cultural inability to cooperate; on the contrary, both countries had fashioned some effective, institutionalized means for cooperation but only over narrow issues or in more distant times in the past. Instead, it was Mexico's choice during the preceding decades to institutionalize cooperation over just a few issues; non-institutionalization otherwise prevailed in bilateral relations.

One important motivation for Mexico's participation in institution building in the late 1980s and thereafter was strictly defensive, as neorealists would expect. Joseph Grieco has written with regard to European integration that "weaker but still influential partners will seek to ensure that the rules so constructed will provide sufficient opportunities for them to voice their concerns and interests and thereby prevent or at least ameliorate their domination by stronger powers."[22] This approach fits the origins of NAFTA. Mexico sought a free trade agreement, in part, to ensure that its exports would not be locked out of U.S. markets. In response to fears of protectionism (and fears about the implications for Mexico of the just-signed U.S.–Canada agreement), Mexico sought an institutionalized voice in its relations with the United States and a mechanism to settle disputes.

But the reasons for building institutions, including NAFTA, went beyond such defensiveness for both the United States and Mexico. Both governments sought to facilitate cooperation, not just ward off trouble. The new institutions might not be optimal for either party, but they would be reliable because both governments would consent to them. These institutions would establish stable mutual expectations about patterns of bilateral interaction. Second, the prohibitions against discriminatory practices (including in the trade area) would lower transaction costs. Compliance became rational. The transaction costs of lawful behavior dropped; the transaction costs of misbehavior rose. The main insurance against wholesale violation of the agreed upon rules would become the growing linkage among issues and the inter-penetration of economies. It became cheaper for governments and firms to reach agreements and make deals once a new international regime had been instituted. Firms could begin to take advantage of economies of scale. Third, international institutions reduced uncertainty and facilitated the transfer of information. In the 1990s, both the United States and Mexico would gain extraordinary access to each other's government agencies, officials, associations, and business firms. They would find it much easier to cooperate in times of crisis to ward off panic, as happened most notably during Mexico's 1994 election year and 1995 financial crash.[23] To be sure, each successful instance of cooperation deepened the incentives for further collaboration. The two partners learned to look for joint gains. Despite these good reasons to create international institutions, Mexico and the United States had eschewed such practices until the 1990s.

We next consider why this had been so, and why the historic shift occurred near the century's end.

ECONOMIC STRATEGIES AND PERFORMANCE: FOUNDING INSTITUTIONS

Since the 1930s, Mexico pursued a rather autarkic policy of import-substituting industrialization as its engine for economic growth; it had also implemented "nationalist" policies to control, regulate, and at times prohibit certain trade and investment relations. Mexico was also reluctant to design or join key international economic institutions. For example, Mexico long refused to join GATT; President López Portillo explicitly considered joining GATT but, in 1980, reaffirmed the decision not to join. Nonetheless, in the course of deciding how to proceed, it became evident that there were two contending factions at the top of the government. One already advocated joining GATT, and the second opposed such a step.[24] López Portillo agreed with this second faction; he believed that Mexico could use its new petroleum wealth to facilitate other Mexican exports. The oil weapon was thought to be superior to GATT as a means to advance Mexican trade interests.[25] Mexico had not been the only country to remain outside the GATT system, but no other such country had a long physical border with the United States and none consistently concentrated two-thirds of its international trade with the United States. The stakes for Mexico were incomparably higher than they were for other GATT non-participants.

In the first half of the 1970s, the rate of exports of Mexican manufactured products to the United States increased significantly, often by reliance on export subsidies. In the second half of the 1970s and in the early 1980s, Mexican manufactured exports stagnated in part as a consequence of the overvaluation of the peso.[26] This outcome increased the political demand in Mexico for export subsidies, and these, in turn, rendered Mexican exports politically vulnerable to retaliation in the U.S. market and triggered a bilateral trade crisis. Until 1985, a U.S. producer simply had to show that Mexico had subsidized an export product to trigger the imposition of a U.S. countervailing duty; the U.S. complainant did not have to prove that Mexico's subsidized exports had injured the U.S. producer. Nonetheless, Mexico persevered in subsidizing exports, because in the first half of the 1970s, exports contributed to the growth of manufacturing output more than import substitution. In 1980, the United States signed the GATT code on subsidies; henceforth, injury would have to be shown provided the alleged subsidizer was a GATT member. Because Mexico remained outside GATT, however, it did not benefit from the U.S. agreement to the GATT code. Mexico's subsidized exports remained vulnerable to easy U.S. retaliation. From the 1970s to the mid-1980s, U.S.–Mexican trade disputes escalated.[27]

Among the many effects of Mexico's economic debacle of the early 1980s was the demise of its past trade policies. Petroleum prices weakened, so the edge of the oil weapon was dulled. Subsidized Mexican exports provoked trade disputes with the United States and insufficient gains to Mexico. Mexico still lacked the means to resolve bilateral trade disputes with the United States.[28] But in the immediate aftermath of the 1982–83 crisis, it had to generate more exports to meet its international financial obligations. The economic crisis weakened many of the economic and political opponents of trade liberalization. And in 1982, de la Madrid, who as budget and planning minister had advocated joining GATT in 1980, replaced López Portillo as president of Mexico. Mexico opened trade negotiations with the United States to construct new bilateral institutions—NAFTA's antecedents.

In April 1985, Mexico and the United States signed an agreement on bilateral subsidies and countervailing duties. In return for a staged elimination of subsidies of Mexican exports to the United States, the United States agreed to provide Mexico the benefit of an injury test under U.S. countervailing duty law. This was the first comprehensive trade agreement between the United States and Mexico since the expiration in 1950 of the wartime Reciprocal Trade Agreement signed in December 1942. (No bilateral trade treaty would be signed until 1975, when a narrow bilateral treaty on textiles and apparel trade was agreed to.) In August 1986, Mexico joined GATT. Under GATT practices, the countries most affected by the trade behavior of a candidate for membership have the greatest say in the GATT negotiations. In the case of Mexico, of course, this general GATT rule empowered the United States to shape Mexico's terms of entry to GATT. Thus, Mexico's decision to join GATT stimulated the continuing construction of bilateral institutions with the United States. In November 1987, the two governments signed a bilateral framework agreement for trade and investment, establishing a consultative mechanism for dispute resolution; soon, there followed bilateral agreements over the steel and textile sectors. The Mexican government dismantled its trade protectionist policies. It abolished official reference prices and import licensing requirements, and it slashed its tariff rates to match those prevailing among the industrial democracies of the North Atlantic world.[29] On the eve of the NAFTA negotiations to free trade across North America, Mexico had already transformed itself from protectionism to trade openness. And it had chosen to build bilateral economic institutions to fill the institutional voids.

Mexico had also transformed its foreign investment policies, partly through explicit agreements with the United States. Until the 1980s, Mexico had regulated foreign direct investment closely and prohibited it from some key economic sectors. Mexico responded to its financial debacle of 1982 to 1983, after some delay, by significantly liberalizing foreign investment regulations. Changes adopted between 1984 and 1986 greatly eased the rules for approval of foreign direct investment. Further changes adopted in 1989 opened the entire economy to foreign direct investment. The privatization of state enterprises begun in the second half of the 1980s was also a vehicle for substantial foreign direct investment. And

NAFTA itself further liberalized the terms for investment across most sectors of the economy. Indeed, attracting such investment was one of Mexico's principal objectives in NAFTA.[30] The main exceptions to these policies regarding privatization and foreign investment were the state-owned petroleum and electricity sectors; their prospective opening in some way to private foreign investment ranked high on the public agenda for U.S.–Mexican relations at the start of the twenty-first century.[31]

In the same vein, starting in the late 1980s, Mexico welcomed portfolio investment in its stock and bond markets and greatly fostered and increased the international financial ties of the Mexican government and private financial institutions. This shift in Mexican policy coincided with a global trend toward financial liberalization and significant interest in what came to be known as "emerging markets." President Salinas and his economic cabinet became the leading salesmen of Mexican financial instruments worldwide, contributing perhaps to excessive, imprudent, and wasteful investments in what was, nonetheless, for the most part a salutary and constructive financial process.[32]

By the end of the 1980s, Mexican government elites had decided on and were in the process of engineering a major change in Mexico's economic strategies. The worldview of Mexican elites with the power to shape policy had changed dramatically. This intellectual change was itself the product of a quiet revolution in the training of prospective Mexican economic policy-making elites who, as young graduate students, studied in U.S. universities, especially in departments of economics. The decisions to study abroad were, of course, individual, but some institutions—especially the Bank of Mexico and the U.S. Fulbright Commission (more recently known as the U.S.–Mexico Fulbright García Robles Commission)—played decisive roles in identifying bright young Mexicans, supporting them during their time of graduate study in the United States, and in some cases helping them find good jobs upon their return to Mexico. These individual connections and new modes of thinking began to have an impact on U.S.–Mexican relations during de la Madrid's presidency, with particularly active roles for Mexico's treasury ministry (led first by Jesús Silva Herzog) and the Bank of Mexico.

The political impact of these highly, technically trained young leaders grew immensely during the Salinas presidency. The Salinas economic cabinet was certainly an impressive team. Salinas himself had a Ph.D. in political economy from Harvard. Treasury Minister Pedro Aspe had a Ph.D. in economics from M.I.T. Commerce Minister Jaime Serra and Budget and Planning Minister Ernesto Zedillo had Ph.D.s in economics from Yale. And Chief NAFTA Negotiator Herminio Blanco had a Ph.D. in economics from the University of Chicago. All of them received their U.S. doctorates in the late 1970s.[33] Together, as *The Economist* called them, they were "probably the most economically literate group that has ever governed any country anywhere."[34]

Under the guidance of these leaders, the economy would henceforth be open to world trade and investment, and much more liberally regulated than in the past.

Mexican business elites followed this lead. The Mexican government signed agreements with the United States, NAFTA above all, to crown and consolidate the new course of Mexican economic history. Mexico also sought to ward off the wave of U.S. protectionism that, rightly or wrongly, Mexican elites believed was about to overwhelm them if they did not reach this entente with the United States.

So marked was the ideological change in Mexico that many aspects of the U.S.–Mexican negotiations over NAFTA and, later on, the Mexican financial bailout in early 1995 could be described as a conversation among members of the same team. To be sure, the representatives of each country were instructed to advance their respective national interests, but the overall conceptual approach to the subject, the character of the analysis and argumentation, the common technical language, and the standards of evidence were agreed upon and shared. U.S. and Mexican elites had thus come to partake in what Peter Haas has called an "epistemic community." Shared ideas, and the means of assessing them, facilitated communication and agreement between national elites.[35] Moreover, thanks in part to their education in the United States, the key Mexican elites were fluent in English, familiar with U.S. culture, and often knew personally their U.S. counterparts in the Treasury Department, the Office of the Special Trade Representative, and the Federal Reserve Board. These personal networks, intellectual values, and modes of technical thinking were key building blocks for the institutionalization that NAFTA would exemplify and accelerate.

NAFTA is not as institutionalized as the EU, but it created a panoply of institutions and practices of consultation such as had never existed to connect the United States and Mexico and address common problems. By the late 1990s, some 50 different bilateral commissions were at work on such problems as agriculture, transportation, rules of origin, industrial and health standards, customs cooperation, dispute resolution in trade and investment, labor, and the environment, among others. Presidents, cabinet ministers, and other high officials from both governments met frequently, regularly, and routinely.[36] As theory would predict, the new international institutions lowered formal barriers to cooperation and transaction costs for business firms, which proceeded to establish strategic alliances to foster efficiency and generate growth.[37] And, as we will read in the chapters that follow, these new international institutions helped the United States and Mexico cope with economic adversity in the mid-1990s and develop their economic relations significantly throughout the decade.

In short, in the late 1980s and in the 1990s, four factors converged to help explain the shift toward bilateral institutions as a means to address joint economic problems and opportunities. First, the structural transformation of the international system, and its effects on U.S.–Mexican relations, removed the barriers that had hitherto prevented close bilateral collaboration. Second, Mexico's severe economic crisis in the 1980s forced the Mexican government to abandon the old economic model and adopt a new one. Third, the economic crisis in Mexico, and domestic political processes in both the United States and Mexico, brought forth new leaders atop each government who were ready to accept ideas about market liberalization and bilateral cooperation under the rubric of North American free trade. And fourth, a set of ideas about politics, markets, institutions, and cooperation, long available among scholars, could be seized upon by these new leaders, in this more permissive international and more urgent Mexican domestic economic context, to construct a bilateral partnership at long last.

Security, Political, and Societal Strategies and Performance: Founding Institutions

The institutional void between Mexico and the United States was, of course, not limited to the economic realm but was quite typical of most issue areas. Arguably, the process of economic cooperation seems to have spilled over to facilitate the construction of other new institutions and practices to cope with various thorny topics in the bilateral relationship.

Despite being neighbors, Mexico and the United States lacked institutionalized means for security cooperation. Despite the serious disputes that emerged with regard to drug trafficking in the 1980s, the two governments lacked institutional procedures to address these problems. During the Cold War, Mexico never signed a defense assistance treaty with the United States. Mexico participated at the lowest possible level in inter-American security institutions such as the Inter-American Defense Board. The Joint Mexican–United States Defense Commission, founded and effective during World War II, became merely a social forum for the decades that followed. In contrast, as will be shown in chapter three, substantial bilateral cooperation over security matters (not just limited to military issues) developed in the 1990s.

Despite having a very long land border plagued with environmental problems, the United States and Mexico had no comprehensive agreement to cope with joint environmental problems until the La Paz Agreements in 1983. Not until 1992 did the two national governments establish border commissions to manage routine local-level issues across the physical border. As the 1990s progressed, however, formal and informal institutional links developed in the border region not only between the national governments but also between some state and municipal governments on both sides of the border.

With regard to international migration, circumstances were more complex. In 1942, the United States and Mexico signed the first of what came to be known as the Bracero Agreements, whereby Mexicans would obtain temporary permits to work in the United States as their contribution to the war effort during World War II and the Korean War. These agreements helped both governments to manage migration relations jointly. For U.S. domestic reasons, the last of this series of agreements was allowed to expire in 1964. Also for domestic reasons, it would remain difficult for the United States to articulate its "national interest" concerning immigration from Mexico until the enactment of the Immigration Reform and Control Act (IRCA) of 1986, when U.S. policy turned restrictionist. The Mexican government had opposed the demise of the Bracero Agreements but, by the early 1970s, had come to prefer that migration relations not become part of the bilateral governmental agenda and certainly not come under the authority of a bilateral institution. The Mexican government feared that the United States would pressure Mexico to control emigration as a condition for making some concession to Mexico in some other foreign policy issue area.[38]

From the late 1980s through the 1990s, the Mexican government gradually shifted from its position of deliberate non-engagement on migration matters to a stance of increasing dialogue with its U.S. counterpart. Mexico did not even comment officially when IRCA was under consideration. In contrast, in the mid-1990s, the Mexican government communicated its views clearly to the U.S. executive branch concerning the migration legislation then under discussion in the U.S. Congress; this legislation would be enacted into law in 1996.[39] In 1994, the United States and Mexico strengthened the Working Group on Migration and Consular Affairs of the Binational Commission. Later on, they created a border liaison entity focused on the activities of the U.S. Immigration and Naturalization Service and of Mexican consulates in the United States and signed a Memorandum of Understanding to protect the rights of Mexican citizens in the United States.[40] They were learning to cooperate over migration for the first time since 1964.

Our view is that the construction of bilateral institutions in these issue areas followed from a "spillover" from the previous processes that we have sketched.[41] The "chain of explanation" begins with the transformation of the international system, moves on to the domestic crises in Mexico, the circulation of national elites, and the availability of new institutionalist ideas about problem solving. The next step in the analysis takes account of the significant change in the behavior of the U.S. and Mexican governments in the late 1980s and early 1990s as they increasingly cooperated over economic issues and institutionalized that cooperation. As presidents met again and again, the conversation moved from trade to other issues in bilateral relations. Subsequent chapters will show that each of these issues had its own structure and dynamics. But, by the late 1990s, the bilateral institutionalist approach had become the standard answer whenever the two governments reached an impasse that had to be overcome in their relations. The habits and mechanisms for institutionalized cooperation in the economic arenas spilled over to security issues (especially drug trafficking), the border, and migration.

CONCLUSION

The United States and Mexico have a long history of conflict, punctured by occasional moments of cooperation. In the late 1980s and early 1990s, the pattern shifted. As the twentieth century ended, the two countries had established strong foundations for institutionalized cooperation over various issue areas, punctured by moments of conflict. In this chapter, we have explained how concurrent changes in the international system far from North America, as well as specific changes in Mexico, in the United States, and in their relations with each other, account for this historic shift.[42] In particular, we have focused on the configuration of four factors:

1. The change in the international system removed barriers to U.S.–Mexican cooperation.
2. The severe structural domestic crises in Mexico in the 1980s compelled its political leaders to re-orient national strategy dramatically.
3. The simultaneous accession to the presidencies of Mexico and the United States of Salinas and Bush (in the context of the other factors) enabled them and their advisers to refashion relations. Especially important were young, U.S.-trained Mexican economists and a set of Texas politicians.
4. A pool of ideas about the utility of international institutions had long been available. With the end of the Cold War in Europe, these ideas could be adopted and tested in the economic realm, where the worldwide record suggested they foster market-based trade and investment. Once this process was under way, the habits and fora of institutionalized cooperation spilled over to other issue areas.

"Yes, yes, yes: how fortunate that our ideals coincide with our interests," Carlos Fuentes's Artemio Cruz recalled on his deathbed, once having spoken mendaciously to his U.S. partner.[43] Feelings of joint interests, hopes, and deceit have long coexisted in U.S.–Mexican relations, defining the varied connections between the two countries. Those themes persisted as the twentieth century ended. Elites at the pinnacle of power in each country still wonder whether their counterpart is telling the truth. And, no matter what the elites say, many people in each of these two countries have too little trust for the other. Many Mexicans and U.S. citizens believe, for example, that their governments fooled them when NAFTA was signed.

Mendacity remains a serious threat to the continued good relations between the United States and Mexico, because it threatens the core functioning of international institutions on which their relationship has come to rest and the public support within each country for the relationship and its instruments. And yet, there is the millennial recognition that U.S.–Mexican relations were markedly better as the twenty-first century began than they were at most points during the twentieth century. There was certainly the millennial hope that the learning of the past century's last decade would be the basis for continuing betterment in the years to come.

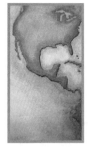

INTERNATIONAL
SECURITY III

F OR MUCH OF THE TWENTIETH CENTURY, THERE HAS BEEN ONLY one source of credible threat to Mexico's international security: the United States. Despite the extraordinary changes in the bilateral relations analyzed in the previous chapter, international security concerns remained an important issue between the United States and Mexico as the twenty-first century began. In this chapter, we examine the evolution of security relations between the two countries and, in particular, focus on the changes in Mexico's security situation and strategies in the 1990s.

During the twentieth century, Mexico had been unable to employ some of the strategies that other states had adopted to address security threats—namely, alliance with other states to balance the threat from the neighboring superpower or the development of internal military and economic capacities to resist on its own. The range of options available to Mexico to protect its international security had been narrower: from open alliance with the United States, at one end, to abnegation, on the other.[1] The problem with aligning with the United States was that this strategy required permitting the United States substantial influence over security and other issues in Mexico. The problem with the abnegation strategy was that it was unable to address some of Mexico's own security concerns that stemmed from its complex relations with the United States. Mexico's security dilemma, therefore, was that it must cooperate to varying degrees with the only source of threat to its international security, and that, in so doing, it must compromise some of its security goals for the sake of achieving others.

During the same decades, U.S. security interests in Mexico had been clearer and easier to implement. For the United States, the optimal outcome was for Mexico to be its ally across all security issue areas; the minimally acceptable outcome was for Mexico to have no military allies and to be incapable of posing a security threat to the United States.

Despite these differing perspectives, Mexico and the United States developed a stable and cost-effective security relationship from the early 1940s to the late 1960s. Mexico practiced, and the United States tolerated, the abnegation strategy. Mexico's international security strategy of abnegation had five characteristics. Mexico:

1. eschewed alliances with any U.S. rival;
2. pursued no foreign policy interest that the United States might construe as a threat to its own security interests;
3. failed to develop a military capability that could resist the United States;
4. relied on many different international suppliers of weapons; and
5. cooperated little or not at all with the United States over international security issues.

At the end of the 1960s, however, the bilateral relationship was destabilized for various reasons, one of which was increased illegal drug consumption in the United States and the attempts of the U.S. government to battle drug trafficking outside its own boundaries. In the decades that followed, Mexican and U.S. security policies would gradually edge toward a security alliance, but the process of convergence over security issues was delayed and made difficult by two factors. First, Mexico differed strongly with U.S. policies toward Central America and Cuba, especially during the 1980s, thereby preventing a closer alliance sooner. The end of the Cold War in Europe and in Central America removed this obstacle, as we indicated in the previous chapter, facilitating a U.S.–Mexican alliance in the 1990s to combat drug trafficking. Second, the security relationship over drug trafficking was punctured by repeated crises that were settled by reluctant Mexican decisions to permit greater U.S. influence over security matters in Mexico. The Mexican government found a security problem of this magnitude to be practically unmanageable.

In general terms, in the 1990s, Mexico followed what Stephen Walt has called a "bandwagoning" strategy (a concept developed, of course, without specific attention to U.S.–Mexican relations): "Bandwagoning involves unequal exchange; the vulnerable state makes asymmetrical concessions to the dominant power and accepts a subordinate role. . . . Bandwagoning is accommodation to pressure (either latent or manifest). . . . Most important of all, bandwagoning suggests a willingness to support or tolerate illegitimate actions by the dominant ally."[2] Mexico adopted a full bandwagoning strategy only during Ernesto Zedillo's presidency (1994–2000), once U.S.–Mexican differences over Central America had ended, although Mexico had been lurching toward a U.S. security alliance since the late 1980s.

Mexico's international security strategy of bandwagoning had six characteristics, the first three of which were common with the abnegation strategy. Mexico:

1. eshewed alliances with any U.S. rival;
2. pursued no foreign policy interest that the United States might construe as a threat to its own security interests;
3. failed to develop a military capability that could resist the United States;
4. built up a substantial military capability to advance joint U.S.–Mexican goals in combating drug trafficking;

5. tilted toward U.S. suppliers of weapons; and

6. cooperated extensively with the United States over international security issues, especially drug trafficking, and tolerated (albeit angrily) unilateral U.S. actions in Mexico as well as U.S. breaches of the bilateral alliance.

The long-term story of U.S.–Mexican security relations in the twentieth century, therefore, has three episodes. Mexico shifted from an attempt to balance U.S. power by contemplating alliances with major powers from other continents (World War I), to an abnegation strategy for most of the century, to bandwagoning with the United States in the 1990s. Mexico's international security declined by the twentieth century's end, threatened by both drug traffickers and U.S. government actions, despite Mexico's significantly larger investment in providing for its own security. Bandwagoning was much less cost-effective for Mexico than abnegation.

The Simplification of Historical Legacies

In the nineteenth century, Mexico faced many credible threats to its international security. It had to fight for its independence from Spain. It lost the northern half of its territory to the United States through defeat at war (1846–48); during the war, U.S. forces conquered and occupied Mexico City. Through coercive diplomacy, Mexico lost another slice of territory in 1853 (the so-called Gadsden Purchase). Mexico was threatened and blockaded at various times by Spain, Great Britain, and France, which, in 1861, jointly invaded Mexico; the French stayed until 1867, seizing Mexico City and sponsoring a short-lived empire under Maximilian of Habsburg.

In the late nineteenth century, one positive development was a definitive boundary settlement between the United States and Mexico. The boundary was settled in the first instance by the Treaty of Guadalupe Hidalgo (1848), which ended the U.S.–Mexican War, as modified by the Treaty of Mesilla, often called the Gadsden Treaty (1853). For much of the length of the boundary, the marker was the middle of the stream (following the deepest channel) of the Rio Grande or Río Bravo. However, the river often changed course. In 1889, the two governments founded the International Boundary Commission to investigate and adjudicate all boundary disputes and implement all of its decisions; these decisions could not be appealed to the courts of either country. Over the years, the commission eliminated all transfers of sovereignty caused by the river's erratic behavior and settled all related disputes. The last one was a piece of land called the Chamizal, which was transferred to the U.S. side of the border when the river changed course in 1864; it was adjudicated in 1911 as belonging to Mexico, but the United States agreed to return it only in 1963. All boundary issues were finally settled by the end of the 1960s.[3]

The Mexican revolution, which unfolded during the second decade of the twentieth century, also featured U.S. military intervention at the port of Veracruz in 1914 in an attempt to overthrow General Victoriano Huerta's rule in Mexico. In 1916, General John J. Pershing led thousands of U.S. troops deep into Mexico to pursue General Pancho Villa, while tens of thousands of additional U.S. troops patrolled the U.S.–Mexican border. Pershing's troops withdrew from Mexico in February 1917, just on the eve of U.S. entry into World War I.[4]

In February 1917, the German government offered Mexico a military alliance. In exchange for military collaboration during the world war, Germany would support Mexico's recovery of the lost northern territories, what the United States had come to call Texas, California, Arizona, and New Mexico (and parts of Colorado and Nevada). Mexican president Venustiano Carranza understood, however, that not even Germany could successfully block U.S. military harm to Mexico, much less assist Mexico on an irredentist quest. Carranza rejected Germany's bid and thereby inaugurated the pattern of Mexican international security policies along the narrow range between alliance with the United States and abnegation, which, as noted at the outset of this chapter, would characterize Mexican security policies for the remainder of the century. During World War I, Mexico remained neutral between the United States and Germany.[5]

In 1938, the Mexican government led by President Lázaro Cárdenas expropriated the foreign-owned petroleum companies. This dramatic act was the culmination of Mexico's revolutionary nationalism. The U.S. and British governments, and especially the oil firms, imposed economic sanctions and exerted other forms of pressure. In December 1941, the United States declared war on Germany, Italy, and Japan. In April 1942, the United States and Mexico agreed that Mexico had the sovereign right to expropriate these firms, and that it would also compensate the expropriated oil companies, though for far less than the companies had claimed. In May 1942, German submarines sank two Mexican tankers. Mexico joined the war against Germany and, for the first time in its history, became a formal wartime ally of the United States. Germany's defeat in 1945 ended the last credible international threat to Mexican security from a source other than the United States.[6] At long last, the historical legacy was simplified: the United States had become the only credible source of threat to Mexico's international security.

MEXICO'S INTERNATIONAL SECURITY STRATEGY OF ABNEGATION

From the end of World War II until the late 1960s, Mexico and the United States had a stable security relationship. It was marked by a Mexican international security strategy of abnegation. Mexican governments since the revolution recognized that Mexico was a weak state incapable of confronting the United States on its own. International alliances to balance U.S. power proved impractical ever since the United States emerged victorious from its war with Spain in 1898 and became the world's leading power after victory in two world wars—a point that two revolutionary presidents, Carranza and Cárdenas, recognized. Thus the first four elements of the abnegation strategy, sketched earlier, embodied the "realism" of a small, weak state. The fifth item—non-cooperation with the United States—was Mexico's innovation to this strategy and set it apart from the international security policies pursued by most other Latin American countries.

As David Mares has aptly pointed out, from their wartime alliance and ever after, Mexico and the United States constituted a "pluralistic security community."[7] The use of military means to resolve threats that one country might pose for the other became unthinkable. The military defense of Mexico in the remote possibility of an extra-continental attack on its sovereignty fell upon the United States. Mexico gave up any pretense of confronting the United States militarily and, in practice, disarmed. The boundary between the two countries became demilitarized. The cross-border movement of goods, services, and people became quite free and frequent. The security community remained "pluralistic," as is the case of the relationship between the United States and Canada, or among the members of the European Union, because there was no territorial amalgamation leading to a new state.

But Mexico was not a U.S. "ally" for most practical military purposes. It cooperated remarkably little with the United States over security matters. U.S.–Mexican international security and other relations remained uninstitutionalized, just as we noted in the previous chapter was the case with regard to trade. In August 1942, the two governments signed a wartime agreement to permit and recruit Mexican workers to work temporarily in the United States as part of Mexico's contribution to the war effort. This so-called Bracero Agreement was the first of a series; it was renewed during the Korean War and the early Cold War years. The Bracero Agreements expired in 1964, never to be renewed.

In February 1942, the United States and Mexico created the Joint Mexican–United States Defense Commission (JMUSDC) as a staff to administer $40 million lend-lease assistance to Mexico and coordinate planning for joint defense along both coasts. These security relations culminated in the deployment of a Mexican air squadron to the Philippines in 1945. This was Mexico's first military collaboration with the United States; the number and size of U.S. technical liaison teams deployed in Mexico were controlled tightly. After World War II and until the early 1990s, the commission remained in existence but mainly as a social forum; it issued its last updated combined defense plan in 1955.[8]

Mexico refused to sign a defense assistance treaty with the United States in 1951. Mexico was the only Latin American country other than Cuba not to host a U.S. Military Assistance Advisory Group during the Cold War. During the Cold War years, Mexico preferred to purchase weapons and equipment from the United States than to accept U.S. military assistance. (Its first major commercial purchase of a U.S. military system was its acquisition of F-5 aircraft in 1981.) Mexico relied on multiple suppliers for its weapons and equipment, among them Belgium, Brazil, France, Israel, the United Kingdom, the United States, and Spain. Mindful of how the United States had used security assistance toward other Latin American countries,

Mexico curtailed U.S. influence over Mexican defense and security policies. It pursued an overt and deliberate effort to build nationalist armed forces free from foreign influences. Mexico did accept grant International Military Education and Training (IMET) funds. About a thousand Mexicans attended U.S. military courses between 1950 and 1980; another thousand did so from 1980 to 1993.[9]

Mexico participated at the lowest possible level in inter-American security institutions such as the Inter-American Defense Board, the Inter-American Defense College, or the meetings of service chiefs such as the Conference of American Armies. Mexico condemned the U.S.-supported invasion of Cuba at the Bay of Pigs in 1961, declined to participate in the naval blockade of Cuba in 1962 during the so-called Missile Crisis (but it did call for the removal of Soviet missiles from Cuba), and refused to implement the collective hemispheric sanctions imposed on Cuba in 1964 and 1967 (because of Cuban support for insurgencies) under the Inter-American Treaty for Reciprocal Assistance. Mexico also opposed U.S. military and other forms of intervention in Central American wars from the late 1970s through the early 1990s, and it opposed the U.S. invasion of Panama in 1989.

Given such extensive non-collaboration, Mexico managed carefully its relations with the Soviet Union and Cuba to reassure the United States that Mexico's international security policy was truly one of abnegation, not one seeking to balance U.S. power. Mexico had correct and uninterrupted diplomatic relations with the Soviet Union since the 1920s. While these relations were typically cordial, both the Mexican and Soviet governments limited their scope. The only issue in that relationship of some significant concern to the United States was the presence of a large Soviet embassy in Mexico City that could serve as a base for intelligence gathering. The Soviet Union never posed a credible security threat to Mexico, however. Mexican-Soviet economic relations were always modest. And Mexico and the Soviet Union certainly never became allies.[10]

Mexico also had generally correct diplomatic and economic relations with Cuba's communist government; it was the only Latin American government that never broke such relations with Cuba. But the Mexican and the U.S. governments well understood the limits of Mexico's relations with Cuba and, indeed, occasionally exchanged information on various matters pertaining to Cuba that were useful to the United States. Mexico and Cuba were never allies, although at times since the 1970s their relations were quite cordial and, occasionally, economically significant. Mexico's policy toward Cuba served Mexican security interests well and, indirectly, even those of the United States. At the heart of the relationship was the commitment of both the Mexican and the Cuban governments not to intervene in each other's domestic affairs. The Cuban government refrained from supporting the domestic opposition in Mexico even when it could have done so easily, such as in 1968 when university students in Mexico City led large-scale protests against the national government and were repressed violently by the Mexican army and police.[11]

Only during the presidency of José López Portillo (1976–82) did Mexico pursue some international security policies that concerned the United States. As noted in the previous chapter, Mexico provided material assistance to the Sandinista insurgents in their eventually successful effort to overthrow the Nicaraguan government of General Anastasio Somoza in 1979. It gave significant economic and political support to the Sandinista government, especially in the early 1980s. And, jointly with the French government, it provided important political support to the Salvadoran insurgency also in the early 1980s. The U.S. government was unhappy about these three Mexican policies, and it strongly opposed the third. It was Mexico's objective that "the United States should acknowledge that Mexico is a force" in Central America. It was the precise objective of the United States not to do that.[12]

Mexico's international security strategy of abnegation had worked well. It had contained U.S. influence on defense and security matters in Mexico. It did not entangle Mexico in severe international disputes far from its shores. It did not require the allocation of large sums from the national budget or the maintenance of large armies. Consequently, it facilitated the consolidation of civilian supremacy over the military; there have been no Mexican presidents with a military background since 1946. Mexico was the only Latin American country to experience no military coups or other irregular or unconstitutional transfers of presidential authority after World War II. And, except briefly in the 1970s and early 1980s, international security abnegation served well to manage relations with both the United States and other countries. Abnegation was cost-effective.

There was one problem. As the consumption of illegal drugs increased in the United States in the 1960s and thereafter, transnational criminal groups began to operate in Mexico on a larger scale. These operations began to threaten Mexican security, in part intrinsically so and in part from growing U.S. concerns about drug trafficking in Mexico. Reluctantly, these issues would lead the Mexican government eventually to become an ally of the United States across an array of international security issues.

Toward Bandwagoning: A U.S.–Mexican Alliance over Drug Trafficking

The United States has long been an exporter of security problems to Mexico. The enactment of the first U.S. drug control law in 1909, subsequent similar laws, and then the Eighteenth Amendment to the U.S. Constitution prohibiting alcohol consumption provoked serious social and security problems along the Mexican side of the U.S. border throughout the 1920s. U.S. drug consumption has long affected Mexico. The first Mexican national campaign involving Mexican federal troops in eradicating the cultivation of plants that could be used to produce illegal drugs occurred in 1948; one of its principal military objectives was to "depistolize" the countryside. But the modern era in drug traffic relations began in 1969 when the U.S. government launched Operation Intercept, the hitherto largest U.S.

peacetime search and seizure counter-narcotics operation. This unilateral offensive, virtually closing the border for 20 days, amounted to economic blackmail, as Richard Craig has put it, to coerce Mexico to cooperate with the United States.[13]

Coercion worked. The United States and Mexico quickly agreed to a joint Operation Condor. Cooperation was excellent for many years. The results in the eradication of marijuana and poppy fields in the 1970s seemed impressive. However, according to Maria Celia Toro, an unintended consequence was to promote cartelization; Operation Condor drove out of business the less daring and smaller traffickers, benefiting the more powerful and better organized. The fittest survivors from Operation Condor resisted enforcement, bought protection, and escalated violence. By the mid-1980s, the international security problem was much worse.[14]

Mexico's response to Operation Condor forever changed aspects of its relations with the United States. Mexico began to accept helicopters, specialized aircraft, spare parts, pilot training, and other forms of U.S. technical assistance in large quantities, which, as we have seen, was utterly unprecedented. The Mexican government agreed to formalize the presence of U.S. police agents in Mexico who had been gathering intelligence information for decades with or without previous notification to Mexican authorities. In 1983, under U.S. pressure, President Miguel de la Madrid greatly increased Mexican military participation in the battle against drug trafficking.

This cooperative relationship exploded in 1985 with the assassination in Mexico of U.S. Drug Enforcement Administration (DEA) agent Enrique Camarena. The United States launched Operation Intercept II, again virtually closing the border for eight days, to coerce Mexico into greater cooperation and greater toleration for unilateral incursions into Mexico by U.S. security operatives. Many U.S. officials also believed that some Mexican government officials, especially some officials from Mexico's police forces, were directly involved in the Camarena murder. As a consequence, U.S. officials responded with outrage, and some U.S. officials publicly insulted Mexican officials. The result made evident Mexico's security vulnerability to the actions of drug traffickers and also to those of the U.S. government.[15]

In the late 1980s, the U.S. government pressed on aggressively with a unilateral strategy to combat drug trafficking. It again sought to force Mexico to cooperate. In 1986, the U.S. Congress enacted a statutory requirement that the executive branch would, every year, without prior international consultation, certify or decertify countries according to the extent of their cooperation with the United States against drug trafficking. The new legislation also extended the reach of U.S. police and legal jurisdiction extraterritorially. The United States expanded intelligence operations in Mexico and began to use increasingly sophisticated military equipment (high-technology radar, night vision equipment, etc.) and military-trained staff. In addition, allegedly "former" U.S. DEA agents in Mexico seized by force, without authorization from the Mexican government, and brought to stand trial in the United States two Mexican citizens accused of complicity in the Camarena murder. The U.S. Supreme Court ruled in these two cases that unlawful searches and kidnapping in other countries, with or without the participation of U.S. agents, did not necessarily lead to the loss of jurisdiction of a U.S. court over those cases. This U.S. Supreme Court decision dismayed the Mexican government, which considered such U.S. actions a kidnapping. Other governments and international organizations and many international lawyers also criticized the decision. U.S. policy seemed based on the willful disregard of the sovereignty of other states.[16]

Alarmed, the Mexican government unveiled new policies aimed at countering the double threat to its international security. One threat came from drug traffickers; the second, from the unilateral actions of the U.S. government. The strategy was to combat the drug traffickers and, through these actions, reassure and thereby contain the United States. In early 1988, President de la Madrid declared drug traffic a threat to Mexico's "national security," a view that his successor Salinas would amplify. Mexican officials had avoided language referring to national security; this symbolic referent signaled a major shift and an accommodation to U.S. approaches to the problem. Mexico relaunched a "permanent campaign" against drug trafficking and drug cultivation. But it also sought to limit the actions of U.S. security agencies in Mexico. Mexico proposed new international agreements to the United States (adding to over 60 such agreements signed in the previous two decades). The most important were the Mutual Legal Assistance Treaty (in effect in 1991) and the modification of the 1980 U.S.–Mexican Extradition Treaty (in effect in 1994). New guidelines were set to regulate the work of DEA agents in Mexico and the terms for U.S. overflights in Mexico in pursuit of traffickers.[17]

President Zedillo defined well Mexico's security priorities in this area. The first priority, the president insisted, was to safeguard Mexican national security, protecting national sovereignty, the effective jurisdiction of the Mexican state throughout the national territory and the strength of the nation's private and public institutions. The second objective was to protect the health of Mexican citizens. The third goal was to foster international bilateral and multilateral cooperation based on the principle of co-responsibility.[18] In this triple phrasing, the president signaled that the security threat from the United States retained its double character: one was the threat from drug traffickers, the other was the threat from the U.S. government to Mexico's sovereignty and institutions. And yet, as a practical matter, President Zedillo found it increasingly difficult to address security threats simultaneously. In the years that followed, his administration increasingly permitted U.S. operations in Mexico.

The Zedillo administration took extraordinary measures in its anti-drug campaign. Thousands of police officials were dismissed; over a third of the members of the Federal Judicial Police were fired. Mexican authorities arrested top- and middle-level leaders of the Gulf of Mexico and Tijuana cartels. Hundreds of Mexican officers died in this literal drug "war." The level of violence remained extraordinarily high and rose in the mid- and late 1990s, rendering ordinary Mexican citizens fearful and apprehensive. For example, the number of reported violent crimes per day in Mexico City tripled in the mid-1990s. Mexico was second only to Colombia in the number of kidnappings (about 1,500 per year). And about a third of Mexico's commercial establishments were robbed annually. Levels of corruption reached high into the upper echelons of the Mexican government. Especially notorious was Mexico's General Jesús Gutiérrez Rebollo's appointment in December 1996 to direct the national institute to combat drugs. In February 1997, drug czar General Gutiérrez Rebollo was dismissed from this post, charged with benefiting from relations with drug traffickers.[19] In the late 1990s, Mexico's relative success against drug trafficking was modest at best, therefore, and its record of performance in the anti-drug campaign remained mediocre.[20] And in September 1997, President Zedillo informed the nation that in the previous year, 1.5 million crimes were reported and that many more were unreported; however, only 150,000 arrest warrants were issued and only 85,000 were carried out. Impunity was the norm.[21]

And yet Mexico's *effort* was impressive in many respects, and certainly costly. By 1998, at strong U.S. urging, on average 20,000 soldiers of the Mexican army were involved in the crop eradication program. (The size of the entire Mexican army was about 170,000 troops.) They worked from 330 operational bases and were supported by 68 aircraft and 90 helicopters from the Mexican air force and the attorney general's office.[22]

The Bush and Clinton administrations, as we have seen, responded constructively to Mexico; their predominant response was to foster and institutionalize economic cooperation. The pattern in security relations, however, had remained uninstitutionalized and marked by cyclical crises. These conflict-ridden patterns persisted into the mid-1990s. For example, in late 1994, the U.S. embassy in Mexico City delivered to President-elect Zedillo a list of 18 current and former high-ranking officials suspected to be tarred by corruption. The list included a former interior minister, a former defense secretary, a former attorney general, and three heads of Mexico's counter-narcotics programs, among others.[23] On the other hand, in October 1995, U.S. defense secretary William Perry visited Mexico to discuss a wide array of bilateral security issues—the first U.S. secretary of defense ever to do so—and specifically to foster collaboration in combating drug trafficking. There had been virtually no operational military-to-military collaboration prior to this visit. The visit and its follow-up set the foundations for increased U.S. military training for Mexican officials and for the transfer of U.S. military helicopters to assist in Mexico's counter-narcotics efforts.[24] Yet, in January 1996, the U.S. government unilaterally beefed up law enforcement along the southwestern border to combat drug trafficking and illegal immigration (Operations Gatekeeper and Safeguard). From Fiscal Year 1993 to Fiscal Year 1997, the Clinton administration increased the number of border patrol agents on the southwestern border from 3,389 to 6,213 to combat drug trafficking and illegal migration.[25]

Moreover, since early 1995, the Republican-controlled U.S. Congress used the annual certification procedures embedded in law since 1986 as a means to monitor and challenge the White House and other countries with regard to their efficacy in controlling drug trafficking. The 1986 Omnibus Act contained a provision that required the president annually to certify to congress whether countries involved in the drug trade were cooperating fully with the United States. If the president decertified a country, he would have to stop aid, vote against loans in the international development banks, and impose trade sanctions, unless he declared it in the national interest not to do so. If the president certified a country, congress had a 30-day period to assess and reverse that decision by means of a joint resolution. This certification policy proved to be an annual source of tension in the relationship between the United States and Mexico.[26] In 1996, the certification debate in the U.S. Congress was particularly heated and offensive to Mexican public officials and institutions. In 1997, the scandal provoked by General Gutiérrez Rebollo's connection to drug traffickers subjected Mexico to two episodes of certification during the same year.

In order to break these noxious cycles, the two governments created bilateral institutions to help them coordinate the anti-drug campaigns. In February 1995, the attorneys general from the United States and Mexico founded the Plenary Group on Law Enforcement to outline strategies to expedite information exchanged and anti-drug legal cooperation between the two countries. The Plenary Group meets four to five times per year.[27] More important, in March 1996, in part in response to the U.S. congressional debate over Mexican drug cooperation certification, the United States and Mexico established a cabinet-level forum for policy coordination: the High Level Contact Group for Drug Control (HLCGDC).[28] In subsequent years, this entity would meet in plenary session approximately twice per year. In May 1997, the two governments published the *United States–Mexico Bilateral Drug Threat Assessment*. The joint threat assessment was the first ever; hitherto, the United States had diagnosed the issue unilaterally, as, on its own, did Mexico. The joint assessment made it possible to develop collaboration between experts in both countries and helped to deepen political collaboration. It served as the basis for the *Declaration of the U.S.–Mexico Alliance Against Drugs*, issued by Presidents Clinton and Zedillo also in May 1997 during a bilateral presidential summit in Mexico City. This declaration sketched a binational strategy to which both countries contributed.[29] In February 1998, the two governments issued the *U.S.–Mexico Bi-National Drug Strategy;* working groups followed up to develop performance measures of effectiveness in its implementation.

The HLCGDC was the first entity created at the highest level of both governments to coordinate and manage bilateral security relations from the policy to the operational level. It marked the end of the strategy of abnegation and the flowering of a bandwagoning alliance, no longer hindered by Cold War-related disagreements over Central America. Its establishment was a culmination of the process of dismantling Mexico's attempts to impede, deter, and limit direct U.S. influence and activity on security matters in Mexico, and a prelude to further steps toward the same end, to wit:

1. Mexico agreed in July 1996 to deploy personnel for a Bilateral Border Task Force to cooperate with its U.S. counterparts; it agreed to training in the United States for these task force members. The first full course of training was completed in August 1997. Bilateral Border Task Forces had not existed before.

2. Mexico agreed to establish a bilateral working group for military issues generally, including counter-drug cooperation. At the United States' request, it agreed to training for Mexican navy and other anti-narcotics forces within its armed forces. Some 300 Mexican military officers were trained in fiscal year 1996; another 1,500 were trained in Fiscal Year 1997. Mexico agreed to coincidental maritime operations between the U.S. coast guard and the Mexican navy. Heretofore, as already shown, military-to-military relations were virtually nonexistent.

3. Mexico agreed to standard operating procedures for permitting U.S. ships and aircraft to enter Mexican territory to conclude detection and monitoring missions. Flexible refueling and overnight stay procedures were formalized. Prior to this agreement, Mexico had required a 30-day advance request and diplomatic clearance for overflight, refuel, and overnight stay for U.S. ships and aircraft in counter-narcotics missions.

4. The United States delivered, and Mexico accepted, dozens of UH-1H helicopters and spare parts to improve the mobility of Mexican security forces for manual drug eradication and move troops engaged in operations against traffickers. The first 20 helicopters were delivered in November 1996, and another 28 in July 1997. Eventually, 73 helicopters would be delivered. Mexico also approved another 12 resident U.S. law enforcement agents and granted consular immunity for 22 more Border Task Forces. Mexico had not hitherto accepted U.S. equipment for counter-drug operations, and it had strictly limited the number and activities of U.S. law enforcement agents.

The significance of these agreements for counter-narcotics results was unclear, however. As the 1990s closed, the U.S. government believed that Mexico remained the principal transit route for up to 60 percent of the South American cocaine sold in the United States. Both the volume of cocaine seizures (measured in metric tons) and the number of counter-narcotics arrests per year during 1996 to 1999, that is, the years under the HLCGDC, were substantially lower than in 1992 to 1993, for example.[30]

Not all of this bilateral cooperation went smoothly, moreover. Consider the case of the UH-1H helicopters.[31] The U.S. government had lobbied the Mexican government to improve military-to-military collaboration; warily, the Mexican armed forces had resisted. In the mid-1990s, President Zedillo and Foreign Minister José Angel Gurría sought to induce the Mexican armed forces to improve their collaboration with the U.S. armed forces; one way to do so was to accept the UH-1H helicopters from the United States. Under long-established U.S. laws wholly unrelated to U.S.–Mexican relations, the helicopters could not be donated, however. They could only be leased; yet, the United States has never asked to take back the equipment it has loaned to other countries, because such equipment is usually war surplus, often obsolete and no longer in use by the U.S. military. The UH-1H helicopters were about 30 years old, dating from the Vietnam War. The Mexican army remained suspicious, nonetheless, that the United States would take the equipment back and, therefore, invested little in the maintenance and operation of these helicopters. But because these helicopters were old, the Mexican army did have normal problems of repair and some difficulty in finding repair pieces. The Mexican army's suspicion was fueled by U.S. specifications that the helicopters had to be used only for counter-narcotics, not counterinsurgency operations. These U.S. specifications, in turn, showed that the U.S. government, too, was suspicious of the Mexican government and especially of the Mexican army.

In 1998, the U.S. General Accounting Office found that airplanes, helicopters, and ships sent to Mexico by the United States were often inoperable, inadequate, and certainly ineffective.[32] This helped to explain why Mexican counter-narcotics operations were often ineffective. Mexico, too, reached the same conclusion. In April 1998, the Mexican National Defense Ministry grounded 72 U.S.-donated UH-1H helicopters that had been assigned to counter-narcotics operations. Having explored possible repair options, the ministry decided that such maintenance would not be cost-effective and, in late 1999, decided to return the aircraft to the United States. The United States agreed to take back all the helicopters, repair 20 of them, and ship these back to Mexico. But as soon as the last helicopter left Mexico, the Mexican government announced that it wanted none back. The U.S. Department of Defense was furious, believing that this was an example of bad faith and breaking a commitment. In December 1999, Mexico purchased 73 Cessna (TXT) 182 Skylab airplanes for reconnaissance and drug plantation eradication operations to replace the returned helicopters.[33]

Moreover, notwithstanding the decisive changes in Mexican strategy, the U.S. government still believed that corruption in Mexico remained widespread, that drug violence continued to increase, and that major traffickers had become bolder in challenging the Mexican state. One manifestation of this persistent view was the insistence of members of the U.S. Congress to micro-monitor Mexico's use of the equipment and training it had received through this bilateral cooperation—a degree of intrusion that Mexico found unacceptable.[34] Mexico's security alliance with the United States was not protecting its interests, but the entanglement was stronger than ever.

Mexico did succeed in placing some items of particular concern on the bilateral agenda. Mexico got the U.S. government to discuss firearms trafficking as a major threat to international security; work began in 1997 to increase information sharing, investigative training, and binational coordination in investigations on this issue. Mexico requested that U.S. export licenses for firearms and munitions be reduced from four years to one year and that the U.S. government should monitor firearms exports more closely.[35]

Above all, Mexico valued the trend toward the institutionalization of relations with regard to counter-narcotics operations. As Mexico's foreign secretary, Rosario Green, put it in November 1999, her government hoped that this process of institutionalization and cooperation would be deepened. Specifically, Mexico hoped that both governments would work to "avoid surprises," compartmentalize segments of the relationship so that a deterioration in one arena would not affect others, and "agree to disagree sometimes" so that some specific disagreement would not jeopardize the overall relationship.[36]

As is inherent in a bandwagoning strategy between unequals, however, Mexico unwillingly had to put up with "surprises"—namely, unilateral U.S. actions that violated their presumed alliance and the newly institutionalized coordination. On May 18, 1998, the U.S. attorney general informed her counterpart that the U.S. Customs Service and the U.S. DEA had concluded a covert operation, begun in 1995, code-named Casablanca. The United States had arrested 22 Mexican bank officials from 12 Mexican banks, issued 100 arrest warrants, and confiscated $35 million, two tons of cocaine, and two tons of marijuana. Eventually, some $110 million was implicated in Operation Casablanca. These are small amounts, however, given the huge drug trafficking business and the scope of the U.S. effort. Nonetheless, the United States willingly put its "alliance" with Mexico at risk. The United States had kept Operation Casablanca secret from its Mexican ally, even during the two years following the foundation of the HLGCDC. The Mexican government was furious. It lodged an official diplomatic protest. It noted that Operation Casablanca was a flagrant U.S. violation of the very international and bilateral agreements that the United States had promoted.[37] Mexico launched an investigation of U.S. agents who operated in Mexico without authorization. (In the end, the Mexican government closed its investigation of U.S. agents involved in Operation Casablanca, alleging that it had no evidence.)[38] President Clinton expressed public "regret that better prior consultation had not been possible in this case."[39] Under bandwagoning, weaker states tolerate illegitimate actions by the dominant ally.

As Mexico deepened its security alliance with the United States, it had to permit greater U.S. influence and activity within Mexico. Inherent in a security alliance with the United States was greater Mexican insecurity with regard to the United States.

COUNTERINSURGENCY AND DOMESTIC SECURITY: IS THERE A U.S.–MEXICAN ALLIANCE?

On January 1, 1994, the Zapatista National Liberation Army (EZLN) opened an insurgency in the state of Chiapas. It quickly seized six towns. On January 12, 1994, the Mexican government offered a cease-fire, the EZLN accepted, and the fighting ended.[40] The army launched an offensive against the Zapatista guerrillas only one other time in February and March 1995. As Raúl Benítez has stated, "unlike Latin American countries that confront guerrillas with military measures, the Mexican government sought a cease fire as a unique pragmatic means to avoid the unforeseeable outcome of military confrontation."[41] The Zapatista insurgency had not ended as the century ended, however. The Zapatista insurgency posed also the question whether the United States and Mexico would be allies in a counterinsurgency war.

The Mexican military and police proved remarkably unprepared for this insurgency. Hundreds of Zapatistas had been training for years. The army came in for sustained criticism for all sorts of mistakes, ranging from its manifest lack of sufficient information to allegations about human rights abuses in the conduct of military operations.[42]

In response to the Zapatista insurgency, the Mexican defense budget rose by several hundred million dollars and U.S.–Mexican indirect military cooperation became closer. Mexican spending on operations, maintenance, procurement, and construction increased sharply. In 1994, Mexico ordered and received 263 armored personnel carriers from Belgium and another 28 from the United States. Mexico also increased its rate of acquisition of helicopters from the United States. Mexico had ordered four UH-60 helicopters in 1992 (delivered in 1995). It accepted a U.S. donation of 73 UH-1H helicopters in 1995 (delivered in 1997), although, as noted earlier, it would return them in late 1999, replacing them with a purchase of 73 Cessna 183 Skylab planes. Much of this equipment would be dedicated to anti-drug operations. The Mexican army formally increased its counterinsurgency cooperation with the Guatemalan army at the border. Mexico also accepted increased U.S. International Military Education Training (IMET) assistance; this U.S. contribution rose from less than a half-million dollar budget in fiscal year 1995 to $9 million in 1998. The United States justified this increased budget as part of the counter-narcotics effort; Mexico understood it, of course, as assistance to its national security.[43] In 1997, the number of Mexican officers in the United States for military training was 305 in the School of the Americas, 260 in the Inter-American Air Forces Academy, and 192 under other IMET arrangements, for a grand total of 757 officers—a stunningly high number by historical standards.[44] And, as noted earlier, twice that number was under training in 1997 under the counter-narcotics budgets. Also in 1997, the U.S. government provided about $37 million in military assistance to Mexico.[45] Although the number of Mexican officers being trained in the United States declined somewhat as the century closed, clearly the new intensity and level of cooperation in military training in the late 1990s were unprecedented and more institutionalized. As Stephen Wager has written, the Mexican government long pursued "an overt and deliberate effort to build nation-alist armed forces free of foreign influences."[46] In the 1990s, that long-held strategy was gradually eroding.

More generally, the Mexican National Defense Ministry greatly increased the training of Mexican officers in other countries. From 1978 to 1998, 4,173 Mexican officers were trained to some extent outside Mexico; 62 percent of these received their international training just between 1995 and 1998. Although the United States trained by far the largest number of Mexican officers, Mexico sent its military officers for training to 20 other countries, including Russia, Ukraine, and Israel.[47] In a similar spirit, although Mexico in the 1990s came to rely much more on U.S. military equipment, it continued to purchase some military equipment from other sources. For example, in the mid-1990s, it purchased 36 Russian heli-copters that operated successfully.[48]

In June 1996, a new security shock was felt. The Popular Revolutionary Army (EPR) began operations in the states of Guerrero and Oaxaca. Unlike the Zapatis-tas, whose military operations have been confined to regions within the state of Chiapas, the EPR ranged more widely and never reached a truce with the Mexican government. From 1996 to 1999, the EPR carried out 44 recorded attacks in seven states and Mexico City.[49] The Mexican government responded to the EPR through a combination of army and police actions, with much lower reliance on political instruments than marked its response to the Zapatistas.[50]

The Mexican government's response to the Zapatista and other insurgencies was quick and rational. The government improved its military capacities, but it also rec-ognized that the army was probably not up to the rigors of an effective and sustained counterinsurgency operation. Nor did the Mexican government wish to be involved in protracted warfare against guerrillas. Thus the government halted the counterin-surgency campaign against the Zapatistas quickly and, in the years that followed, emphasized strategies of political and security containment, isolation, and targeted disruption that gradually weakened the Zapatistas' grip on the popular imagination. The government combined this military strategy with intermittent efforts to nego-tiate a political solution with the Zapatistas; many of these efforts were aimed at weakening popular support for the insurgents. Moreover, the increase in defense expenditures was reasonable, given the size of the Mexican economy: the military budget increase in response to the Zapatista insurgency amounted to one-tenth of one percent of gross domestic product (GDP). By the end of the 1990s, Mexican defense expenditures were about eight-tenths of one percent of GDP.[51]

A more complex question is the role of the Mexican armed forces during the process of democratization. As Raúl Benítez has noted thoughtfully, democratization in southern South America and in Central America contributed directly to demilitarization. Yet, in Mexico, the process of democratization was associated with the breakdown of order in parts of southern Mexico and with instances of social protest in other parts of the country. As a result, the size of the armed forces grew approximately from 166,000 in 1986 to 232,000 in 1999.[52]

The election in 2000 of opposition candidate Vicente Fox posed delicate questions concerning civil-military relations. The armed forces quickly pledged institutional loyalty to the new president, but political jockeying broke out within the military as some officers sought to displace other officers with deep ties to the defeated Institutional Revolutionary Party (PRI) regime. In that context, President Fox upheld the tradition of appointing an officer as defense minister even though some civilians argued that Mexico should have a civilian defense minister.

Relations between the armed forces of the United States and Mexico remained weakly institutionalized during the 1990s apart from counter-narcotics cooperation. The Joint Mexican–United States Defense Commission was still moribund. The most active contacts were private meetings between the chiefs of the respective armies and calls by the U.S. navy to Mexican ports. Perhaps the most institutionalized military relationship occurred at the border where, since 1990, the border commanders have met in formal conference every year.[53] The United States did not wish to be drawn into counterinsurgency operations, but it found it difficult to control the Mexican military's absorption of equipment and training that was delivered for counter-narcotics efforts.

For the Mexican armed forces, in turn, nationalist suspicions remained strong and had been kept alive by the misunderstandings between the two military institutions that dotted the 1990s. One risk to the future U.S.–Mexican military-to-military relations is that instances such as the joint mismanagement of the incident regarding UH-1H helicopters would revive Mexican military nationalism, thereby impeding collaboration in other areas.

CONCLUSION

By the end of the 1990s, the U.S.–Mexican bilateral relationship featured many more security problems than at any time since the days of the Mexican revolution. Both governments were committing more resources to security aspects of their relationship than they had since the 1930s. The days when Mexico could pursue a cost-effective abnegation strategy that served well its security interests were long past. Instead, Mexico faced major problems of drug traffic–related violent crime and various persisting albeit small-scale insurgencies across a swath of its southern states.

During the 1990s, the extent of high-level official U.S.–Mexican consultation and confidence building over security issues improved. It became most institutionalized over drug trafficking; it was more frequent albeit still mainly personal between the top leaders of the respective military institutions. Consultation and confidence building was much less effective between the lower-level security officers of the two governments. There was no formal cooperation over counterinsurgency operations in Mexico, but Mexico derived some benefit to advance these security objectives from its greater security collaboration with the United States. Nonetheless, none of these relationships was particularly reliable. U.S. Congressional efforts to oversee closely Mexico's use of U.S. security resources soured the bilateral relationship. And the U.S. Operation Casablanca's open violation of bilateral agreements governing drug traffic cooperation set back the prospects for deeper and effective binational institutionalization.

One outcome was clearer, however. As the new millennium opened, the United States had greater influence over Mexican security policy than ever. There were more unhindered U.S. security operations in Mexico than at any time since General Pershing's pursuit of Pancho Villa. Mexican sovereignty had been penetrated by its own consent.

More worrisome was the greater disposition of the United States to use force unilaterally at or near the border to cope with the normal problems of neighborliness. The United States and Mexico had been a pluralistic security community, as noted earlier, for most of the second half of the twentieth century. And yet, as the century closed, the United States greatly beefed up its border patrol with heavier weapons, more high-technology equipment, and more personnel. U.S. drug traffic agents demonstrated again and again their belief that they could act in Mexico without the prior consent of Mexican authorities. And in the mid- and late 1990s, U.S. troops were actually deployed on the border to stop illegal migration and drug trafficking. As the Marine Corps commandant, General Charles Krulak, put it while explaining why he opposed pulling U.S. troops off patrols of the U.S.–Mexican border: "There is a role for the United States military to support and defend the Constitution against all enemies foreign and domestic."[54]

THE EFFECT OF

INTERNATIONAL

INSTITUTIONS IV

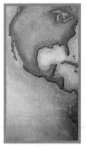

AS WORLD WAR II ENDED, THE UNITED STATES EMERGED AS THE world's premier military, economic, and political power. It exercised global leadership and obtained the international cooperation of other states. For example, in the mid- and late 1940s, the U.S. government led in the creation of new international institutions. These included the United Nations (UN), the International Monetary Fund (IMF), the World Bank (formally known as the International Bank for Reconstruction and Development), the General Agreement on Tariffs and Trade (GATT), and, in the Americas, the Organization of American States (OAS). The United States also built various international military institutions, some of which were discussed in the previous chapter.

Mexico addressed many international issues through its involvement in these international institutions, or through its explicit decision not to join or to be relatively inactive in others. These institutions, therefore, were important arenas for U.S.–Mexican relations, and they were key for the remaking of U.S.–Mexican relations from the late 1980s until the end of the twentieth century. This chapter focuses on the evolution of U.S.–Mexican relations in these institutions. The first section is dedicated to two political organizations: the UN and the OAS. The second section addresses the economic organizations, namely, the World Bank, IMF, and GATT, and the emergence of the North American Free Trade Agreement (NAFTA).

We argue that Mexico followed a relatively consistent foreign policy position in the UN and OAS, which could be characterized as pragmatic autonomy relative to the United States. The Mexican government used the multilateral political institutions to calibrate the extent of desired and feasible Mexican independence from the United States. This foreign policy matched closely Mexican security strategies evident from the 1940s to the 1980s, discussed in the previous chapter. This aspect of Mexican foreign policy responded directly to the positions of each incumbent president. The autonomy obtained was greater in the 1970s and early 1980s, albeit at a substantial cost to the quality of relations with the United States; there was, however, greater pragmatism, more accommodation to the United States, and consequently less autonomy in the 1990s. Mexico's periods of greatest autonomy coincided with the erosion of the international economic arrangements created in the aftermath of World War II, especially evident in the breakdown of the system of relatively fixed exchange rates in the early 1970s and in the growing U.S. disenchantment with GATT. In the 1980s, Washington's disenchantment with GATT allowed North American trade regionalism to emerge, leading to NAFTA's birth in the 1990s.

We also argue that the IMF, the World Bank, and the U.S. government enabled Mexico to pursue its chosen economic development strategies both from the 1940s to the early 1980s and again from the late 1980s through the end of the century. These external agents constrained the economic choices of the Mexican government only to a limited degree during these years. Only during the severe economic crisis in Mexico in the early to mid-1980s did the U.S. government, followed by the IMF and the World Bank, push the Mexican government into changing the course of economic policy. Yet only when Mexican government elites themselves reached this conclusion—midway through the administration of President Miguel de la Madrid (1982–88)—did the pace of domestic and international economic change accelerate in Mexico. Thus, Mexican elites enjoyed substantial discretion in their relations with the international political and financial institutions most of the time after World War II, except for the early 1980s when the Mexican economic debacle permitted external actors to help reshape the course of Mexican foreign and domestic economic policy.

Finally, we argue that the decision of the Mexican and U.S. governments to institutionalize their trade relations was a practical solution to a central problem in their bilateral relations. The key issues were how to foster the growth of trade, adjust both economies to such dynamic growth, and fashion the means for the peaceful resolution of disputes. Both countries entered the 1980s without a single comprehensive trade treaty to assist them to cope with these challenges. The burst of institutional creativity from the mid-1980s to the early 1990s, culminating in NAFTA, successfully addressed these practical issues, unleashing the growth potential of their bilateral trade.

MEXICAN PARTICIPATION IN MULTILATERAL POLITICAL INSTITUTIONS

Mexico's position in the UN and the OAS could be characterized as pragmatic autonomy. These two organizations enabled Mexico to develop a foreign policy that sought to retain substantial independence from the United States, while aligning firmly with the United States on the fundamental issue of Soviet activities in the hemisphere. For example, in the OAS in 1962, Mexico decided not to break off relations with Cuba but, nonetheless, to condemn the Soviet military presence in Cuba during the missile crisis.

Pragmatic autonomy sought to reconcile two competing positions in Mexican policy toward the United States—namely, the belief in the value of non-intervention and the need to accommodate fundamental U.S. interests. Mexico consistently voted for non-interventionist policies in the UN and the OAS, albeit not necessarily intending to vote against the United States. Mexico employed its juridical expertise to inform its decisions in the multilateral organizations. For example, Mexico's decision in 1962 to vote against Cuba's expulsion from the OAS was based on a detailed juridical argument that the inter-American accords did not contain a clause to apply such a sanction.[1] This autonomy, however, has always been constrained by the need to accommodate the United States and confront it only when necessary. Therefore, Mexico has chosen to stand for election to the UN Security Council only infrequently to avoid having to make decisions at odds with U.S. preferences. As stated by Ambassador Andrés Rozental: "Mexico has been a member of the Council just on two occasions (1946 and 1980–81) mainly because the prevailing view has been that most issues considered there are not important enough to Mexico to risk frictions with the great powers, especially not with the United States."[2]

Mexico's continued effort to balance U.S. power within the UN and the OAS has been demonstrated by its persistent call to redistribute the authority within the organizations. Mexico tried to mitigate what it saw as excessive U.S. weight in the multilateral organizations by calling for greater pluralism. Mexico advocated the creation of international economic institutions as well as new rules to bridge the differences between rich and poor nations. Indeed, when the OAS was created in 1948, Mexico had expected that the United States would contribute resources to encourage economic and social development within the hemisphere.[3]

Mexico's policies evolved from pragmatism and moderation during the first years after World War II to a search for greater autonomy in the 1970s and early 1980s. In these latter years, Mexican initiatives in the UN engendered frequent conflicts with the United States, particularly during Mexico's membership in the UN Security Council in 1980 to 1981. During the 1990s, there was greater convergence between the United States and Mexico. Both governments displayed greater pragmatism. The United States was free from combating communism. Mexico became less combative and less vociferous in expressing its differences with the United States. Mexico dropped its search for an economic order tilted to benefit underdeveloped nations once it fully embraced market-oriented economic policies. An example of U.S.–Mexican post–Cold War convergence in the UN system was their collaboration in the Salvadoran peace process in the early 1990s.

The United Nations

Mexico participated actively in the establishment of the UN, even presenting its own proposal for the organization's design. From the outset, Mexico opposed the concentration of power in the five permanent members of the UN Security Council at the expense of the General Assembly, but it understood that this compromise would be necessary to found the UN. Nonetheless, Mexico continued to insist on a more democratic UN decision-making process. Even on the fiftieth anniversary of the UN, Manuel Tello, Mexico's UN representative, still argued for a better balance of power between the assembly and the council.[4]

Mexico's experience in the UN differed substantially from that of other Latin American countries. Mexico was elected to the UN Security Council in 1946, but thereafter it would not stand for election again until 1980. This pattern contrasted sharply with those of Brazil, Argentina, Colombia, and Panama, all of which were elected frequently to the UN Security Council.[5] This Mexican decision served two purposes. First, it avoided unnecessary confrontation with the United States. Second, it was consistent with Mexico's principled judgment about the flawed design and functioning of the Security Council. Mexico preferred to focus on its self-assigned role of developing and improving the UN.[6] In 1980 and 1981, however, Mexico was elected to the Security Council. This adventure climaxed the period known in Mexico as "the active foreign policy"—namely, the presidencies of Luis Echeverría (1970–76) and José López Portillo (1976–82).[7]

These two presidents embarked on an assertive foreign policy to enhance Mexico's standing in world affairs, especially among underdeveloped nations. In order to diversify its relations and mitigate its excessive reliance on the United States, Echeverría sought to increase Mexico's international ties. During his six-year term, the number of countries with which Mexico had bilateral diplomatic relations rose from 67 to 131.[8] To combat global poverty and dependence, Echeverría advocated a New International Economic Order (NIEO). He actively promoted the NIEO through the Charter of the Economic Rights and Duties of States, a Mexican motion approved by the UN General Assembly in late 1974 by a vote of 120 to 6 (with 10 abstentions); the highly industrialized nations either abstained or voted nay.[9] In 1975, with Venezuela as a co-sponsor, Echeverría moved to establish the Latin American Economic System (SELA). Echeverría's frenzied foreign policy and assertions of sovereignty and economic independence provoked stinging criticism within Mexico. The business community became suspicious both of Echeverría's statist domestic economic policy and his active foreign policy. The end of his term was tainted by a serious economic crisis.

In the mid-1970s, Mexico discovered that it had vast petroleum reserves. Crude oil began to flow in large quantities during López Portillo's presidency. This oil bonanza helped Mexico to overcome the economic crisis inherited from the previous administration, but it also prompted the government to continue an activist foreign policy. López Portillo promoted various multilateral initiatives in the UN, especially with respect to energy, migration, multinational corporations, and global development issues. In 1979, Mexico proposed a World Energy Plan to the UN General Assembly.[10] Yet Mexico refrained from joining the Organization of Petroleum Exporting Countries (OPEC) even though it would at times coordinate its petroleum policies with those of OPEC countries.

This activist foreign policy, seeking autonomy from the United States, had direct implications for Mexico's UN participation because it led its government to seek election to the Security Council. Alas, the traditional argument that participation in the Security Council would provoke frictions with Washington proved correct. In January 1980, the United States presented a resolution to the Security Council to impose economic and diplomatic sanctions on Iran in retaliation for the taking of hostages at the U.S. embassy in Tehran. Mexico abstained on the grounds that developments in Iran did not jeopardize international security.[11] In 1981, South Africa's involvement in Angola provoked Mexico to co-sponsor a UN Security Council resolution imposing sanctions on South Africa, but the United States vetoed the measure.[12] Most U.S.–Mexican conflicts in the Security Council, however, revolved around the situation in the Middle East. Mexico condemned almost every Israeli action in Lebanon, the Gaza Strip, Iraq, and Syria, while the United States supported Israel. Consider, for example, the case of the Israeli decision in 1981 to expand its jurisdiction over the Golan Heights. Mexico and the United States were at odds regarding Resolution 497, which sought to impose economic sanctions on Israel. Mexico backed the resolution; the United States vetoed it.[13]

In contrast, the administration of Carlos Salinas de Gortari (1988–94) decided in 1991 that Mexico should forgo the opportunity to stand for election for the two-year UN Security Council seat traditionally reserved for a Latin American country. By this time, Mexican policy had reverted to the pragmatism that had once characterized it to avoid unnecessary frictions with the United States. A Mexican diplomat from the 1990s argued, for example, that it was inconvenient for Mexico to participate in the UN Security Council because Mexico was actively promoting the council's reform. Consequently, "we avoided being judge and jury."[14]

Mexico's voting coincidence with the United States in the UN General Assembly provides another way to assess U.S.–Mexican relations in the UN. According to the U.S. State Department, Mexico's voting patterns were once closer to Cuba's than to such U.S. allies as Canada, the United Kingdom, and Israel.[15] In 1985, only 14.5 percent of Mexico's UN General Assembly plenary votes matched those of the United States, while 6.2 percent of Cuba's votes and 69.8 percent of Canada's matched U.S. voting patterns (see Table 4.1). The voting coincidence between the United States and Mexico rose in the 1990s to a peak of 41.6 percent in 1995, the year after NAFTA went into effect, though it dropped to 32.8 percent in 1998. Mexico's voting record in the 1990s resembled Brazil's more than Cuba's.

Mexican diplomat Miguel Marín-Bosch cautions against excessive reliance on the official U.S. analysis, however. He argues that the U.S. State Department's accounting, shown in Table 4.1, is skewed because it fails to take abstentions and absences into account; it exaggerates the extent of agreements and disagreements thereby.[16] Marín-Bosch's findings are reported in Table 4.2. These alternative calculations present a stronger basis for the claim that Mexico retained substantial autonomy from the United States even in the 1990s.[17] In both tables, Mexico is shown to have become closer to the United States in the 1990s than in the 1980s,

TABLE 4.1

**Mexican Voting Coincidence with the United States
in UN General Assembly Plenary Votes
(percentage)**

	1985	1986	1987	1988	1989	1990
Mexico	14.5	17.6	14.8	11.1	12.0	15.2
Israel	91.5	89.9	80.0	91.0	87.5	88.2
United Kingdom	86.6	88.2	79.2	83.1	77.8	81.8
Canada	69.8	72.0	67.9	62.8	60.9	60.0
Argentina	16.4	16.4	12.4	10.0	13.3	12.5
Brazil	16.0	18.5	13.3	8.8	11.8	14.9
Cuba	6.2	6.8	5.0	4.2	5.9	9.2

Source: U.S. Department of State, *Voting Practices of the United Nations—1998*. Note: These data do not take into account abstentions and absences.

TABLE 4.2

**Mexican Voting Coincidence with the United States
in UN General Assembly Plenary Votes
(percentage)**

	1981–1988	1989	1990	1991	1992	1993	1994	1995	1996
Mexico	26.5	21.7	23.8	25.0	28.4	32.8	37.5	39.1	39.1
Canada	63.7	52.2	56.0	58.3	57.4	60.2	62.5	62.3	62.8

Source: Adopted from Miguel Marín-Bosch, *Votes in the UN General Assembly* (Boston: Kluwer Law International, 1998), 212.

but the inclusion of abstentions and absences attenuates the difference between the two time periods. The NAFTA spirit of cooperation between the United States and its North American neighbors had only a modest impact in the UN arena.

The Organization of American States

The Cold War had a comparably significant impact on Mexico's position and actions at the OAS and related inter-American political and security institutions, although it caused Mexico to adopt different tactics. Mexico developed a defensive and disengaged role in the OAS during the Cold War. In the post–Cold War period, however, Mexican diplomats worked to strengthen the OAS to fulfill its potential for improving inter-American relations.[18]

In the 1950s and 1960s, Mexico confronted the U.S. anti-communist agenda in the OAS more than in any other multilateral organization. The cases of Guatemala, Cuba, and the Dominican Republic convinced Mexico that the OAS had become a U.S. tool to undermine governments that Mexico deemed reformist but that the United States perceived as communist threats.[19] For example, the

TABLE 4.1 continued

1991	1992	1993	1994	1995	1996	1997	1998
20.6	20.3	28.3	33.3	41.6	38.8	37.5	32.8
87.5	92.3	93.5	95.2	97.0	95.0	93.3	94.1
79.6	73.6	80.0	84.4	85.1	79.1	79.4	74.5
69.6	60.0	66.7	74.5	73.5	73.0	71.7	67.3
41.0	44.4	53.8	67.9	68.8	60.7	56.1	50.0
22.7	22.7	28.0	39.1	41.1	42.4	42.6	41.7
7.8	11.1	6.3	15.5	14.5	14.5	13.2	15.9

Tenth Inter-American Conference, held in Caracas in 1954, served to legitimize the coup against the reformist constitutional government of President Jacobo Arbenz in Guatemala. The Inter-American Conference held at Punta del Este in 1962 suspended Cuba from its membership in the OAS. And in 1965, the OAS created an inter-American peace force to legitimize U.S. military intervention in the Dominican Republic after it had already occurred. Consequently, Mexico lost interest in the OAS and behaved defensively within it.[20] In the 1980s, Mexico avoided OAS attempts to find peaceful solutions to the wars in Central America. Instead, in 1985, it helped to create the Contadora Group along with Colombia, Venezuela, and Panama. Contadora was an alternative forum for some Latin American governments to collaborate in the search for peace in Central America.

In 1982, the inter-American response to the war between Argentina and the United Kingdom over the Falkland/Malvinas Islands further diminished the value of the institutions of the regional system for Mexico. Mexico believed that the Inter-American Treaty for Reciprocal Assistance (TIAR, also known as the Rio Treaty) should have been applied to this war. Signed in 1947, one year prior to the establishment of the OAS, the treaty states that an external aggression against one member of the inter-American region would be considered an aggression against the entire hemisphere. The United States supported the United Kingdom, not Argentina. The United States did so, however, because Argentina had been the aggressor and thus TIAR did not apply under international law.

In the post–Cold War period, Mexico came to believe that the OAS increased its credibility and capacity to play a positive role. The OAS benefited from the Cold War's end, in Mexico's view, because U.S. anti-communist pressures subsided (except with regard to Cuba), enabling OAS members to defend the principle of non-intervention more effectively. Thus, in 1989, most OAS members refused to support the U.S. invasion of Panama. In 1996, the OAS General Assembly approved a resolution to demand a juridical assessment of the "Helms-Burton" Act (the U.S. statute that codifies and expands U.S. unilateral sanctions on Cuba); only the United States voted against.[21] The Cold War's end also allowed the UN Security Council to overcome the gridlock once caused by the East-West confrontation. This change facilitated joint UN–OAS operations in Haiti in the early and mid-1990s.

Two additional factors, in the official Mexican view, help to explain the strengthening of the OAS in the 1990s: Canada's entrance into the organization in 1990 and the Summits of the Americas held in Miami in 1994 and in Santiago de Chile in 1998.[22] The Canadian presence in the OAS helped to counterbalance the overwhelming U.S. presence; it also energized the OAS to address such issues as environmental protection, democracy, and human rights. The Miami Summit of the Americas established OAS mandates concerning trade, human rights, and illegal drugs. The OAS became the leading organization for the advancement of a regional trade agreement known as Free Trade for the Americas. At the Santiago Summit of the Americas, the Inter-American Drug Abuse Control Commission (CICAD), created in 1986, was given the mandate to develop a means for the multilateral assessment of inter-American cooperation in the fight against drugs.[23] Mexico participated in this CICAD work because it was an alternative to one of the major irritants in U.S.–Mexican relations in the 1990s—namely, the U.S. unilateral process known as drug certification, which was discussed in the previous chapter.[24]

Mexico's renewed interest in the OAS was accompanied, however, by a heightened caution toward the organization's increased focus on promoting democracy and human rights.[25] As we will see in chapter six, in the 1990s, Mexico became concerned that the inter-American human rights and democracy-promotion institutions might interfere within Mexico itself. Mexico thus accepted the resolutions to help with the restoration of democracy in Haiti in 1991, Peru in 1992, and Guatemala in 1993, but it did not participate in the missions to those countries. In 1993, Mexico agreed to take to the UN Security Council the question of military intervention to restore democracy in Haiti because it continued to believe in the primacy of the UN over the OAS. Nevertheless, Mexico did not agree to the Security Council's decision to intervene militarily in Haiti, because, in Mexico's view, the interruption of democracy in that country did not threaten international peace and security.[26]

THE PERMISSIVE WORLD FINANCIAL SYSTEM

Mexico participated in the creation of the new international financial institutions in the mid-1940s, the IMF and the International Bank for Reconstruction and Development (better known as the World Bank). Mexico's delegation at the UN Monetary and Financial Conference, held in Bretton Woods in July 1944, submitted a successful amendment to the Articles of Agreement that assigned to the World Bank the dual tasks of reconstruction and development. This amendment

expanded the Bank's focus from simply rebuilding Europe to promoting development in Latin America and the other underdeveloped regions.[27] Mexico's real
weight in the emerging financial institutions, however, would be minimal. Twenty
of the forty-four countries represented at Bretton Woods were from Latin America and the Caribbean, but they accounted for less than five percent of the Bank's
voting power.[28] The United States would become the largest shareholder.

The Bretton Woods system flourished in the 1950s and 1960s and achieved one
of its main goals, the reconstruction of Western Europe. Japan, too, emerged as a
financial powerhouse. The prosperity of those years coincided with Mexico's early
strategies of import substituting industrialization (ISI); from the mid-1940s to
about 1970, ISI delivered steady gross domestic product (GDP) growth of about
six percent annually. Mexican finances, nevertheless, experienced some turbulence
during this period. Mexico requested loans from the IMF five times; twice in the
1940s, twice in the 1950s, and once in the 1960s. Mexico received a significant
number of World Bank loans in the 1950s and 1960s. Most of these loans were
either for electrical power development or for irrigation projects.[29]

Mexico's reliance on the World Bank increased in the 1970s as its economy
entered a more difficult phase of ISI. Both presidents Echeverría and López Portillo challenged the United States, distancing Mexico City from Washington
through their emphasis on ISI rather than the market-oriented policies that the
United States promoted. However, both presidents developed close relations with
World Bank President Robert McNamara. McNamara came to the Bank in 1968
with a special interest in combating poverty. The World Bank's financing of Mexico greatly expanded during Echeverría's term, funding programs in rural
development, seaports for tourism, and steel complexes. By the end of Echeverría's presidency, the World Bank's share in Mexico's long-term debt reached
almost 17 percent, while Mexico's share in total World Bank loans was above ten
percent.[30] At the end of Echeverría's administration, however, chronic budget
deficits resurfaced; inflation accelerated. The peso was devalued in August 1976.
(Henceforth, there would be an economic crisis at the end of each presidential
term for the next two decades, a cycle that not even the enactment of NAFTA was
able to break.) Mexico signed a three-year Extended Fund Facility agreement for
about $1 billion with the IMF and, as usual, the U.S. Treasury provided a stabiliza-
tion fund.[31]

López Portillo inherited a country in economic crisis though with a hidden
asset: the newly discovered oil reserves. The rapid exploitation of oil reserves
allowed Mexico's economy to grow at unprecedented levels, over eight percent in
1978, 1979, and 1980.[32] Mexico became the darling of foreign commercial banks,
and it borrowed very heavily. During its oil boom, Mexico called the shots with
the IMF, the United States, and the foreign commercial banks. The relationship
with the World Bank remained friendly. All of these international actors failed to
assess the risks of the oil boom and acquiesced in Mexico's heavy indebtedness.

Mexico's foreign debt quadrupled during Echeverría's term from $6.6 to $25.9 billion, of which 75 percent was public debt. At the end of the López Portillo administration in 1982, Mexican debt reached $85 billion.[33] Commercial banks then turned their backs on Mexico. To make matters worse, oil prices declined sharply in 1981. In 1982, the Mexican economy was in a free fall; the peso was devalued twice in an attempt to stabilize the economy. In August, Mexico was on the brink of declaring a debt moratorium. Mexico's treasury minister, Jesús Silva Herzog, went to Washington to meet with IMF Managing Director Jacques de la Larosière, Chairman of the Federal Reserve Board Paul Volcker, and U.S. treasury secretary Donald Regan. Silva Herzog returned to Mexico with a rescue package.[34] The United States assisted in ameliorating this Mexican financial crisis as it had in previous crises since 1947. In 1982, however, U.S. officials took a tough stand vis-à-vis Mexican financial needs. Out of the $2 billion that Mexico received from the treasury, one billion was lent against future oil purchases. U.S. officials also attempted to set the price of the Mexican oil $5 per barrel below market prices. President López Portillo did not accept these terms at first, but his bungled negotiating skills left Mexico with a lower oil-price equivalent at the end of the bargaining than at the beginning. In the end, the U.S. loan had an implicit interest rate of about 38 percent.[35] The U.S. loan was complemented by $1.85 billion from members of the Bank for International Settlements and by $4 billion from an IMF three-year Extended Fund Facility. The IMF agreement conditioned its loan on the commercial banks' lending $5 billion to Mexico.[36]

From the summer of 1982 to the spring of 1990, external indebtedness became the number one problem for the Mexican economy. Mexico's relations intensified with the IMF, the World Bank, and U.S. financial officials, both in the treasury and the federal reserve. Most of the ideological clashes between the IMF, U.S. Treasury officials, and Mexican officials ended, however, with the inauguration of de la Madrid in December 1982. President de la Madrid's economic team believed in the economic discipline of the market; it was more receptive to IMF and U.S. Treasury advice. Yet the social impact of the austerity was draconian; during President de la Madrid's term, real wages fell 41.5 percent.[37]

Despite the new administration's fiscal and budgetary discipline, Mexico needed debt relief. In 1985, the Baker Plan, named after U.S. treasury secretary James Baker, provided some help. It called for more funds, contingent on further structural reforms; it acknowledged that debtor countries needed GDP growth in order to service their debts. The Baker Plan fell short of providing debt relief, but it was a step in the right direction. In 1989, the Brady Plan, named after President George Bush's (1989–93) secretary of the treasury, Nicholas Brady, explicitly incorporated the goal of debt service relief. Mexican officials welcomed the initiative. The debt negotiations that followed were complicated, taking almost a year to reach agreement. When Secretary Brady came to Mexico City in March 1990 to sign the new deal, Mexico was ready to move beyond the debt issue. As put by

José Angel Gurría, Mexico's leading debt negotiator, it removed from the Mexican psyche the burdensome problem of debt. It prepared the country for the new decade of free trade.[38]

President Salinas accomplished remarkable economic reforms, with NAFTA as the crowning glory of his administration, as we will soon see. Yet, for the fourth consecutive time at the end of a presidential term, Mexico suffered a financial panic either just before or just after a presidential transition. Twenty days after President Ernesto Zedillo's inauguration (1994–2000) on December 1, 1994, a financial crisis erupted; the peso's value plunged. In response, the Clinton administration prepared a financial package of unprecedented size, over $50 billion. In comparing the U.S. response to the Mexican crises of 1982 and 1995, Nora Lustig concluded that the first U.S. rescue package barred Mexico from participating in international financial markets for seven years while the second succeeded in bringing Mexico back into these markets in less than seven months. These results were related to the size and the conditions of the packages and the effectiveness of Mexican macroeconomic policies. The 1982 deal was designed to prevent Mexico from defaulting; the 1995 package was large enough for Mexico to address its liquidity crisis.[39] NAFTA had created a special bond between the Clinton and Zedillo administrations, which allowed the White House to prepare a huge financial package and sidestep congressional opposition.

From GATT to NAFTA,
from Multilateralism to Regionalism

NAFTA enabled the two countries to bridge the wide chasm between them. Indeed, few things were more divisive in U.S.–Mexican relations during the post–World War II period than trade policy. The United States was the principal international force behind trade liberalization and the strongest supporter of GATT. Mexico developed a highly protectionist trade regime and did not join GATT until four decades after its creation. These divergent trade policies were a constant source of mutual recrimination and misunderstanding between the United States and Mexico. As stated by Sidney Weintraub, "trade conflict between the United States and Mexico was the result of these two world views. As long as both countries prospered, as they did until the 1970s, the conflict was muted."[40] In the 1980s, the U.S.–Mexico trade arena became a battleground: from 1980 to 1986, Mexico faced 35 U.S. countervailing duty and anti-dumping suits seeking to impose U.S. penalties on Mexico for unfair trade practices.[41]

Paradoxically, while Mexico was opening its economy in the mid-1980s, the United States was showing signs of increased protectionism in response to what it considered unfair trade practices by many foreign countries. U.S. trade policy was also moving away from an almost exclusive reliance on multilateralism toward regionalism; the United States was increasingly frustrated with the lack of progress in the Uruguay Round of GATT. This crossroads between U.S. and

Mexican trade policy would eventually lead to the creation of NAFTA. Mexican officials soon realized that the only way to secure the country's new outward-oriented economy was to seek a special agreement with its number one market, the United States. From 1985 to 1990, Mexico would attempt to achieve this special accommodation through bilateralism and multilateralism and, after 1990, through North American regionalism, NAFTA.

Ironically, for a country that had been the driving force behind trade liberalization since the creation of GATT in 1948, protectionism gained popularity in the United States in the early 1980s. Throughout the Cold War, free trade and peace had been seen as intertwined. Washington promoted free trade both as a tool for obtaining greater economic efficiency and increasing national wealth and also as the optimal way to guarantee international peace.[42] This vision was obscured in the 1980s by U.S. accusations of unfair trading practices and the rising fears that U.S. dominance in the world economy was eroding. U.S. public officials watched as the country's trade deficit grew to $160 billion in 1987.[43] U.S. manufacturers' share of world markets dropped sharply from the golden years of the 1950s.[44] The emergence of many new competitors, such as the newly industrializing countries, also challenged U.S. economic might. In addition, the dollar was seriously over-valued, which undermined U.S. competitiveness in international trade and contributed to the soaring trade deficits of the early 1980s, even though the economic recession of those years should have caused a trade surplus.[45]

Rising U.S. protectionism was manifested primarily through contingent measures and, to a lesser extent, new non-tariff barriers such as voluntary export restrictions and orderly market agreements. Ambassador Rodney Grey, a Canadian trade negotiator, coined the phrase "contingent protection" to describe anti-dumping and countervailing duty measures and other import-limiting actions imposed on a semi-discretionary basis.[46] Contingent measures, employed mostly by U.S. producers facing foreign competition, either limited imports or imposed supplemental duties in retaliation for what were considered unfair trade practices. U.S. legislation proscribes two trade practices as unfair: foreign subsidies and dumping. From 1980 to 1984, there was an explosion in the volume of U.S. unfair trade cases: 249 countervailing duties and 217 anti-dumping investigations were initiated.[47]

Both trade remedy legislation and non-tariff barriers had an impact on U.S.–Mexican bilateral trade in the 1980s. U.S. producers used countervailing duties repeatedly against Mexican products. As argued in chapter two, Mexican exports were an easy target for U.S. investigations, because U.S.–Mexican trade relations were literally in a state of anarchy. When Mexico started to dismantle its protectionist economy in 1985, no bilateral agreement had governed trade relations between the two countries since 1950 (except for a textile and apparel sectoral accord in 1975) when the Reciprocal Trade Agreement of 1943 expired. Moreover, Mexico was not a member of GATT, nor a signatory of its anti-dumping–countervailing duty code.

Mexico would not become a member of GATT until 1986. In addition to dozens of complaints of unfair trading practices, the U.S. imposition of a voluntary export restriction on Mexican steel in 1985 exemplified Mexican vulnerability; this voluntary export restriction limited Mexican exports to the United States to 0.32 percent of U.S. domestic consumption.[48]

Mexico had its own complex system of trade barriers. De la Madrid launched an unprecedented trade opening during the last three years of his presidency, moving Mexico away from licensing to limit import quantities and imposing high tariffs for most products. In 1985, when this unilateral trade opening began, 83.5 percent of all imports required licenses.[49] There were ten tariff levels; the maximum tariff was 100 percent and the production-weighted average tariff was 23.3 percent. By 1988, Mexican import licenses settled at about 20 percent and the production-weighted tariff fell to 11 percent.[50]

Mexico began to adhere to international trade rules created by GATT and sought a special agreement with the United States to bring order to the chaotic bilateral trade. Mexico sought to create a trade framework to keep the U.S. market open to Mexican exports. It used both multilateralism and bilateralism. From 1985 to 1989, Mexico and the United States signed six bilateral trade agreements. This strategy commenced with the 1985 agreement on subsidies and countervailing duties and ended in 1989 with the Legal Trade Framework II. In 1986, Mexico joined GATT, which was an unequivocal sign for U.S. trade officials that their southern neighbor was committed to further economic liberalization.[51] At the end of 1987, one of de la Madrid's economic reformers, Budget Minister Salinas, became the Intstitutional Revolutionary Party (PRI) presidential candidate, ensuring that Mexican economic reforms and adherence to international trade rules would remain on course.

In the meantime, U.S. trade policy was undergoing a dramatic change. The trade policies of regionalism and multilateralism were no longer seen as being diametrically opposed. This new co-existence of multilateralism and regionalism in U.S. trade policy proved to be a key element in opening the way to NAFTA.[52] Three reasons explain this change in U.S. policy. The first was dissatisfaction with the pace of multilateral trade negotiations. Most analysts agree that the United States became dissatisfied with the progress of trade liberalization in negotiations during GATT's Uruguay Round, begun in Punta del Este, Uruguay, in 1986.[53] This was especially true in areas where GATT had no real track record, such as trade in services, protection of intellectual property, and investment matters, and in those sectors in which GATT had achieved minimum results such as agriculture.[54] Some U.S. officials came to believe that more rapid progress could be made in regional negotiations than in the multilateral framework. In 1990, an influential Washington-based trade analyst, Gary Hufbauer, wrote: "If sector agreements are the 'dark prince' of trade policy and retaliation is the 'avenging angel,' then free trade areas are the 'white knights.'"[55]

The second important motivation for the U.S. shift toward trade regionalism was the consolidation and expansion of the European Community under its new name, the European Union. Regionalism in Europe was deepening and expanding to other countries. The traditional argument used to persuade the U.S. Congress that the United States should not embark on regional trade agreements because of their inherent discrimination against non-members was weakened by the realities of the European Community's discrimination against imports from the United States. The European Community had become an enormous exception to GATT's bedrock principle of non-discrimination. By definition, European regionalism could not be purged by U.S. insistence on multilateralism. Influential voices would be heard in Washington arguing that North American regionalism would be the best way to deal with European regionalism.

A third and final reason for GATT's weakening was, ironically, the enormous success of the previous multilateral tariff-cutting negotiations. The Kennedy Round (1964–67) and the Tokyo Round (1973–79) successfully lowered tariffs among the industrial nations. The weighted-average tariff reductions on manufacturing products made by major industrial countries in the Tokyo Round amounted to 34 percent of the pre-Tokyo Round rate, leaving an actual weighted-average tariff of 4.7 percent.[56] So long as the trade policy issues revolved around the traditional barriers—tariffs and quotas—GATT negotiators could focus on limiting and reducing them. This made for efficient GATT rounds because national delegations had clear and measurable targets, such as tearing down tariffs, to negotiate with each other. The remarkable success with post–World War II tariff reductions forced negotiators in the Uruguay Round to move to the more difficult issues of non-tariff barriers, which were "harder to negotiate, more intertwined with issues of domestic policy and national sovereignty, and not well defined in the original GATT rules."[57]

The first example of the shift in U.S. trade policy was seen in U.S.–Canadian affairs. From 1985 to 1988, the Canada–United States Free Trade Agreement (CUSFTA) was negotiated; it went into effect in January 1989.[58] Canada typically received about 20 percent of U.S. exports; it was by far the largest U.S. trade partner. The investment and production links between the two countries are also extensive. U.S. foreign direct investment (FDI) to Canada was second only after the United Kingdom. While U.S. foreign direct investment in the United Kingdom was concentrated in the banking and financing sectors, in Canada half of U.S. foreign direct investment was in manufacturing.[59] More important, the composition of merchandise and services traded between the United States and Canada pointed to economic integration: approximately 70 percent of Canadian exports to the United States were either intra-firm trade (40 percent) or the result of licensing and strategic alliances (30 percent) between Canadian and foreign corporations.[60]

The Bush administration came to office in 1989 with a clear international trade policy objective: to conclude the Uruguay Round of GATT. Although Mexican president Carlos Salinas would come to Washington in June 1990 to seek a free trade agreement, the Bush administration continued to consider the Uruguay Round far more important as a trade policy issue, and it was scheduled to conclude before NAFTA talks could seriously begin. Carla Hills, U.S. trade representative, the leading U.S. official for international trade negotiations, was committed to completing this major round of GATT. She had, nevertheless, inherited the central problem of the Uruguay Round: trade in agricultural products. Since the Kennedy Round, the United States had struggled with the Western European governments to reduce protection and lower their subsidies in agriculture.

Ironically, it would take a trip to a European capital, as it did for Carlos Salinas almost a year earlier, to convince Carla Hills that North American regionalism ought to be one of the Bush administration's top trade priorities. The Uruguay Round ministerial meeting in Brussels in December 1990 had given rise to great expectations in U.S. trade policy circles for overcoming the impasse on agriculture. As stated by I. M. Destler, "Carla Hills flew to Europe, accompanied by a large inter-agency support cast, observers from the Hill, and a strong delegation of U.S. private-sector representatives."[61] Contrary to U.S. expectations, the agriculture negotiations could not even reach a consensus on the framework for an agreement. This induced Hills to shift her policy priorities from the multilateral Uruguay Round of GATT to the regional agreement, NAFTA.

The decision to seek a free trade agreement was momentous for Mexico. It is widely believed that President Salinas reached the decision to seek a trade accord with the United States during a trip to Davos, Switzerland, in February 1990.[62] After little more than a year of promoting foreign investment and economic opportunities in Mexico, Salinas, as we argued in chapter two, realized that Western Europe was absorbed with its own transformation and that of Eastern Europe. Japan was focused on economic growth in East Asia. Latin America could not provide Mexico with the necessary foreign investment or markets. Salinas's trade strategy was redirected toward Mexico's northern neighbor.

ACHIEVING A NEW PARTNERSHIP:
THE NORTH AMERICAN FREE TRADE AGREEMENT

NAFTA was made possible, therefore, by several concurrent changes in the policies of the United States and Mexico. The United States abandoned its almost exclusive reliance on multilateralism by entering into free trade with Canada, its most important trade partner. Mexico, following the costly breakdown of its import substitution development model in the early 1980s, unilaterally reduced its import barriers and pursued a series of market-opening reforms, which accelerated when Salinas entered office in December 1988. An astute tactician, President Salinas presented NAFTA as a way to lock in these market-oriented reforms. Mexican resolve also motivated U.S. policy-makers.[63]

TABLE 4.3

Mexican Exports by Main Destinations, 1970–1994

(million dollars)

Year	Total	U.S.	EEC[a]	Other Europe[b]	LAC[c]	Japan	Other[d]
1970	1,290	880	101	33	172	79	35
1980	15,132	9,892	1,047	1,420	1,077	681	1,015
1985	21,866	13,388	2,245	1,849	1,269	1,719	1,398
1990	24,273	17,151	2,965	269	1,762	1,291	834
1991	27,120	18,345	3,292	228	2,131	1,241	1,883
1992	27,521	18,911	3,252	252	2,784	879	1,453
1993	51,886	43,068	2,600	228	3,058	700	2,231
1994	60,833	51,688	2,756	n.a.	3,180	798	2,404

(percentage of total)

Year	Total	U.S.	EEC[a]	Other Europe[b]	LAC[c]	Japan	Other[d]
1970	100	68.2	7.8	2.5	13.3	6.1	2.7
1980	100	65.3	6.9	9.3	7.1	4.5	6.7
1985	100	61.2	10.3	8.4	5.8	7.9	6.4
1990	100	70.6	12.2	1.1	7.3	5.3	3.4
1991	100	67.6	12.2	0.8	7.8	4.5	6.9
1992	100	68.7	11.8	0.9	10.1	3.2	5.3
1993	100	82.9	5.1	0.4	5.9	1.3	4.3
1994	100	84.9	4.4	n.a.	5.1	1.3	3.3

[a] Since 1990, Spain, Greece, and Portugal are included because they became a part of the European Economic Community (EEC).
[b] Includes Eastern Europe.
[c] Latin American and Caribbean countries.
[d] Includes Canada as a main "other" market.

Source: 1990–1993 *Revista de comercio exterior*. Based on data from the work team INEGI-SHCP-Banco de México for the information on foreign trade; Banco de México, *Informe anual, 1994*.

Mexico's approach to U.S. trade policy in 1990 resembled Canada's in 1985. Mexico as well as Canada relied heavily on the U.S. market. In 1990, the year NAFTA negotiations were launched, 70 percent of Mexican exports went to the U.S. market and 65 percent of Mexico's imports came from the United States. Japan was Mexico's second most important single-country market for exports, but it accounted for only 5.3 percent of total exports. The European Union and Latin America, each as a whole, received 12 and 7 percent of total exports respectively (see Tables 4.3 and 4.4).

President Salinas's initiative to negotiate a free trade agreement with the United States made it imperative for Canada to join. If the United States and Mexico were to form a free trade area, a hub-and-spoke arrangement would

TABLE 4.4

Main Sources of Mexican Imports, 1970–1994
(million dollars)

Year	Total	U.S.	EEC[a]	Other Europe[b]	LAC[c]	Japan	Other[d]
1970	2,463	1,567	633	n.a.	142	105	16
1980	18,832	12,604	2,583	874	1,072	1,018	681
1985	13,212	8,970	1,744	605	634	735	524
1990	26,963	17,428	4,175	842	1,365	1,279	1,872
1991	38,184	25,032	5,712	1,052	1,970	1,783	2,636
1992	48,138	30,365	7,109	1,168	2,380	3,025	4,091
1993	65,367	46,467	7,288	1,140	2,546	3,369	4,556
1994	79,375	54,749	8,498	1,413	2,984	5,080	6,626

(percentage of total)

Year	Total	U.S.	EEC[a]	Other Europe[b]	LAC[c]	Japan	Other[d]
1970	100	63.6	25.7	n.a.	5.8	4.3	0.6
1980	100	66.9	13.7	4.6	5.7	5.4	3.6
1985	100	67.9	13.2	4.6	4.8	5.6	4.1
1990	100	64.6	15.4	3.1	5.1	4.7	6.9
1991	100	65.5	14.9	2.7	5.2	4.7	6.9
1992	100	63.1	14.8	2.4	4.9	6.3	8.5
1993	100	71.1	11.1	1.7	3.9	5.1	7.1
1994	100	68.9	10.7	1.8	3.8	6.4	8.3

[a]Since 1990, Spain, Greece, and Portugal are included because they became part of the European Economic Community (EEC).
[b]Includes Eastern Europe.
[c]Latin American and Caribbean countries.
[d]Includes Canada as a main "other" market.
Source: 1990–1993 *Revista de comercio exterior*. Based on data from the work team INEGI-SHCP-Banco de México for the information on foreign trade; Banco de México, *Informe anual, 1994*.

result: the United States would be the hub and Canada and Mexico the spokes. Only the United States would have free trade across North America.[64] Since 1985, Canada had already concluded that protection of its domestic market was no longer optimal and that a free trade agreement with the United States would not destroy the nation's sovereignty. Canada thus joined the NAFTA negotiations.

NAFTA differed from other integration agreements because it brought together an economic powerhouse—the United States—and an emerging economy, Mexico's, one-twentieth the size of the U.S. economy, along with Canada's midsized economy. (The European Union has GDP disparities among its members, but they are narrower than those that prevail in North America.) Each country came to the negotiation with fixed constraints. Mexico's reluctance to open its oil sector barred serious negotiations about oil. The United States was not willing to discuss difficult issues such as labor migration. These limitations explain, in part, NAFTA's shortcomings. There were other concerns over sovereignty. For example, in 1985, Canada decided that creating a customs union with the United States was not politically viable because it would have unacceptably subordinated Canada's sovereignty by imposing the U.S. external tariff and trade policy on Canada; Canada consequently preferred to negotiate a free trade agreement. When Mexico suggested free trade negotiations with the United States, and Canada chose to join the process, CUSFTA was used as a model for the new agreement. There may one day be a common external tariff among the three countries—the competitive pressures for external tariff equalization are substantial—but a common commercial policy among the three countries was not feasible in the 1990s.

The NAFTA text is a massive document of thousands of pages. Much of the verbiage deals with exceptions to free trade. In some sectors, such as textiles and apparel, agriculture, and automotive goods, complex and lengthy legal contortions were needed to move from protection on a global scale to less onerous restrictions applicable to trade within North America. The FTA formula, with the separate external tariffs of the three countries, necessitated rules of origin. For example, the complicated rules of origin for automotive goods required a regional value content of 62.5 percent to make a vehicle eligible for free trade under NAFTA.[65] This, by itself, need not be a major impediment to trade among the three countries, but the rules have been used in some sectors to divert trade from other countries.

Mexico received more quantitative and qualitative exemptions and reservations than the United States and Canada combined.[66] Energy is a fixed exemption; most other Mexican reservations are transitory. This was the case in automotive trade and investment and the provision of financial and other services, regarding which Mexico gradually would open its doors to free trade during the 1990s and would continue to do so in the new century's first decade. In addition, Mexico's tariff reduction schedule was slower to drop than those of the other two countries. These differences in trade and investment openings reflected Mexico's less-developed status coupled with a more closed economy on the eve of the transition to NAFTA. For the most part, all three countries will be at equal levels in trade liberalization when the transition period ends in 2005, although some agricultural products will remain exempted until 2010.

Each country retains its own laws and procedures for anti-dumping and countervailing duty measures, which contradicts the "free" trade promise. Yet chapter nineteen of NAFTA, based on chapter nineteen of CUSFTA, creates a unique procedure for dispute settlement. NAFTA signatory countries may use binational panels to challenge final anti-dumping and countervailing duty measures issued by the investigating administrative authorities of the other NAFTA parties. These panels act as a substitute for judicial review by the national courts of the three countries.[67] The inclusion in NAFTA of a mechanism with these characteristics represented a significant change in Mexico's long-standing nationalist legal tradition of the Calvo Doctrine.[68] According to the doctrine, foreigners are not entitled to any rights or privileges that are not available to nationals; thus, foreigners must submit any claims involving property to the jurisdiction of their national courts and waive any right of diplomatic protection from their governments.

President Salinas managed the politics of NAFTA carefully. In spring 1990, when a *Wall Street Journal* article alerted Mexicans that the Salinas administration was seeking a free trade agreement with the United States, President Salinas convoked a "National Consultation on Mexico's Worldwide Trade Relations" through the Mexican Senate.[69] The consultation concluded that Mexico "should incorporate into the new trade and economic world trends."[70] It served to legitimate the president's policy of actively seeking a free trade agreement. The Mexican people took the change in the economic relationship more or less in stride, whereas the U.S. population did not.

Ironically, the United States would become more concerned about sovereignty during the NAFTA debate. First, some U.S. citizens feared what presidential candidate Ross Perot called the "giant sucking sound": that jobs and manufacturers would race across the border to low-wage Mexico. Second, the dispute-settlement procedures for dealing with countervailing duty measures and anti-dumping penalties invoked fears of multinational bureaucracies, because chapter nineteen removes these issues from U.S. courts and places them in the hands of trilateral panels.

NAFTA, unlike the European Union, deliberately did not create a central executive arm. The negotiators wanted to minimize the political content of the agreement. As stated by Sidney Weintraub, "there is an abhorrence of establishing new institutions in the U.S. executive branch and the Congress."[71] The Canadian and Mexican governments had the same preference. All governments worried about how NAFTA institutions would affect sovereignty, as well as about the costs of staffing such institutions. This limited perspective on institution building explains NAFTA's skeletal organizations as compared to the European Union's. Even the NAFTA commission is simply composed of the commerce secretaries of each of the three countries, who meet periodically; these three officials retain for themselves the final decisions over the implementation of the agreement in the absence of a trilateral mechanism.

The NAFTA document established many working groups to deal with the most salient issues for the operation of the agreement. Each of the 20 chapters of NAFTA implies the creation of at least one committee or working group. These groups address such matters as the compatibility of industrial standards; safety and other standards for trucks and buses, which in a number of years will have the right to travel throughout the three countries; sanitary standards for foodstuffs; simplification of rules of origin; acceleration of customs clearances; facilitation of trade in agriculture, textiles and clothing, and telecommunications; and clearing procedures for financial relations among the three countries.[72]

Two U.S. concerns present from the outset of the NAFTA negotiations—the environment and labor standards degradation—would be addressed in 1992 upon the election of a Democrat, Bill Clinton, to the White House. The election defeat of President Bush, with whom the Salinas administration had established a close relationship, forced the Mexican government to learn afresh the new U.S. president's priorities and specific pressures. During the presidential campaign, Clinton had conditioned his support of NAFTA to the negotiation of parallel accords "until we have reached additional agreements to protect America's vital interest" addressing environmental and labor concerns of important groups in the United States.[73]

The North American Agreements on Environmental and Labor Cooperation (NAAEC and NAALC, respectively) were designed to placate the concerns of the labor and environmental movements. The agreements have some "teeth," but not very sharp or effective ones. There are provisions to impose trade penalties for consistent violations of each of the three nations' own standards. But the procedures for imposing penalties are so long and cumbersome that it is almost impossible to impose sanctions under either agreement. For example, if an alleged instance of non-enforcement of a labor law were to arrive at the last stage of the process, which means suspension of NAFTA trade benefits, more than a thousand days would have to pass from the moment of the submission to the imposition of sanctions. The goal of these complicated dispute settlement processes is to encourage independent voluntary improvement in enforcement through the international exposure of problems. Five years after the implementation of the parallel agreements, no trade sanction has been imposed on environmental or labor grounds.

The parallel agreements established institutional arrangements over and above those of NAFTA. Each agreement created a commission, which has a permanent secretariat. The environmental secretariat is located in Montreal; the labor secretariat was initially located in Dallas and moved to Washington, DC, in 2000. The commissions have developed two main functions: to foster cooperation among the participant countries and to oversee the enforcement of labor laws. The implementation of the agreements during their early years helped the United States and Mexico to develop the extent and quality of their official environmental and labor relations from loosely coordinated associations to fairly structured relationships. There are numerous environmental and labor cooperative actions taking place among the three North American countries; the trinational exposure of environmental and labor regulation increased the costs of noncompliance. This is especially true for Mexico, which has been the target of the highest number of non-enforcement allegations in environmental and labor affairs.

Consider two examples. In May 1997, the U.S.-based Human Rights Watch and the International Labor Rights Fund along with the Mexican Democratic

Lawyers' Association filed a complaint under the NAALC. They alleged a pattern of widespread Mexican government–tolerated discrimination against women who were being subjected to pregnancy tests and denied employment if they tested positive. Companies named as offenders through their Mexican operations included General Motors, Zenith, Siemens, Thomson, Samsung, Sanyo, Matsushita, Johnson Controls, and other multinational firms. The U.S. National Administrative Office investigating under NAALC found evidence of discrimination. In March 1999, Mexican government officials acknowledged the unlawfulness of employee pregnancy testing under Mexico's own laws and the failure of Mexican officials to halt it. Mexico promised new regulations and better enforcement. Some firms voluntarily changed their practices in response to the unusual visibility.

In July 1998, a coalition of independent Mexican union, farmworker, and human rights groups backed by the United Farm Workers, the Teamsters, and the International Labor Rights Fund filed a complaint under NAALC alleging the failure of U.S. law to protect workers' rights in the entire Washington State apple industry. This transnational coalition of labor unions and human rights activists from both sides of the U.S.–Mexican border made effective use of NAALC, generating a great deal of attention in both countries. In May 2000, the secretaries of labor for the United States and Mexico reached an agreement on addressing these labor union complaints. It was the first agreement that covered both U.S. and migrant agricultural workers. Thus, though the NAALC relies principally on gathering information and making it public, its capacity to shame firms and governments that break established law is already significant. It has brought about an unprecedented increase in exchange, communication, and collaboration among labor rights advocates in the NAFTA countries.[74]

CONCLUSION

The NAFTA negotiations represented an extraordinary period of cooperation among the three participating nations. Because of the comprehensive nature of the negotiations, the teams representing the three countries encompassed an array of officials that went well beyond trade authorities to include members from each country's most prominent business organizations. The creation of NAFTA revolutionized U.S.–Mexican relations in three fundamental ways.

First, it changed the governmental perception of bilateral affairs in both Washington and Mexico City from a relationship based on geography to an economic partnership. The U.S. and Mexican governments, for the first time in history, would foster economic integration instead of repressing it. This would lead U.S. and Mexican policy-makers to abandon ideological rhetoric and adopt a more pragmatic conflict-solving approach.

Second, the NAFTA negotiations and the agreements themselves institutionalized inter-governmental trade affairs and, to a lesser extent, environmental and labor affairs. Institutionalization was an effective response to shared practical problems. These agreements would order inter-governmental affairs, establish a set of rules, and create a series of commissions and working groups. Institutionalization in trade affairs improved policy decision-making by providing abundant information and increasing governmental technical capacities. This institutionalization spilled over into the Mexican government, which began to pursue a strategy of formalizing its dialogue and establishing consultation mechanisms in other difficult and complicated bilateral issues such as migration and drug trafficking.

Third, the NAFTA negotiations intensified contacts between government officials from all three levels (federal, state, and local) and also between business executives, non-governmental organizations, and media organizations. This intensification of contacts deepened the decentralization of bilateral relations, loosening the respective central governments' management of U.S.–Mexican affairs, a topic to which we turn in the next two chapters. NAFTA improved coordination between trade officials on both sides of the border; it also increased the burden on those officials who must deal with intensified trade and economic transactions at the border itself.

This chapter showed how the political and economic institutions of the post–World War II era shaped U.S.–Mexican relations, and how the emergence of North American regionalism in the 1990s substantially altered governmental behavior in economic matters. During the Cold War, bilateral disagreements were hard to resolve. This was especially the case in trade policy, where Mexico and the United States lacked institutionalized means for dispute resolution. The international financial system ordinarily enabled Mexico to pursue its preferred economic strategy, but it was the locus of severe U.S.–Mexican disputes in the early 1980s. Coinciding with the end of the Cold War, U.S.–Mexican economic relations converged and blossomed into a new regional institution, NAFTA. This economic convergence had important spillovers in other areas of the bilateral relationship. It returned Mexican diplomats to their tradition of not seeking election to the UN Security Council in order to avoid a possible source of friction between Mexico and the United States. More important, it fashioned new means in old international political and economic institutions for the two governments to coordinate their policies over many issues and even, at times, to differ more amicably over important topics.

THE DOMESTIC CONTEXT
FOR FOREIGN POLICY
DECISION-MAKING V

THE RELATIONS BETWEEN THE UNITED STATES AND MEXICO WERE
not limited to the interactions between the two national governments. Bilateral
relations also featured two other levels of interaction. First, the respective bureaucracies within the national governments as well as the U.S. Congress developed
their own independent impact on bilateral relations. Second, the respective societies
(including political parties, the mass media, various non-governmental organizations, and, more generally, public opinion) affected and constrained the general
course of relations. This multilayered tapestry had long been an aspect of
U.S.–Mexican relations, but it acquired new significance in the 1990s as economic
ties deepened, political interactions multiplied at all levels, societal interchanges
became more complex, and the North American Free Trade Agreement (NAFTA)
was enacted and implemented.

This chapter analyzes the changing domestic context for foreign policy
decision-making in the United States and Mexico in the 1990s and how the two
national governments managed their bilateral relations. It focuses on the
processes of decision-making in the United States and Mexico, and on public opinion, the mass media, and political parties. We note the difference between the
traditionally fragmented U.S. policy process and the centralized decision-making
in Mexico. We analyze the dynamic nature of U.S.–Mexican relations in the
1990s, especially its decentralization at all levels and the multiplication of the
number of non-governmental and governmental actors involved. This greater
depth and intensity in bilateral relations in the 1990s intensified the fragmentation of the U.S. policy process with regard to Mexico, while it edged Mexican
foreign policy processes toward decentralization.

The way both governments approached each other was also transformed; the
respective coordinating roles of the State Department and the Foreign Affairs
Ministry diminished in the 1990s. As a result, the presidents of the two countries
had to take the leadership to initiate some aspects of policy coordination through
their increasingly frequent meetings. In addition, the remarkable and persisting
goodwill in public opinion attitudes toward the "other" country in both the
United States and Mexico provided a reservoir of political stability to fashion

national policies toward each other through the 1990s. Public support for good relations mattered for three reasons. The partisan environment in Mexico became more contentious because of the heightened importance of opposition parties, as Mexico's domestic democratization proceeded. The U.S. mass media adopted a more critical attitude with regard to Mexico. And bipartisan support for internationalism (including free trade) declined in the United States. Another source of stability derived from the gradual convergence of foreign policy views among the three principal political parties in Mexico. By the late 1990s, the main parties agreed on the broad outline for Mexican policies toward the United States, including support for NAFTA, even if they differed on important specific points.

THE DECISIONAL CONTEXTS

The U.S. and Mexican political systems have been only superficially similar; there is a clear contrast in the amount of power wielded by the executive. The Mexican presidency was generally able to centralize decision-making and conduct disciplined policies toward the United States; the White House has been much more constrained. The U.S. Congress limits the president's powers particularly on domestic issues and those foreign policies with domestic implications.[1] Moreover, there are numerous examples in the history of U.S.–Mexican relations when a U.S. agency, such as the Customs Service or the Drug Enforcement Administration (DEA), pursued its own agenda toward Mexico with considerable independence from the preferences of the White House. From 1995 to 1998, for example, the U.S. Customs Service implemented an undercover sting operation, called Casablanca, targeting money laundering in Mexico (see discussion in chapter three). This operation was conducted without the prior knowledge of the White House and the State Department. Its results were announced in May 1998, infuriating Mexican officials as well as U.S. secretary of state Madeleine Albright. Albright protested to her cabinet counterpart, Robert Rubin, who had nominal authority over the U.S. Customs Service.[2]

The lack of a coordinated foreign policy process in the United States in the 1990s was not a new phenomenon nor did it just affect Mexico. Already in 1947, the United States established the National Security Council precisely because the State Department could not control the U.S. national security bureaucracy. The State Department's loss of foreign policy power proceeded apace in the decades that followed as other "domestic" U.S. government agencies developed their own international relations. Certainly with regard to Mexico, since the 1950s, the State Department has had to compete with other U.S. agencies to shape U.S. policy; by the 1990s, all major U.S. agencies had their own representative in the U.S. embassy in Mexico City.

In Mexico, in contrast, the president and his Foreign Affairs Ministry maintained a virtual monopoly over foreign policy through the end of the 1970s. The Mexican Constitution grants the president extensive foreign policy powers. As in

the United States, the Mexican Senate advises the president on world affairs, rati-
fies treaties, and approves the appointment of ambassadors; the Mexican Senate
also approves the appointment of consuls-general. However, in practice, the senate
merely rubber-stamped the president's foreign policy decisions in part because no
opposition party member was elected to the senate before the end of the 1980s.
Even at the end of the 1990s, the official Institutional Revolutionary Party (PRI)
held 77 of 128 seats (60 percent) in the senate.[3] Moreover, Mexico's relative economic autarchy and defensive foreign policy from the mid-1940s until the early
1980s made it easier for the president, his closest associates, and the diplomatic
service to conduct Mexican foreign policy.[4] In sharp contrast with the harsh
debate over NAFTA created in the U.S. Congress, NAFTA breezed through the
Mexican Senate virtually with no debate.

The remarkable centralization of Mexican foreign policy–making toward the
United States began to break down in the 1980s. During Miguel de la Madrid's
administration (1982–88), there was a significant split in attitudes toward Washington between the Foreign Affairs Ministry and the Treasury and Commerce
Ministries. The Foreign Affairs Ministry developed a policy in Central America
that confronted Washington (see chapter two). Treasury and commerce, in contrast, wanted to improve cooperation with the United States. The treasury was
involved in lengthy discussions with U.S. officials to renegotiate Mexico's external debt, while the Commerce Ministry negotiated various bilateral trade
agreements and entry into the General Agreement on Tariffs and Trade (GATT).[5]

These decision-making characteristics—Mexico's centralization and U.S. fragmentation—were accentuated by the asymmetrical attention that each
government conferred on the other. In the United States, benign indifference
toward Mexico often accentuated the fragmented nature of U.S. policy-making, as
the earlier example of Operation Casablanca suggests. In contrast, Mexican atten-
tiveness and sensitivity to U.S. affairs reinforced the centralization of decisions.
Foreign policy–making toward the United States, it seemed, was too important to
leave to anyone other than the president. For example, when the United States
invaded Panama in 1989, the Mexican condemnation of the intervention was
released from Los Pinos, the presidential residence. In the United States, foreign
policy decisions are filtered through many officials before they reach the president; in Mexico, foreign policy decisions are often made and announced by the
president himself.

Prior to 1990, the differences between U.S. and Mexican decision-making
processes contributed to important misunderstandings. When a U.S. agency or
even a *Washington Post* article criticized Mexico, there was a tendency in Mexico
to believe that the action was a White House–orchestrated conspiracy. For example, in 1984, President de la Madrid visited Washington for the first time during
his presidency. *Washington Post* columnist Jack Anderson alleged that de la
Madrid was a millionaire with a secret Swiss bank account. Anderson's article

greatly annoyed Mexican officials who believed that there was a leak by a U.S. agency and that the Reagan administration was unable or unwilling to suppress the article.[6] The conspiratorial explanations were grounded in the erroneous belief that, just as in Mexico, every decision in the United States regarding Mexico involved or was approved by the president.

In the 1990s, Mexican officials and diplomats understood the United States better and overcame this conspiracy thinking. Indeed, once Mexican diplomats became aware of the decisional fragmentation in U.S. foreign policy–making, they started to lobby to advance Mexican interests in diverse and dispersed centers for decision making.[7] For example, in the first three months of 1999, the Mexican ambassador to Washington visited more than 20 U.S. legislators from both parties. He was trying to induce the U.S. Congress not to reverse President Clinton's certification of Mexico's cooperation in the war on drugs (see discussion of the drug certification process in chapter three).[8]

More Actors and Issues in U.S.–Mexican Relations

Many of the issues relevant for U.S.–Mexican relations such as immigration, drugs, the environment, and trade have large domestic components. Thus U.S.–Mexican relations have long been called "intermestic," because they involve international and domestic dimensions.[9] Indeed, most U.S. agencies involved in Mexican affairs have a domestic orientation, such as the Immigration and Naturalization Service (INS), the Federal Bureau of Investigation (FBI), and the Environmental Protection Agency (EPA). Since 1980, but especially in the 1990s, this characteristic has become more pronounced. There has been a wider decentralization of bilateral relations. The number of actors involved in bilateral affairs has increased dramatically thanks to an accelerated pace of bilateral economic integration and the globalization of communications and the process of production. Non-governmental organizations (NGOs) have also heightened their activism regarding bilateral issues, as have the state governments at the border (see also the discussion in chapter seven).

Table 5.1 enumerates the most important actors in the bilateral relationship. Non-governmental actors (including business firms, non-governmental organizations, and organized crime) have imparted a new dynamism to bilateral affairs during the last two decades. Among the governmental actors, the executive branches remain the most important, followed by the legislative branches, particularly the U.S. Congress, and then the state governments, courts, and local governments, especially those of the border cities. The mass media also play a role.

Non-Governmental Actors

The ever-expanding interaction between U.S. and Mexican societies reshaped U.S.–Mexican relations. As a result of NAFTA, relations boomed between business executives, firms, and business federations on both sides of the border. Joint

TABLE 5.1

Most Important Actors Participating in the U.S.–Mexico Bilateral Relationship

Category	Members
Non-governmental actors	Business executives
	Business firms
	Business federations
	Non-governmental organizations
	Organized crime
Governmental actors	Executives
Other branches and levels of government	Congress
	State governments
	Courts
	Local governments
Mass media	Newspapers
	Television and radio

ventures became a popular modus operandi for many Mexican and U.S. firms in search of long-term agreements to better operate in a foreign environment. Through these alliances, U.S. firms obtained access to Mexican resources that otherwise would have been unavailable or too costly—and vice versa. In the 1990s, strategic alliances, Hildy Teegen has argued, became the most effective and fastest formula for economic integration.[10] One example is the large Mexican supermarket chain Aurrera, which has a joint venture with U.S.-based Wal-Mart; the consumer who walks into a Mexican Wal-Mart buys products brought by the U.S. firm as well as familiar Aurrera products.

In the 1970s, Mexican NGOs began to develop linkages with U.S. and other overseas-based NGOs, mainly in the human rights arena. During the second half of the 1980s, Mexican NGOs became stronger. In Mexico City, for example, NGOs took the lead in rebuilding the city after a major earthquake in September 1985. The linkages between NGOs on both sides of the Rio Grande flourished as well during the NAFTA negotiations. U.S. environmental NGOs sought alliances with their Mexican counterparts.[11] By the time NAFTA was approved by the U.S. Congress in November 1993, the similarities between U.S. and Mexican environmental NGOs' positions had greatly increased.[12] In the border region, the environmental degradation provided the incentive to strengthen Mexican NGOs and establish linkages with their U.S. counterparts.[13]

Organized crime is also a key actor in bilateral relations, considering that two-thirds of the cocaine and one-fifth of the heroin available in the United States is smuggled through or originates in Mexico.[14] It is difficult to know, however, what forms of bilateral or international associations have been developed among these criminal bands. According to Thomas A. Constantine, U.S. DEA administrator, criminal organizations have become as sophisticated as multinational corporations; Mexican-based criminal organizations, he has argued, are the primary distributors of drugs to U.S. citizens.[15] These bilateral linkages have grown stronger during the last ten years. As the twenty-first century starts, drug trafficking has become the main source of friction between the two governments and, as shown in chapter three, the greatest threat to Mexico's national security.

GOVERNMENTAL ACTORS

The executive branch of both governments became more decentralized during the 1990s as the range of tasks that both national states had to address in their bilateral relations widened. The number of agencies participating in the bilateral relationship increased; the contacts between them grew stronger and more direct. The new buzzword in U.S.–Mexican inter-governmental relations was specialization: experts in telecommunications conversed, while, independently, law enforcement officials on both sides of the border analyzed how to apply the extradition treaty to a particular case. This posed extraordinary problems for coordination between the two governments. The roles of the foreign ministries in coordination declined; only the respective presidents could perform some coordinating tasks effectively.

The diminishing role of the U.S. State Department and the Mexican Foreign Affairs Ministry in U.S.–Mexican relations was one important consequence of this decentralization of inter-governmental affairs. Formally, both state and foreign affairs remained responsible for the coordination of bilateral affairs. The respective foreign ministers headed the Binational Commission, which was the highest formal interstate coordinating mechanism. However, since its origin in 1981, the commission met just once a year, which explained why the day-to-day coordination was increasingly difficult for state and foreign affairs to manage. Moreover, both the U.S. secretary of state and the Mexican foreign affairs minister generally lacked the domestic political clout required for a more effective coordination; they could not lead their fellow cabinet members, who participated in bilateral relations on their own.

The increasing salience of economic matters and the recent dominance of drug-related issues also diminished the roles of the State Department and the Foreign Affairs Ministry. During the 1980s, the restructuring of Mexico's external debt, its entry into GATT, and the negotiation of numerous bilateral trade accords caused the economic agencies to become central players in U.S.–Mexican relations. This trend became more pronounced in the early 1990s, when NAFTA became a priority for both governments.

During the second half of the 1990s, law enforcement agencies emerged as prominent actors in bilateral relations. Numerous U.S. law enforcement and intelligence agencies participated willingly in the war against drugs, in part, because it

TABLE 5.2

U.S.–Mexico High Level Contact Group for Drug Control

Mexico	United States
Ministry of Foreign Affairs	Office of National Drug Control Policy
Attorney General's Office	Department of State
Ministry of the Treasury	Department of Justice
Ministry of Government	Drug Enforcement Administration
Ministry of Health	Federal Bureau of Investigation
Ministry of Defense	Department of Defense
Ministry of the Navy	Department of the Treasury
	U.S. Customs
	U.S. Coast Guard
	Health and Human Services

was one of the few policy areas where budget expenditures continued to increase rapidly.[16] Consider the High Level Contact Group created in 1996 to improve coordination between agencies involved in counter-narcotics on both sides of the border (see also chapter three). By the late 1990s, ten U.S. and seven Mexican agencies participated in it. (Table 5.2 shows its membership and structure.) In that context, the weight of the foreign affairs ministries was diluted.

In the early 1990s, counter-narcotics efforts opened the prospects for sustained interaction between the U.S. Defense Department and the Mexican Defense Ministry, with the former characteristically urging the latter to become more involved in such efforts. During the Cold War, the two militaries cooperated little; this changed dramatically during the second half of the 1990s as shown in chapter three. The growing role of the Mexican military in counter-narcotics had ramifications both domestically and bilaterally. The Mexican military came to confront a worrisome threat to national security; it was no longer relegated to a secondary activity such as disaster-relief efforts. The Mexican military was also exposed to corruption from drug traffickers. In 1997, the head of the Mexican government's counter-narcotics institute, recently retired General Jesús Gutiérrez Rebollo, was found guilty of protecting the most-wanted Mexican drug lord, Amado Carrillo Fuentes. Understandably, this caused a crisis in bilateral affairs. The United States came close to decertifying Mexico for lack of cooperation in counter-narcotics efforts. The military's deeper involvement in political affairs also increased its visibility and made it more vulnerable to the incumbent administration's political fortunes. As Roderic Camp argued, "the military runs a much greater risk of losing rather than gaining institutional prestige in its current, expanded role."[17]

The prominence of economic agencies in U.S.–Mexican relations affected the ideational context of bilateral relations, as noted in chapter two. The leading economists in both U.S. and Mexican financial and trade agencies shared a common

vision and values that facilitated cooperation. Peter Haas has called this phenomenon "epistemic communities." Epistemic communities are networks of
professionals with recognized expertise in certain issues who share norms, beliefs,
and common standards to gather, test, and evaluate information. These intellectual traits enhance the capacity for coordination and cooperation.[18] For example,
during the NAFTA negotiations the U.S. Special Trade Representative officials and
their Mexican counterparts in the Ministry of Commerce shared the belief that
free trade would enhance the welfare of both nations. They also agreed on procedures to measure and evaluate welfare-enhancing decisions for both countries.
These shared beliefs encouraged and promoted compromise.

In contrast, an epistemic community has yet to develop in drug-trafficking
cooperation between the two countries, although it is conceivable that police professionals from both countries could construct such shared norms and
procedures in the twenty-first century. In the early 1990s, NAFTA dominated the
U.S.–Mexican agenda; bilateral affairs emphasized a cooperative problem-solving
approach. In the late 1990s, confrontation over drug trafficking became more significant, souring bilateral relations.

Fortunately, in the 1990s, the more frequent interaction between the presidents
of the two countries provided another avenue for bilateral coordination because the
two chief executives came to trust each other. From 1989 to 2000, there were 23
presidential meetings, 11 between Carlos Salinas and George Bush, two between
Salinas and Clinton, nine between Clinton and Ernesto Zedillo, and one between
Clinton and Vicente Fox. Table 5.3 lists all the meetings held between the presidents of both countries from 1909 to 2000. The first took place in 1909 between
William H. Taft and Porfirio Díaz, who met at the border between El Paso and Ciudad Juárez. The second meeting was held in 1943 between Franklin Roosevelt and
Manuel Avila Camacho. From then on, presidential meetings have been a recurrent
mechanism for managing bilateral affairs, but their frequency escalated in the
1990s when, on average, there were two meetings per year between the two presidents. Such meetings offer an opportunity to review the state of binational affairs
in general, call attention to specific topics, and resolve disputes. When a bilateral
dispute appears on the agenda of a presidential meeting, it receives considerable
visibility, greatly enhancing the likelihood that both administrations will work to
solve or manage the conflict. This was the case of border violence, for example. It
became part of the presidential agenda in Monterrey in November 1990; several
binational meetings focused on border violence thereafter.

In addition, the U.S. embassy in Mexico City and, in the 1990s, the Mexican
embassy in Washington, in part replaced the respective foreign ministries as the
coordinating bureaucratic centers for bilateral affairs. The decentralization of
inter-executive branch relations and the development of direct contacts between
specific agencies from both countries fostered the emergence of the embassies as
nodes for coordination. In the late 1990s, the U.S. embassy in Mexico represented

32 agencies; the Mexican embassy in Washington represented 14 (see also chapter six). Most of these attachés received direct orders from their respective ministers, but the ambassador was technically their boss. The mere presence of these attachés in the embassies encouraged coordination. It is easier for the ambassador to call a meeting with all the agency attachés under his direct supervision than for the foreign affairs minister in Mexico City or the secretary of state in Washington to call a meeting of cabinet members.

In the Mexican case, two other elements contributed to the embassy's rise as the coordinating center in the late 1990s: direct communication between the embassy and the presidential office at Los Pinos and the hiring of Washington lobbyists. Because Mexico assigns such importance to U.S. relations, the ambassador to Washington is someone trusted and close to the president. He is the only ambassador who reports directly to Los Pinos, in addition to the foreign affairs minister. And the closer the ambassador is to the president, the greater is his access to the various cabinet members in Mexico, and thus the more prominent is his role as coordinator of bilateral affairs. An ambassador to Washington with easy access to the Mexican cabinet becomes the bridge between the two administrations. In addition, the hiring of professional lobbyists increased the resources available to the ambassador. For example, in the spring of 1999, the ambassador and lobbyists became the key actors in lobbying the U.S. Congress to ensure that it would not reverse President Clinton's drug certification of Mexico.

The different roles of the U.S. and the Mexican Congresses in foreign affairs exemplify how the U.S. and Mexican political systems are similar in theory but not in practice. The U.S. Congress competes with the executive branch over the control of relations with Mexico and, in areas such as immigration, it is the predominant voice. In contrast, the Mexican Congress traditionally rubber-stamped executive decisions.

The U.S. Congress has consistently played an important role in U.S.–Mexican relations, though its role varied with the issue and the period.[19] Its role has always been prominent in controversial issues with domestic impact, such as immigration, trade, drugs, and the environment. For example, the Immigration Reform and Control Act of 1986 (IRCA) and the Illegal Immigration Reform and Immigrant Responsibility Act of 1996 (IIRIRA) forced the U.S. executive branch to accept a tougher immigration policy than had been the president's preference or than its agencies wished to implement.

The U.S. Congress generally deferred to the executive branch over security issues when the United States had been at war, but historically it played important roles concerning the use of U.S. force with regard to Mexico. During the U.S.–Mexico war of 1846–48, for example, congress denied President James Polk's request for a formal declaration of war and balked at annexing more of Mexico than Nicholas Trist had negotiated in the Treaty of Guadalupe-Hidalgo. During the U.S. Civil War, congress adamantly backed Mexico's efforts to be free from

TABLE 5.3

U.S.–Mexican Presidential Meetings, 1909–2000

Mexico	United States	Meeting Place	Date
Porfirio Díaz	William H. Taft	Ciudad Juárez and El Paso, TX	October 16, 1909
Manuel Avila Camacho	Franklin D. Roosevelt	Monterrey and Corpus Christi, TX	April 20, 1943
Miguel Alemán	Harry S. Truman	Mexico City, Mexico	March 3–5,1947
Miguel Alemán	Harry S. Truman	Washington, DC	April 29–May 1, 1947
Adolfo Ruiz Cortines	Dwight D. Eisenhower	Falcon Reservoir, Mexico–U.S. border	October 19, 1953
Adolfo Ruiz Cortines	Dwight D. Eisenhower	White Sulphur Springs, WV	March 26–28, 1956
Adolfo López Mateos	Dwight D. Eisenhower	Acapulco, Mexico	February 20, 1959
Adolfo López Mateos	Dwight D. Eisenhower	Washington, DC	October 15, 1959
Adolfo López Mateos	Dwight D. Eisenhower	Ciudad Acuña, Mexico	October 24, 1960
Adolfo López Mateos	John F. Kennedy	Mexico City, Mexico	June 29–July 1, 1962
Adolfo López Mateos	Lyndon B. Johnson	Palm Springs, FL	March 21–22, 1964
Adolfo López Mateos	Lyndon B. Johnson	El Chamizal, Mexico	September 25, 1964
Gustavo Díaz Ordaz*	Lyndon B. Johnson	Johnson Ranch, TX	November 12–13, 1964
Gustavo Díaz Ordaz	Lyndon B. Johnson	Mexico City, Mexico	April 14–15, 1966
Gustavo Díaz Ordaz	Lyndon B. Johnson	Friendship Reservoir, Mexico–U.S. border	December 3, 1966
Gustavo Díaz Ordaz	Lyndon B. Johnson	Washington, DC, and El Chamizal, Mexico	October 26–28, 1967
Gustavo Díaz Ordaz	Lyndon B. Johnson	El Chamizal, Mexico	December 13, 1968
Gustavo Díaz Ordaz	Richard Nixon	Friendship Reservoir, Mexico–U.S. border	September 8, 1969
Gustavo Díaz Ordaz	Richard Nixon	Puerto Vallarta, Mexico	August 21, 1970
Gustavo Díaz Ordaz	Richard Nixon	San Diego, CA	September 3, 1970
Luis Echeverría*	Richard Nixon	Washington, DC	November 13, 1970
Luis Echeverría	Richard Nixon	Washington, DC	June 15–16, 1972
Luis Echeverría	Gerald Ford	Nogales and Magdalena, Mexico–U.S. border	October 21, 1974
José López Portillo*	Gerald Ford	Washington, DC	September 24, 1976
José López Portillo	James Carter	Washington, DC	February 14–17, 1977
José López Portillo	James Carter	Mexico City, Mexico	February 14–16, 1979
José López Portillo	James Carter	Washington, DC	November 28–29, 1979
José López Portillo	Ronald Reagan*	Ciudad Juárez, Mexico	January 5, 1981
José López Portillo	Ronald Reagan	Washington, DC	April 9, 1981

Mexican President	U.S. President	Location	Date
José López Portillo	Ronald Reagan	Grand Rapids, MI	September 17–18, 1981
Miguel de la Madrid*	Ronald Reagan	San Diego, CA	October 8, 1982
Miguel de la Madrid	Ronald Reagan	La Paz, Mexico	August 4, 1983
Miguel de la Madrid	Ronald Reagan	Washington, DC	May 14–16, 1984
Miguel de la Madrid	Ronald Reagan	Mexicali, Mexico	January 3, 1986
Miguel de la Madrid	Ronald Reagan	Washington, DC	August 4, 1986
Miguel de la Madrid	Ronald Reagan	Mazatlán, Mexico	February 13, 1988
Carlos Salinas de Gortari*	George Bush*	Houston, TX	November 22, 1988
Carlos Salinas de Gortari	George Bush	Paris, France	July 14, 1989
Carlos Salinas de Gortari	George Bush	Washington, DC	October 1–6, 1989
Carlos Salinas de Gortari	George Bush	Washington, DC	June 12, 1990
Carlos Salinas de Gortari	George Bush	New York, NY	September 30, 1990
Carlos Salinas de Gortari	George Bush	Monterrey and Agualeguas, Mexico	September 26–27, 1990
Carlos Salinas de Gortari	George Bush	Houston, TX	April 7, 1991
Carlos Salinas de Gortari	George Bush	Camp David, U.S.	December 13, 1991
Carlos Salinas de Gortari	George Bush	San Antonio, Mexico	February 26, 1992
Carlos Salinas de Gortari	George Bush	San Diego, CA	July 14, 1992
Carlos Salinas de Gortari	George Bush	San Antonio, TX	October 7, 1992
Carlos Salinas de Gortari	William Clinton*	Austin, TX	January 8, 1993
Carlos Salinas de Gortari	William Clinton	New York, NY	September 26, 1993
Ernesto Zedillo Ponce de León*	William Clinton	Washington, DC	November 23, 1994
Ernesto Zedillo Ponce de León	William Clinton	Miami, FL	December 10, 1994
Ernesto Zedillo Ponce de León	William Clinton	Washington, DC, New York, NY	October 9, 1995
Ernesto Zedillo Ponce de León	William Clinton	Mexico City, Mexico	May 6–7, 1997
Ernesto Zedillo Ponce de León	William Clinton	Washington, DC	November 13–14, 1997
Ernesto Zedillo Ponce de León	William Clinton	New York, NY	June 8–9, 1998
Ernesto Zedillo Ponce de León	William Clinton	Mérida, Mexico	February 15, 1999
Ernesto Zedillo Ponce de León	William Clinton	Sacramento, Los Angeles, San Diego, San Francisco, CA	May 19–20, 1999
Ernesto Zedillo Ponce de León	William Clinton	Washington, DC	June 8, 2000
Vicente Fox Quezada*	William Clinton	Washington, DC	August 24, 2000

*As president-elect.

Source: Archives, Mexican Ministry of Foreign Affairs, and Ricardo Ampudia, *Los Estados Unidos de América en los informes presidenciales de México* (Mexico, DF: Secretaría de Relaciones Exteriores and Instituto Matías Romero de Estudios Diplomáticos, 1993).

French imperial rule, though well short of committing U.S. resources; this stance can be explained in terms of both U.S. self-interest and the lobbying of the Mexican envoy to Washington, Matías Romero.

In the closing quarter of the twentieth century, the U.S. Congress seldom granted the executive branch unfettered authority. For example, since 1974, congress required the president to renew every three years his "fast track" authority to negotiate and ratify international trade agreements expeditiously (under "fast track," congress limits the amount of debate and permits only a "yes" or "no" vote without allowing amendments).[20] The Drug Control Act of 1986 created the drug-certification process. Through this device, congress reviewed on a yearly basis the extent of cooperation of other countries, including Mexico, in the drug war; congress could reverse the presidential decision on certification and impose sanctions. Other laws also obligated the president to submit various reports to congress; these included, for instance, annual reports on human rights as well as reports on the voting record of all countries in the UN. Congress also asked the president to submit an assessment of NAFTA's progress after three years.

Congressional autonomy and assertiveness in various foreign policy areas illustrate what Robert Putnam calls "two-level games."[21] That is, U.S. officials negotiate simultaneously with Mexican officials and their own congress. When U.S. Special Trade Representative officials were negotiating NAFTA, they had to consider congressional interests in addition to the issues posed by Mexican officials. Similarly, when U.S. officials were developing a strategy with their Mexican counterparts to cope with narcotics, they had to recall that congress assesses the extent of Mexico's cooperation every spring. The analysis of the two-level games generates some hypotheses about bargaining power in U.S.–Mexican interactions.

Putnam's general hypothesis fits well the case of U.S.–Mexican relations: "institutional arrangements which strengthen decision-makers at home may weaken their international bargaining position, and vice versa." The extraordinary power of the Mexican president through the end of the twentieth century to govern and dominate the congress, courts, and bureaucracy weakened Mexico's capacity to negotiate with the United States. The assertiveness of the U.S. Congress before approving NAFTA, for example, allowed the Clinton administration to extract last-minute concessions from Mexican officials, such as the establishment of the North American Development Bank and special protection for the U.S. sugar industry. Thus a White House constrained by congress is generally strengthened when bargaining with Mexico.[22]

Executive-legislative relations were quite different in Mexico. The Mexican Congress played a minor role in U.S.–Mexican relations to the end of the twentieth century. Nonetheless, inter-branch relations were altered somewhat by the 1997 midterm elections, when, for the first time ever, the official party, PRI, lost its majority in the chamber of deputies. Four opposition parties forged a coalition with 11 more seats than the PRI; they organized the chamber, chairing 14 of its 22 committees. The PRI retained a clear majority in the senate. The chamber of deputies discussed how to increase its formal powers with regard to foreign affairs, but little came of it.

A much larger change occurred in the 2000 national elections when Fox from the National Action Party (PAN) won the presidency as an opposition party candidate, defeating the presidential candidate of the long-ruling PRI. Nevertheless, the PRI remained the single largest party in the chamber of deputies with 211 out of 500 seats (42 percent) and in the senate with 60 out of 128 seats (47 percent). PAN had 206 seats in the chamber of deputies (41 percent) and 46 seats in the senate (36 percent), although its allied environmentalist or green party (PVEM) had 17 deputies and 5 senators. The Alliance for Mexico, clustered around the Party of the Democratic Revolution (PRD), elected 66 deputies and 17 senators (of these, the PRD had 16 senators and 50 deputies). This meant that the executive branch would require for the first time, for example, crafting legislative coalitions for the approval of treaties or the confirmation of ambassadors, which are senate prerogatives. Thus Mexico in the early twenty-first century could reap both the policy-making headaches and the international bargaining advantages to be expected from two-level games. The presidency would need to bargain simultaneously with both congress and external partners over how to conduct Mexico's international relations.

The other government actors listed in Table 5.1 (state governments, courts, and local governments) increased their levels of participation in U.S.–Mexican relations in the 1990s, but continued to play minor roles compared with those of the executives and the U.S. Congress. U.S. border state governments, and those with large populations of Mexican-Americans such as Illinois, became outspoken participants in Mexican affairs. Most of these states opened offices in Mexico City to work in liaison with the Mexican bureaucracy and promote business. On occasion, U.S. governors influenced federal policy toward Mexico. In 1994, for example, California voters approved Proposition 187, which sought to deny health and educational services to undocumented immigrants; California's Republican governor, Pete Wilson, was a key advocate for this measure. In turn, Proposition 187 inspired the sponsors of the 1996 IIRIRA federal legislation. A quite different example occurred in 1999. The three Republican governors of the border states Texas, (whose governor was George W. Bush), New Mexico, and Arizona and the new Democratic governor of California called President Clinton's attention to Mexico's efforts in combating drugs and the importance of continued cooperation with the Mexican government. They urged the president to certify Mexico in the war on drugs. (See also discussion in chapter seven.)

There have been continuous meetings between U.S. and Mexican border state governors since 1980; since 1987, they have been known as the Border Governors Conferences. Typically, ten governors, six from Mexico and four from the United States, meet twice a year to discuss common problems and explore and encourage further economic development.[23] Mexico's sustained political opening in the 1990s increased the role played by Mexican state governments in U.S.–Mexican affairs, overcoming the effects of Mexican political centralization to some degree. The opposition governors of some border states (Baja California and Chihuahua) pioneered these wider roles, but they soon extended to PRI border-state governors who gained autonomy from the national government.

The special problems at the border also fostered cooperation between law enforcement institutions at the state and local levels (criminals often flee to the other side of the border). By the 1980s, the state governments of the border region perceived the need to improve coordination of judicial institutions on both sides of the border. In 1986, they created the Border States Attorneys General Meetings to exchange information about common threats in the border region—namely, drug trafficking, money laundering, stolen vehicles, child trafficking, arms trafficking, criminals targeting tourists, and other forms of violence.[24]

In the 1990s, the impact of U.S. courts on U.S.–Mexican relations increased in part because of the prominence of drug-trafficking issues on the bilateral agenda. Two court cases involving Mexican citizens who allegedly participated in the murder of DEA agent Enrique Camarena reached the U.S. Supreme Court.[25] The court's decision in the second case ignited a bilateral crisis. In June 1992, the U.S. Supreme Court ruled that the kidnapping of Alvarez Machaín (a Mexican physician accused by DEA of participating in Camarena's killing) did not violate the U.S.–Mexico Extradition Treaty because kidnapping was not specified in the text of the accord. The Mexican government rejected this interpretation of the agreement, decided to review the extradition treaty, and severely curtailed DEA activities in Mexico.[26] Surprised by the harsh response, Washington sent a delegation to Mexico City to appease the Mexicans. In the end, the Extradition Treaty was revised, and Alvarez Machaín was repatriated to Mexico after a U.S. Ninth Circuit Court judge was unable to find enough evidence for a guilty verdict.[27]

Coping with Decentralization

In the last quarter of the twentieth century, there were three major efforts to improve the managing capacities of the U.S. and Mexican governments regarding bilateral affairs. They were the establishment of a U.S. special coordinator for Mexican affairs at the State Department, the emergence of a key person who served as broker at the highest levels of Washington's bureaucracy, and the institutionalization of inter-governmental affairs. The first two were unilateral Washington efforts to improve the U.S. policy-making process; the last was a bilateral attempt to cope with the increasing demands that culminated in NAFTA.

The most important U.S. review of its policy toward Mexico in the history of bilateral affairs was undertaken during Jimmy Carter's presidency (1977–81). Presidential Review Memorandum 41 included the participation of 14 agencies. Through a series of meetings chaired by the State Department, each agency discussed its main issues in U.S.–Mexican affairs as well as its interaction with other U.S. agencies. The meetings revealed why it was so difficult for the United States to develop a coordinated policy toward Mexico. Every agency made decisions on its own with little regard for other agencies. As a result of the review, the president appointed a special coordinator for Mexican affairs at the State Department, former Texas congressman Robert Krueger. The new position was, according to Robert Pastor, "an ambassador-level 'coordinator' who would advise [Carter] and the Secretary of State, have access to the entire cabinet, and intervene to ensure that various agencies would consider the 'Mexican dimension' before making domestic decisions."[28] This Carter initiative was not successful, however. Krueger faced numerous obstacles in the search for a coherent U.S. policy toward Mexico. His position at the State Department created bureaucratic confusion concerning who was the real ambassador to Mexico. His lack of close ties to President Carter prevented him from speaking with presidential authority. And his tenure in congress had been too short. Krueger was not an expert in the Washington game, nor was he knowledgeable about Mexico. In the end, the hostage crisis in Iran killed whatever momentum there might have been to improve policy coordination toward Mexico by focusing all high-level foreign policy official attention in Washington on Iran, rather than on Mexico.[29]

The Bush and Clinton administrations followed a different approach: a key individual became a broker for U.S.–Mexican affairs. During the NAFTA negotiations in the Bush administration, two sensitive incidents threatened the agreement. One was the DEA kidnapping of Dr. Humberto Alvarez Machaín who allegedly was involved in the murder of DEA agent Camarena. The other was a U.S. embargo on tuna caught by the Mexican fisheries industry. In both cases, Robert Zoellick, undersecretary of state for economic affairs and a close aide to Secretary of State James Baker, became a broker at the highest levels of the U.S. bureaucracy. In the Alvarez Machaín case, Zoellick understood how sensitive this episode was for Mexico; he was able to influence key Bush administration officials who eventually provided a response acceptable to Mexico.[30] In the tuna embargo case, Mexico was forbidden to export tuna to the United States, because the Mexican fisheries caught more dolphins than were allowed under U.S. law. Mexico took the tuna case to GATT, which declared the U.S. embargo illegal. Zoellick convinced President Salinas's chief of staff, Jose Córdoba, that Mexico should not seek to implement the GATT resolution because it would damage Mexico's image in the United States.[31]

In the Clinton administration, the president's longtime friend Thomas F. ("Mack") McLarty served as the president's chief of staff (1993–94), then as counselor to the president, and in 1996, he was appointed special envoy to the Americas. As chief of staff, McLarty worked in fall 1993 to ensure congressional approval of NAFTA, which made him familiar with Mexican affairs. McLarty gradually became another broker for Mexican affairs. He became the Zedillo administration's direct conduit to Clinton in early 1995, during the peso crisis, and in 1997, when General Jesús Gutiérrez Rebollo was found guilty of protecting drug lords just two weeks before the administration released its annual report on Mexico's drug cooperation.[32]

Institutionalization of inter-governmental affairs is the most serious bilateral effort to manage U.S.–Mexican relations. During the late 1980s and early 1990, the U.S. and Mexican governments strengthened and formalized their inter-governmental ties. Existing mechanisms of bilateral consultation were strengthened, such as the Binational Commission, which now includes more than 20 cabinet members and 16 working groups from both administrations (see also chapter six). New mechanisms were created, such as the High Level Contact Group to deal with drug trafficking. Numerous bilateral agreements were signed, such as NAFTA and its side agreements on environmental and labor cooperation. Each of these agreements enhanced the means for communication between both governments and created permanent working groups. Bilateral (the NADBank) and trilateral (the North American Commissions for Labor and Environmental Cooperation) institutions have been established to seek to improve the management of U.S.–Mexican affairs. The institutionalization of inter-governmental affairs improved decision-making in those areas of bilateral affairs, such as trade or environmental protection, where the interests of the two countries converged. NAFTA allowed bilateral trade to boom and permitted both countries to resolve their differences without rancor. Institutionalization was not able to erase some traditional bilateral tensions, however. At the end of the 1990s, there was less bilateral institutionalization over drug trafficking and migration; the existing mechanisms were also less effective in these issue areas.

Mass Media

The media have always played an important role in U.S.–Mexican relations. They helped to form each country's perception of the other and shaped the bilateral agenda. The Mexican media pay more attention to the United States than the U.S. media do to Mexico. NAFTA increased the general coverage of bilateral affairs in both countries.[33] Yet, despite the many changes in Mexico and the United States, and in their bilateral relations, until the mid-1990s the constant that remained was the mass media support for the policies and prevailing views of the governing elites in each country with regard to the principal issues in U.S.–Mexican relations.

U.S. elite media tended to accept as inevitable the coercive structure and perverse workings of the Mexican government as well as corruption and inefficiency in Mexico's private sector. They supported Carlos Salinas de Gortari's presidential campaign in 1988 and his subsequent administration.[34]

U.S. elite mass media acceptance of the structure of Mexican politics, and support for the Mexican government in particular, broke first, albeit temporarily, with the 1982 economic crisis and then, more important, in 1985 to 1986 with the drug trafficking crisis. The U.S. mass media gave Mexico and its government credit for addressing the 1982 economic crisis effectively but harshly criticized their performance regarding counter-narcotics policy.[35] U.S. elite media support for U.S. policy toward Mexico, and for the policies of the Mexican government, reached its apogee during the Salinas presidency. In part, this was the result of an unprecedented and very effective media strategy organized in the United States by the Salinas administration. The U.S. media broke with this past pattern only in 1994 to 1995 in response to the Zapatista insurgency in Chiapas, the assassination of prominent Mexicans including the PRI presidential nominee Luis Donaldo Colosio, and the Mexican financial collapse and subsequent U.S. bailout. Since then, reporting critical of Mexico on these and other issues (including U.S. policy toward Mexico) became frequent in the U.S. mass media; elite media criticism of drug trafficking and corruption in Mexico has been especially severe.[36] This shift in media coverage had consequences for policy. The tough stances toward Mexico's counter-narcotics cooperation taken by U.S. senators Alfonse D'Amato (R-NY) and Dianne Feinstein (D-CA) were probably responses to the increased negative media coverage of Mexico. Drug corruption–related stories in the *New York Times, Washington Post*, and *Wall Street Journal* increased from 338 stories in 1991 to 515 in 1996.[37]

For many years, the Mexican mass media echoed the Mexican government's views and policies; they were alternately critical or supportive of U.S. policies depending on the preferences of the Mexican government.[38] The first Mexican daily newspapers that displayed, in the early 1980s, a sustained independence in their reporting of U.S.–Mexican relations were, first (and only for a few years), *Uno Más Uno* and, then, *La Jornada*. Since that time, the number of independent newspapers and magazines grew, as did the margin of independence of long-established mass media outlets. Nevertheless, the Mexican media at times took out of context what was said in the United States about Mexico. For example, a passing reference to Mexico regarding the financial crisis in Japan made by U.S. treasury secretary Robert Rubin testifying at a senate hearing made headlines in some of the major Mexican newspapers. Moreover, through the end of the twentieth century, caricatures and editorials in Mexican newspapers continued to portray the United States, and especially its government and financial elites, predominantly as "power hungry, hypocritical, and anti-Mexican," as Stephen Morris has summarized it. Although these themes were somewhat attenuated in the 1990s, they continued to persist alongside more favorable images of the United States, especially from official sources.[39]

One of our major arguments in this book—that NAFTA was a catalyst for much more than trade integration between the United States and Mexico, because it increased contacts at most levels—holds true as well for the role of the media in bilateral affairs. NAFTA was a good reason for expanded U.S. media coverage of Mexico and vice versa. The number of foreign correspondents in Mexico increased from 26 in 1975 to 146 in 1993; most of these correspondents worked for U.S. media services.[40] In 1989, only one Mexican newspaper, *Excélsior*, one television network, Televisa, and the Mexican government's news agency, Notimex, had correspondents in Washington. In 1992, four Mexican newspapers and one magazine had correspondents in Washington.[41]

NAFTA expanded U.S. public interest in Mexico and Mexican affairs. Once the NAFTA negotiations and the deliberations in the U.S. Congress became a part of the domestic political debate in the United States, then both the negotiations and domestic Mexican affairs became more relevant to the U.S. public. The CNN television debate in 1994 between Vice President Albert Gore and NAFTA's fiercest critic, Ross Perot, on the popular television show "Larry King Live," illustrates well how NAFTA came to matter for a much wider television audience.

NAFTA similarly transformed Mexican media coverage of the United States. The newly numerous Mexican correspondents in Washington became the first Latin American journalists to obtain permanent passes to the White House and the State Department. These Mexican correspondents were quickly included in the "short list" of journalists to whom the U.S. special trade representative would give privileged information. As argued by Dolia Estévez, Washington correspondent for the Mexican daily *El Financiero*, "it became easier to interview high-ranking policy-makers of the Bush administration."[42]

Mexico's largest and most influential private television network, Televisa, has long broadcast to the Spanish-language audience in the United States. Televisa's subsidiaries dominate the U.S. Spanish-language television market. In contrast to U.S. television networks, Televisa's U.S. subsidiaries broadcast a great deal of information about Mexico, particularly about Mexican sports events. In general, the political and economic information broadcast about Mexico is quite consistent with Mexican government views. Mexican officials are typically cast positively. U.S.–Mexican relations are characteristically described as good and constructive.[43]

In the late 1990s, moreover, the Internet facilitated ready access to information as well as communications between a growing number of U.S. and Mexican citizens. Neither national government made much effort to regulate the Internet. The rapid changes in telecommunications altered interactions among all elite actors in U.S.–Mexican relations. E-mail facilitated direct and daily contact between Mexican and U.S. officials in every agency and every hierarchy; this rendered absurd the long-held belief of the Foreign Affairs Ministry and the State Department that they are the privileged intermediaries between the two governments. The Internet tremendously facilitated communications among business firms, academics, and non-governmental organizations.

In conclusion, by the end of the 1990s, the U.S. and Mexican mass media had adopted a more critical role toward the two governments and their management of U.S.–Mexican relations. This change in mass media coverage in both countries generated a more complex political environment to manage the bilateral relations.

TABLE 5.4

U.S. Mass Public Attitudes toward Mexico, 1978–1998

	1978	1982	1986	1990	1994	1998
Favorable rating[a]	58	60	59	56	57	57
Favorable rating ranking[b]	5	3	5	6	4	4
Vital interest percentage[c]	60	74	74	63	76	66
Vital interest percentage ranking[d]	15	7	7	9	4	8
Sample size	1,546	1,546	1,585	1,662	1,546	1,507

[a]Favorable rating. Respondents are asked to rate countries on a "feeling thermometer" ranging from zero to 100.

[b]Favorable rating ranking. This is the country's ranking among the thermometer scores.

[c]Vital interest percentage. This is the proportion of the public agreeing that the United States has a "vital interest" in a particular country.

[d]Vital interest percentage ranking. This is the country's ranking among the vital interest scores.

Note: In all cases, respondents are men and women age 18 and above.

Source: John Rielly, ed., *American Public Opinion and U.S. Foreign Policy* (Chicago: Chicago Council on Foreign Relations), as follows: 1979, 16, 18; 1983, 16, 19; 1987, 17–18; 1991, 19, 21; 1995, 20, 22; 1999, 13, 28.

But, above all, the mass media were much likelier than ever to cover "the other" country professionally.

PUBLIC OPINION AND BILATERAL RELATIONS

During the last quarter of the twentieth century, U.S.–Mexican relations changed dramatically. Yet, surprisingly, certain fundamental aspects in the structure of public opinion changed much less: Mexican and U.S. citizens have thought well of each other's country, on balance, for a long time.[44] The citizens of both countries were more ready for intense collaboration well in advance of their respective governments or most of their leading politicians. U.S. and Mexican citizens held positive attitudes toward "the other" country even when bilateral relations between their governments deteriorated or the mass media turned sour.

Consider some evidence for the United States. The Chicago Council on Foreign Relations polled U.S. citizens and elites on various international questions from the 1970s to the 1990s.[45] The council repeatedly used a "thermometer reading" (from zero to 100) to gauge the extent of "warmth" toward various countries (see Table 5.4). In 1978, Mexico's score was 58 (in contrast, Cuba's score was 32, ranking last); in late 1994 and in late 1998, Mexico's score was 57. In 1978, Mexico was the fifth most popular country for the U.S. public; in 1994 and 1998, Mexico tied for fourth place as most popular. In the intervening years, Mexico's thermometer score never dropped below 56 and never rose above 60. Canada and the United Kingdom consistently outranked Mexico, but Mexico's popularity was about the same as that for Italy, Germany, France, and Israel. Mexico's popularity with the U.S. public never ranked higher than a tie for third place (in 1982) and never lower than a tie for sixth place (in 1990). Over time, U.S. public attitudes toward Mexico

TABLE 5.5

Mexico City Mass Public Attitudes toward the United States, 1956–1979

	1956	1964	1965	1972	1/1979	8/1979
Opinion of the United States						
Percent positive	61	79	61	54	63	68
Percent negative	4	3	5	15	15	13
Basic interests of U.S. and Mexico						
Percent saying similar	--	75	64	--	59	56
Percent saying different	--	16	22	--	37	41
Sample size	1,455	506	493	500	500	501

Source: William J. Millard Jr., "Mexico City Public Opinion Prior to the Presidential Visit," R-10-79 (Washington: Office of Research, International Communication Agency, 1979), 30, 33; William J. Millard Jr., "Mexico, Reluctant Friend of the U.S.: Mexico City Opinion on Bilateral and International Issues," M-34-79 (Washington: International Communication Agency, 1979), 34, 41.

most resembled the public's attitudes toward France. U.S. citizens liked Mexico and France but, in each case, they were probably aware of difficulties and complexities in the respective bilateral relations.

Consider evidence for Mexico (see Table 5.5). The United States Information Agency polled the opinion of the citizens of Mexico City starting in the 1950s. The approach and actual wording of the question were the same. In 1956, 61 percent of Mexico City respondents had a good or very good opinion of the United States; in late 1979, 68 percent held the same opinion. The same question was asked in 1964, 1965, 1972, and early 1979. The results were remarkably consistent, though good opinions of the United States were highest in 1964 and lowest in 1972 (when 54 percent of respondents had a good opinion of the United States).

During the 1980s, the manifold conflicts between Mexico and the United States took a toll. In 1986, 48 percent of Mexicans in a national sample had favorable views of the U.S. government, and 47 percent had a favorable view of the people of the United States; in each case, the proportion of favorable to unfavorable views was about two to one. Mexicans were also asked to give their opinion of other countries on a scale from one to ten "like in school" (the top grade in Mexican schools is a ten). They rated the United States 7.9, second only to Japan at 8.0 and ahead of all Latin American and European countries.[46] At the time of the 1988 presidential election, Mexicans rated the United States as 8.2, still slightly behind Japan but ahead of all Latin American and European countries.[47] Mexican public attitudes toward the United States became less positive than ever in the 1990s. In 1995, only 41 percent of Mexicans had a positive general opinion of the United States; the next category, "so-so", garnered 31 percent.[48]

In short, the public in both the United States and Mexico had positive attitudes toward the other country for decades. In the United States, the level of positive attitudes toward Mexico remained constant. In Mexico, it was constant from the

1950s through the 1970s, but then the positive attitudes dropped a bit in the 1980s and 1990s; by far the largest plurality of Mexicans retain positive attitudes of the United States, despite sometimes troubled official bilateral relations.

Attitudinal Bases for Bilateral Conflict and Cooperation

Beyond these broad views, there is considerable complexity. In the United States, as the polls of the Chicago Council on Foreign Relations show, the public overwhelmingly believed that Mexico was of "vital interest" to the United States (see Table 5.4). In 1978, 60 percent of the public and 90 percent of the elites held that view. In 1982, fueled by fears of communism in Central America and the Caribbean, 74 percent of the public and 98 percent of the elites held that view. In 1978, Mexico ranked fifteenth in the public's estimate of its importance to the United States; in 1982, it ranked seventh. Thereafter, the estimate of Mexico's significance remained fairly steady, though it reached its lowest level (63 percent) in 1990. In late 1994, the year when NAFTA went into effect, and the Zapatista rebellion was launched, 76 percent of the public and 98 percent of the elites thought that Mexico was a "vital interest" to the United States; Mexico tied for fourth place. By 1998, 66 percent of U.S. respondents thought of Mexico as a "vital interest"; fears of a negative impact from NAFTA or the early 1995 financial crisis had faded. Mexico tied the United Kingdom for eighth place in its relative importance for U.S. interests.

Perhaps because Mexico was deemed such a "vital interest," in 1990 the Chicago Council's polls showed that 48 percent of the U.S. public (though only 19 percent of the elites) favored using U.S. troops "if the government of Mexico were threatened by a revolution or civil war." In 1994, 34 percent of the public and 46 percent of the elites thought that the United States should be spying on Mexico secretly, although over half of both the public and the elites opposed such espionage. Public attitudes also provide some context for the prospects for cooperation. Various polls indicate that U.S. public support for NAFTA was positive throughout the 1990s except during 1992 to 1994, the period of active debate over ratification. By 1994, NAFTA commanded more support than opposition.[49] In 1998, only three percent of respondents to the Chicago Council poll explicitly expressed concerns about the possible adverse effects of the NAFTA on jobs in the United States; a much larger proportion of the U.S. public expressed fears about economic competitiveness and jobs that could include worries about Mexico.

The attitudinal complexity was evident as well in Mexico. From the 1960s through the 1970s, despite the high and relatively constant positive views of the United States, there was a steep slide in the proportion of Mexicans who believed that the "basic interests" of the United States and Mexico were "very much" or "fairly well" in agreement. That proportion fell from 75 percent in 1964 to 56 percent in mid-1979 (see Table 5.5). That trend probably contributed to weakening the overall positive views about the United States. In the mid-1980s, Mexicans believed that they enjoyed fewer political freedoms and had fewer opportunities of becoming rich without working harder than U.S. citizens, but that they were much closer to their children, had stronger values, were more religious, and were just as likely to be as happy as U.S. citizens.[50]

Three-quarters of Mexicans supported NAFTA in 1990 but, in 1995 at the time of the severe economic crisis, a majority of Mexicans turned against NAFTA. As the Mexican economy recovered in 1996, a slight plurality of Mexicans came to back NAFTA again. Volatile as these attitudes were, two explanations account for much of the variation in opinion about NAFTA. Prior to NAFTA's enactment, attitudes toward President Salinas and the United States were the strongest explanations for support for freer trade. Over a longer time span, including the Salinas and Zedillo administrations, the most persistent explanation for opinion on freer trade was individual attitudes toward the United States.[51] In addition, in 1995, 57 percent of Mexicans believed that foreign investment was good for Mexico versus 27 percent who thought that it was not. That was wider support than the 52 versus 33 percent split on a similar question in 1988.[52]

By the mid- and late 1990s, there were also some important similarities between U.S. and Mexican public opinion. In 1994, the Times Mirror Center for People and the Press found modest levels of political information in both countries and a markedly higher attention to popular culture than was evident in other countries. Only 50 percent of U.S. respondents and 42 percent of Mexican respondents could identify Boris Yeltsin as the Russian president, and only 14 percent of Mexicans and 13 percent of U.S. respondents could identify Boutros Boutros-Ghali as UN secretary general. Yet 51 percent of Mexicans and 49 percent of U.S. respondents had followed the pop singer Michael Jackson's personal problems, a much higher proportion than in the other six major countries surveyed.[53]

U.S. and Mexican citizens in the 1990s also shared attitudes toward some of the major economic issues that affected bilateral relations. In 1998, 79 percent of U.S. respondents and 70 percent of Mexicans favored free trade, but only 31 percent of U.S. respondents and 29 percent of Mexicans believed that NAFTA had been good for "you and your family." These joint findings reflected both a substantive reality and the enormous importance of questionnaire wording in discerning these attitudes. Moreover, 91 percent of U.S. respondents and 98 percent of Mexican respondents believed that drug trafficking was a serious world problem. Fifty-three percent of U.S. citizens and 47 percent of Mexicans thought that countries that sell drugs are "guiltier" with regard to drug trafficking than countries whose citizens purchase drugs. Finally, though the U.S. and Mexican governments disagreed in their respective approach toward Cuba's government, the public agrees. Forty-four percent of U.S. respondents and 43 percent of Mexicans believed that increased trade and investment is the policy most likely to bring about the end of communism in Cuba. In each country, the larger plurality favored a policy of engagement toward Cuba.[54]

Nonetheless, in 1998, the public in the two countries also differed on some important issues. About 44 percent of Mexicans thought that the United States was a trustworthy commercial partner, but only 26 percent of U.S. respondents thought so of Mexico. (See substantive analysis in chapter seven.) Moreover, 72 percent of U.S. respondents but only 54 percent of Mexicans favored the imposition of U.S. sanctions on countries involved in drug trafficking; this difference over a principal U.S. foreign policy instrument reflects as well major differences between the two governments. Finally, 74 percent of U.S. citizens thought that U.S.-style democracy was "a model to be followed," but only 47 percent of Mexicans agreed.[55]

Mexican Americans View Mexico and the United States

Many Mexican-origin people live in the United States. Until the early 1970s, official Mexico tended to disdain this diaspora as lost citizens and wished them good riddance. By the early 1990s, in contrast, the Mexican government courted its diaspora in the United States in search of allies to help reshape U.S. policy toward Mexico.[56] What were the views of Mexican Americans? The attitudes of Mexican Americans most resembled the attitudes of Italian Americans, Rodolfo de la Garza and Louis DeSipio have argued. Both groups exhibit minimal political interest in the homeland of origin while maintaining a cultural identity in the adopted country.[57] Mexican-American iconography and cultural practices celebrate many dimensions of Mexicanness—holidays, religious symbolism, the Spanish language, food festivals, and so forth—but Mexican Americans have sought inclusion in the United States as full citizens for their own sakes, not to advance the interests of the Mexican government.

The Latino National Political Survey (carried out in 1989 to 1990) is the only survey that includes a nationally representative sample of Mexican Americans. Its results show that Mexican Americans had much more positive attitudes about the United States than they did about Mexico. Moreover, about 90 percent of Mexican Americans were principally concerned with U.S. politics, while only one in ten had a significant interest in Mexican politics. About 85 percent of Mexican Americans thought that corruption in Mexico was a principal cause of that country's problems, while fewer than one out of six Mexican Americans blamed U.S. policy for Mexico's problems. Three-quarters of Mexican-Americans agreed that there were "too many immigrants in the United States"—perhaps the clearest mark of identification for someone who has truly arrived in the United States! Subsequent research through smaller or regional surveys confirmed these findings. In particular, contrary to the preferences of the Mexican government, most Mexican Americans opposed NAFTA's enactment; pluralities of Mexican Americans in Texas and California supported NAFTA implementation, however. In short, for most practical purposes regarding U.S.–Mexican relations, Mexican Americans were best seen as Americans of Mexican origin.

U.S. and Mexican Attitudes toward Migrants

As the paragraph above indicates, immigrants to the United States are unpopular even among Mexican Americans. They are certainly unpopular with the wider U.S. public and, perhaps more surprisingly, they are not well regarded in Mexico either. Research by Thomas Espenshade and Maryann Belanger shows the broad outlines of the attitudes of the U.S. public toward migrants. Asked in 1993 about the group of recent immigrants to which "you feel most favorable," 18 percent of the public identified Mexicans. Asked about the group of recent immigrant to which "you feel least favorable," 28 percent of respondents in the same survey said Mexicans. In another poll conducted also in 1993, the U.S. public was asked with regard to various immigrant nationalities "whether you believe their presence has generally benefited the country or generally created problems for the country." Twenty-nine percent responded that Mexican immigrants brought more benefits, while 59 percent believed that they brought more problems. (In 1985, the U.S. public had held a much more favorable view of Mexican immigrants by a 44 percent to 37 percent margin.) The public in the United States also overwhelmingly favored greater U.S. government efforts to keep illegal immigrants out of the country, including adding more border patrol agents and building fences in high-traffic areas to discourage illegal immigrants who crossed the border on foot. However, in 1993, two-thirds of the public opposed building a fence or wall along the entire U.S.–Mexican border. In short, the U.S. public did not like immigrants from Mexico, especially if they entered the United States illegally. The public supported various measures to control such immigration but not building fences or walls to seal the entire U.S.–Mexican border.[58]

The view of Mexican emigrants is no rosier from Mexico City, however. In 1997, Mexico City's leading newspaper, *Reforma*, polled residents of the city about their attitudes toward "Mexicans who go to work in the United States." Forty-seven percent of these respondents had a "very bad or bad" opinion of such people versus 27 percent who said they had a "very good or good opinion."[59] Thus, it turns out that the Mexico City public has an opinion of Mexican emigrants that is approximately as unfavorable as the U.S. public has of Mexican immigrants. Neither public likes migrants. At the attitudinal level, there is in fact no conflict between the U.S. and Mexican public. The conflict derives from the actual process of migration.

Implications of Public Attitudes

The popular press at times depicts irreconcilable differences, misunderstandings, and conflicts between ordinary folk in the United States and Mexico. No doubt that is often the case. There is evidence, however, of abundant goodwill among the citizens of each country toward those in the other. There is also a very broad agreement between the two publics on some fundamental issues, including support for freer trade, even if the respondent has yet to benefit (a consensus that

Mexican Americans eventually joined), and dislike of migrants. Nevertheless, there is also evidence of some long-term secular trends that have generally reduced the attitudinal bases for cooperation, although a preference for cooperation remains the predominant opinion, as well as some volatility in attitudes toward trade. Finally, the public in both countries, and the politicians who claim to represent their values and interests, differ substantially over three issues: how to manage their bilateral trade, U.S. international policy toward drug trafficking, and U.S. policies to "export" its democratic model to Mexico.

POLITICAL PARTIES IN U.S.–MEXICAN RELATIONS

In the 1990s, the domestic politics of foreign policy were transformed in both the United States and Mexico over many issues, certainly including those in U.S.–Mexican relations. In Mexico, the key transformation was the growth of inter-party competition over the conduct of the nation's international relations; in the United States, it was the drop in domestic support for international engagement.

The Mexican Party System

In Mexico, the transformation of the party system and its relationship to international relations began during the campaign leading to the 1988 presidential and congressional elections, the principal effect of which was the breakdown of a virtual one-party system of rule. Three-way party competition strengthened; opposition party representation in congress grew. From the 1988 campaign onward, Mexican political parties competed over various issues, including their proposed policies toward the United States. Mexico shifted from near unanimity in the domestic political backing for its foreign policy to partisan contentiousness in assessing its international relations. This process climaxed in the national elections in 2000, when an opposition candidate won the presidency and no party obtained a majority in either congressional chamber.

In 1988, the leading opposition challenger for the presidency was Cuauhtémoc Cárdenas. During the campaign, Cárdenas argued, "I think that this administration has been letting foreigners take over our fundamental decisions. It has acted not in the interest of the country but of foreigners who are against Mexico." Cárdenas also argued that Mexico would "have to declare a moratorium on the [international] debt," although this should be done, in his judgment, in order to reach a more favorable agreement with creditors. PRI candidate Salinas responded that "the fundamental decisions of Mexico's economic policy have been taken by Mexicans . . . for the interests of our fellow Mexicans." Salinas also believed that "it is better to negotiate than to enter into confrontation" with international creditors over the debt. Yet, during that election, Salinas also opposed a free trade agreement with the United States: "Listen—on the record— . . . The U.S. and Mexico have very dissimilar economies, it's so uneven the relationship that that's the reason why I have rejected the idea of entering a North American common market."[60] (Despite these differences between politicians, voters took foreign and foreign economic policies into little account in making the electoral choices between presidential candidates in 1988.[61])

By the 1991 nationwide congressional elections, the NAFTA negotiations were under way. Cárdenas opposed a U.S.–Mexican free trade agreement because, he believed, it would leave Mexico as a "low wage, high unemployment economy, with large impoverished sectors, high concentration of income in the hands of a few, and an overwhelming subordination to the U.S. economy."[62] He criticized the increase in imports whose effects, in his estimation, would dismantle Mexico's industrial capacity. On the other hand, Cárdenas and his party, the PRD, did not reject a free trade agreement outright. The PRD proposed a "social charter as a fundamental part of NAFTA." It would emphasize dispute settlement procedures, labor mobility, environmental protection, compensatory investments, and so forth. The PRD's concepts drew from the European Community's treatment of its less economically developed members—Portugal, Spain, Greece, and Ireland.[63]Moreover, Cárdenas no longer proposed a debt moratorium, although he and his associates continued to criticize the terms reached in the Mexican government's public debt settlement with its creditors.

For the 1994 presidential elections, Cárdenas modified his position on NAFTA: "It is now the law of the country. If I am elected I intend to enforce it and assume full responsibility for the implementation of this trilateral commitment of my country." He still thought that NAFTA could be improved, but he would seek to make those improvements "working within the existing framework of NAFTA." His remaining critiques of NAFTA resembled those of much of the Democratic party majority in the U.S. Congress: the need for stronger protection for labor and the environment, better compensatory financial assistance to ease labor and community adjustment to trade-originated economic disruptions, and a more democratic Mexico.[64]

Mexico had thus developed a viable three-party system. The parties debated the fate of the country across many issues including its relations with the United States. The gap among politicians in policy attitudes toward the United States narrowed considerably from the late 1980s to the mid-1990s, however, mirroring the much more collaborative disposition of the Mexican public. Salinas led the PRI and his government to reverse previous policies in order to align with the United States. The opposition PAN supported NAFTA's enactment, giving it bipartisan endorsement in Mexico from the outset. Equally important was the evolution in the attitudes toward NAFTA and the foreign debt evinced by Cárdenas and the PRD.[65] By the mid-1990s, the three main parties supported the fundamental institutional framework and key policies in U.S.–Mexican relations, even if, appropriately, they continued to differ on many specifics. All three political parties had also begun to raise funds among Mexican-origin and other communities in the United States; Mexican presidential candidates typically visited Washington to establish their own credibility during the campaign. Greater democracy, it turned out, had been good for Mexico, not just intrinsically but also because democracy made it possible to establish more firmly and with a broader base the support for the foundations of Mexican relations with the United States.

Some of the key themes in Vicente Fox's successful presidential campaign in 2000 illustrated how Mexican political parties had developed converging views on U.S.–Mexican relations. In 1991, as we noted, Cárdenas and the PRD compared NAFTA unfavorably to the European Community in part because NAFTA, unlike the European Community, failed to provide for transborder labor mobility, more effective environmental protection, and a compensation fund to develop Mexico's poorest regions. In 2000, Fox favored amending NAFTA to create a North American common market to allow a freer flow of merchandise and workers while adhering strictly to standards for the protection of the environment, law enforcement, and workers' rights. Fox also favored the creation of a compensation fund to develop Mexico's poorer regions. "The United States' goal has been to put up walls, police, and soldiers to fight immigration. That can't work," argued Fox.[66] Fox's proposals differed from the PRD's 1991 statement on a fundamental dimension, of course. Fox was a strong supporter of NAFTA, but Fox's specific proposals to widen and deepen NAFTA echoed the PRD's earlier calls for a European-like social charter for NAFTA. (One reason for this inter-partisan convergence was that the same person advised Cárdenas in 1991 and Fox in 2000 regarding U.S.–Mexican relations: Jorge G. Castañeda.) Fox's views on NAFTA amendments facilitate building domestic support within Mexico to fashion new policies toward the United States, even if some of the objectives—free labor mobility in North America—would remain for the time being only a hope.

The U.S. Party System

In the United States, the drop in domestic support for international engagement developed gradually from the 1960s to the 1990s, but it accelerated after the collapse of the Soviet Union with the disappearance of the "cause" of prior sustained U.S. engagement beyond its borders. One example of the decline in U.S. support for internationalism during those decades was the Democratic party's turn toward protectionist policies. In the 1960s, President John Kennedy and the Democrats launched an important worldwide process of trade liberalization, which came to be known as the Kennedy Round of GATT. In 1991, President George Bush asked the U.S. Congress to authorize so-called fast track legislation in order to proceed with NAFTA discussions with Mexico and Canada; approximately 85 percent of the "no" votes in the U.S. Senate and House of Representatives came from Democrats. Opposition was strongest from states with old manufacturing plants and strong labor unions, mainly from the northeast and midwest.[67]

Fortunately for NAFTA's enactment, the agreement was negotiated and signed by a Republican president and it fell to a Democratic president, Bill Clinton, to secure its ratification by the U.S. Congress. On November 17, 1993, the U.S. House of Representatives ratified NAFTA with the votes of three out of four Republicans and four out of ten Democrats.[68] Although the Republicans were the minority party in both chambers in the U.S. Congress, more Republicans than Democrats voted for NAFTA in both the U.S. Senate and the House of Representatives.[69] Despite this inter-party difference in the United States, democratic procedures worked to fashion the bases for broad bipartisan support for NAFTA's fundamental features. The futures of both countries had been joined by the consent of the people's parliamentarians.

The final negotiations over NAFTA also illustrated the complex relationship between political regime, political partisanship, and foreign policy bargaining strength, as already noted earlier in this chapter. Four decades ago, Thomas Schelling described a key tactic of an effective negotiator. Negotiating power, Schelling argued, depends on an evident inability to make concessions: the more constrained I am in my capacity to yield in negotiations, the more credible will be my statements that I cannot yield. Thus, the stronger the domestic political support for a government, the weaker this government's international negotiating leverage, because it will be literally incredible when it claims that it can make no concessions. This has often come to be known as a two-level game, that is, the consequences of domestic politics for international politics and vice versa.[70]

President Salinas had a disciplined command of PRI majorities in both chambers of the Mexican Congress. President Clinton had to construct pro-NAFTA majorities in both chambers of the U.S. Congress drawing from both political parties. There was no automatic internationalist majority in the U.S. Congress, as there once was in the 1960s; Clinton did not command a majority even in his own party. At first blush, this made the Clinton administration seem weaker. And yet, explicitly and implicitly, the Clinton administration played on its weakness to obtain additional concessions from Mexico to modify the NAFTA text negotiated by the Bush administration. The Mexican president was strong enough to impose concessions on his supporters, concessions deemed necessary to enable the "weaker" U.S. president to obtain ratification of the agreement. Even though Mexico was, objectively and structurally, the weaker country, Clinton's political weakness was more credible politically. Mexico had to agree, first, to formal labor and environmental side agreements, and, later, to many last-minute concessions to enable the Clinton administration to secure the votes in the U.S. Congress. Mexico's future negotiating strength relative to the United States should have increased as a result of a deepening of its own democratization following the elections in 2000, when no political party obtained an outright majority in either congressional chamber.

The disappearance of an internationalist majority in the U.S. Congress, and the drop in bipartisan support for international engagement, became clearer in the response to the Mexican financial crisis of late 1994 and early 1995. President

Clinton sought congressional support to bail out Mexico from a major crisis that could threaten the U.S. financial system. The Democrats had become the minority in both chambers of the U.S. Congress, having lost the November 1994 congressional elections. Recalling also that majorities of Democrats had opposed NAFTA's enactment, Clinton turned for support, therefore, to the hitherto more internationalist party, the Republicans. Yet the Republican leaders of the U.S. Senate and the House of Representatives could not deliver a majority of their party to prevent the Mexican financial crisis from deepening and spreading, nor could President Clinton secure a majority among his own Democrats.[71] The U.S. bailout of Mexico in early 1995 occurred thanks to a risky statesmanlike decision by President Clinton to assist the Mexican government on his own authority despite the lack of congressional support.

The decline of U.S. international engagement was evident in other issues as well. The post-1994 Republican majority in the U.S. Senate and House of Representatives distrusted immigration, especially from Mexico. It enacted legislation to increase the frequency of deportations of illegal aliens, including many who were in the process of regularizing their status in the United States, and deny a number of welfare benefits to legal residents of the United States. In particular, the U.S. government accelerated deportations of illegal aliens who had committed crimes; deportations of criminal aliens jumped from 36,967 in Fiscal Year 1996 to 50,165 in Fiscal Year 1997, when on average more than a hundred criminals per day were deported to Mexico.[72]

Several of these acts of congress had unintended consequences. The policies against legal residents generated a huge jump in their applications for U.S. citizenship; many of these were immigrants from Mexico who had been living lawfully in the United States for years but came to feel newly vulnerable. These policies may also have galvanized many naturalized citizens in California (many of whom were also Mexican by origin)—the state where these issues were felt most acutely—to defeat the Republican party in the 1998 elections for governor, the state legislature, and the U.S. Congress. Moreover, criminal deportees newly arrived in Mexico brought with them acquired skills. They were more likely to know English, retain transborder connections to gangs in Los Angeles and other cities, and know better how to use assault weapons than when they first emigrated from Mexico. Thus, the criminal deportations policy could be described as if it were the "U.S. International Criminal Network Enhancement Act"! The shift in partisan control in the U.S. Congress certainly reshaped U.S. international policies, including those that affected Mexico.

The tide of opinion on immigration among U.S. political leaders changed somewhat, however, in time for the U.S. presidential election in 2000. Sustained economic growth in the United States in the 1990s and the drop in the U.S. unemployment rate to low single-digit levels by decade's end facilitated this political change. In the 2000 presidential elections, both major-party candidates, Albert

Gore Jr. and George W. Bush, opposed punitive policies on immigration and courted the U.S. Latino vote.

Implications of Changes in the Party Systems

Both the Mexican and the U.S. party systems were transformed in the 1990s. In Mexico, the new party system, born from the democratic opening, set the foundational framework for a new relationship with the United States. In the United States, the newly configured party system provided less support for international engagement. Support for NAFTA's enactment required hard political work; there was also little support for the financial rescue package, and there was in the mid-1990s punitive legislation toward legal and illegal immigrants, many of whom were Mexicans.

The future of bilateral U.S.–Mexican relations will require steadiness in the Mexican party system and readjustment in the U.S. party system to Mexico's new circumstances. Neither outcome is certain. The best chance for the future of U.S.–Mexican relations lies with public opinion, where convergence in U.S.–Mexican opinions and preferences seems all the more remarkable in the light of this analysis. Perhaps just as Mexican party politicians came to see the worth of good U.S.–Mexican relations in part because that is what voters supported, so too will U.S. politicians come to represent the positive U.S. public attitudes toward Mexico.

CONCLUSION

In the 1990s, the salience of U.S.–Mexican relations rose for both countries. Business firms profited, as did organized crime. Ordinary citizens crisscrossed the border legally and illegally. Non-governmental organizations established transnational links to shape policies in both countries. This increasingly important and complex relationship multiplied the number of actors that sought participation and gain. This process led to a decentralization of decision-making from the public to the private arenas, from the capital cities to the states and local governments, from the executives to the legislatures and courts, and even within the executive branches of the respective national governments away from the foreign ministries. Political parties fractured over their views concerning this bilateral relationship; the mass media became suspicious and at times hostile toward the government and institutions of the other country. And yet, Mexico and the United States became closer and prospered more in the 1990s than at previous times in their shared history. One key to this successful outcome was the role of the presidents of the two countries in creating new means for policy coordination. Another key was the surprising statesmanship of U.S. and Mexican citizens who, better than those who claim to represent their interests, understood that these two peoples had much to gain from each other.

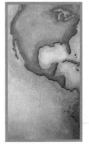

CONTENT AND CONDUCT

OF FOREIGN POLICY VI

PRINCIPLES, PROFITS, AND POWER WERE AT THE HEART OF U.S.–Mexican relations in the 1990s. In this chapter, we examine some aspects of each of these three concepts. We first consider the internationalization of important aspects of Mexican domestic politics—namely, the structure of its political regime and its observance of the human rights of its citizens. Mexico had long sought to create an impermeable barrier to external influence over these domestic characteristics. That barrier broke in the 1990s. International organizations, transnational alliances of non-governmental organizations, U.S. political organizations, and even the U.S. government exercised direct impact on these aspects of Mexican politics.

Second, we analyze aspects of U.S.–Mexican relations in the areas of finance, trade, and investment. We argue that the North American Free Trade Agreement (NAFTA) succeeded in fostering the growth of trade and investment, promoting efficiencies and economies of scale. NAFTA also made it easier to settle trade disputes through agreed-upon routine procedures. And NAFTA provided the necessary political underpinning for the Clinton administration's decision to rescue Mexico from its financial collapse in late 1994 and early 1995. NAFTA did not, however, meet the hyperbolic expectations of many of its strongest advocates prior to its enactment. Nor did NAFTA in the 1990s address Mexico's severe problems of poverty and maldistribution of income.

Finally, we explore the exercise of diplomatic power. How did each government advance and represent its interests in its normal diplomatic interaction with the other? We argue that both the United States and Mexico changed their respective strategies of diplomatic representation toward each other in the 1990s. The United States set aside its active interventionist practices of the 1980s; Mexico departed from a longer tradition of low-profile diplomacy. Their respective diplomatic practices converged toward active but professional and respectful representation of each country's interests. In forgoing the crude exercise of its power, the U.S. government gained greater influence. And in abandoning its excessive diplomatic self-restraint, the Mexican government came to represent its own interests more effectively.

These three trends connected the United States and Mexico much more intimately in the 1990s, as their business firms, human rights activists, diplomats, labor unions, election observers, government officials, and others pursued their interests. In so doing, they exercised effective power to earn profits, defend the rules, and advocate the principles that govern this deeper and increasingly complex bilateral relationship.

MEXICAN DEMOCRACY AND HUMAN RIGHTS IN U.S.–MEXICAN RELATIONS

"The perfect dictatorship is not communism, nor is it the Soviet Union, nor is it Fidel Castro: it is Mexico." So alleged the Peruvian novelist and presidential candidate Mario Vargas Llosa in August 1990 during a series of round tables convoked in Mexico City by the dean of Mexican letters, the late Octavio Paz.[1] Vargas Llosa noted that the long-term permanence of a single party in power, the manipulation of elections, and the suppression of domestic criticism marked this dictatorship.

Mexico had long escaped international criticism of its political system. The Latin-American political left (especially that in Argentina, Chile, El Salvador, and Nicaragua) was grateful to Mexican governments of the 1960s through the 1980s for having granted asylum to those fleeing from military dictatorships. The Cuban government appreciated that Mexico's was the only government that never broke diplomatic or economic relations with Cuba. Latin-American right-wing governments welcomed Mexico's respect for, and defense of, their sovereign rights to shield their domestic political systems from external critique. The U.S. government feared communist influence much more than Institutional Revolutionary Party (PRI) dominance in Mexico; it long eschewed disparaging remarks on Mexico's lack of democracy.

By the time of Vargas Llosa's criticism, much of the world had changed, and it had changed suddenly. In 1989, communist regimes had tumbled across Eastern Europe; only a very weakened Soviet Union lingered. Military dictatorships had ended throughout South America, most satisfyingly so earlier in 1990 in Chile. In early 1990, an important precedent had been set in Nicaragua's presidential elections: the United Nations (UN) and many international non-governmental organizations deployed a large number of election observers, with the consent of Nicaragua's Sandinista government, to help ensure the fairness of the electoral process. In late 1990, Mexico had yet to meet minimum standards of democratic constitutionalism, that is, its political regime did not ensure effective rights for the opposition to contest and win power, nor was it governed by effective rules to conduct campaigns and elections fairly.[2]

In May 1990, the Inter-American Human Rights Commission published its report in response to the complaint filed by Mexico's National Action Party (PAN), protesting irregularities in elections held in 1985 and 1986 in the states of

Durango and Chihuahua. The commission found that the civil rights of Mexican citizens had been violated. When Mexico's foreign ministry sought to deny the commission's right to comment on domestic elections, the commission shot back that Mexico itself had defended that very right for the commission's work in other countries. In June 1990, Americas Watch, a U.S.–based human rights non-governmental organization, released an even more critical report about human rights violations in Mexico, in particular holding the federal judicial police accountable. The international press began to criticize Mexico's poor record on democracy and human rights. Indeed, only the U.S. government remained a steadfast ally on these issues. The Reagan administration congratulated Carlos Salinas de Gortari even before the votes were counted (and evidence of fraud presented) on his presidential election in 1988; the Bush administration remained mum on the deficiencies of the Mexican political system while NAFTA negotiations were under way. Yet, in 1990, faced with a barrage of international criticism, the Mexican government made a first concession: President Salinas created the first National Commission on Human Rights.[3]

The lack of democracy in Mexico became an international issue both because of changes in the international system and also because of changes in Mexico. As noted above, PAN internationalized its dispute with the PRI over the 1985–86 state elections in Durango and Chihuahua. PAN took its protest to the Inter-American Human Rights Commission, to individual U.S. senators, including the ranking Republican on the Senate Foreign Relations Committee, Jesse Helms (R-NC), and to representatives of Washington think tanks; PAN also held a press conference at the National Press Club in Washington, DC. Other Mexicans in 1984 had founded the Academia Mexicana de Derechos Humanos as a civic organization. But these voices within Mexico had gone unheard until the international context changed. In 1990, President Salinas wanted to alter the character of U.S.–Mexican relations, leading eventually to the signing and ratification of NAFTA. Salinas believed that his government's foreign economic policy goals could only succeed if Mexico's "image" were better. Thus, for the sake of foreign economic policy goals, the Mexican government gradually became more vulnerable to domestic and international pressure on human rights and democracy.

After the hotly contested 1988 presidential election, the left-wing candidate, Cuauhtémoc Cárdenas, also internationalized his dispute with the PRI. Cárdenas toured the United States in search of support especially among the Mexican-origin population in Chicago and Los Angeles. On behalf of their Party of the Democratic Revolution (PRD), Cárdenas and leading PRD senator Porfirio Muñoz Ledo (1988–94) argued that Mexico should democratize before signing NAFTA. Muñoz Ledo made his case to the U.S. Congress, too, principally to the Democrats. U.S. representative Robert Torricelli (D-NJ), chairman of the U.S. House of Representatives' Western Hemisphere Subcommittee, held two hearings on human rights and elections in Mexico. Mexican human rights organizations at long last became stronger; they sought alliances with their counterparts in the United States and other countries as part of their strategy of organizational development. In short, Mexican opposition parties across the ideological spectrum, and human rights organizations, publicly sought international and, specifically, U.S. pressure on the government of Mexico, breaking the taboo of non-intervention that had long prevailed in Mexican politics consistent with a traditional notion of sovereignty.[4]

The Mexican government responded strategically to these events. In 1990, it created the Program for Mexican Communities Living in Foreign Countries to strengthen its ties with the Mexican diaspora in the United States. As part of the new program, the Mexican Foreign Ministry increased the number of consulates in the United States and expanded their services to assist Mexican-origin communities.[5] The Salinas administration was not about to let the Mexican opposition monopolize relations with Mexican-origin people in the United States. And, cleverly but also appropriately, the Mexican government launched a democratizing international program of its own—namely, a new endeavor to protect the human rights of Mexican migrant workers in the United States, seeking the help of U.S. non-governmental organizations (NGOs) to this effect.[6] These Mexican government activities benefited from convergent concerns from U.S. NGOs about violations of the rights of migrants by U.S. agencies at or near the U.S.–Mexican border.[7]

Continued international and, specifically, U.S. pressure on the Mexican government contributed to other important changes in Mexican electoral laws in time for the 1994 presidential elections. The principal explanation for these changes lies, of course, in Mexican domestic political processes, including the Zapatista insurgency that broke out in the state of Chiapas in January 1994. The main change with international repercussion was to permit "international visitors," though officially not "election observers," to be present in Mexico while the campaign and election were under way. Until early 1994, the Mexican government had defiantly resisted any international presence at all in Mexico during election time. Prior to the election, the Mexican government also invited the UN to provide technical assistance for better election administration. On election day, the Mexican government permitted, indeed promoted, exit polling and quick-counts as means to assess the fairness of the electoral process; in the 1988 presidential election, the Mexican government prohibited exit polling on election day.[8]

The most important electoral reforms were approved in 1996. The Federal Electoral Institute (IFE) became strikingly independent. The president surrendered his right to appoint any councilors. The IFE would henceforth be led by citizen councilors chosen by a two-thirds vote of the chamber of deputies (this super-majority requirement ensured that at least two of the three largest parties had to vote to appoint them). The IFE was given a significant budget and large professional staff. The new electoral law also allocated large funds for the public financing of electoral campaigns. In the 2000 national election, each of the two opposition coalitions clustered around PAN and the PRD received approximately $100 million in public financing. These changes strengthened the Mexican opposition, making possible its unprecedented and successful victory in the July 1997 elections, wresting control of the national chamber of deputies and the government of Mexico City from the PRI, and promoting the even more decisive presidential victory by Vicente Fox, PAN candidate, in the 2000 elections.

A turning point in U.S.–Mexican relations over democracy took place in May 1997 during President Bill Clinton's visit to Mexico. Clinton met officially with the leaders of the principal Mexican opposition parties across the ideological rainbow, namely PAN and the PRD. This was the first time a president of the United States had had such meetings.[9] President Clinton thus signaled that the U.S. government no longer had a preferred partisan interlocutor in Mexico.

A more belated international pressure pushing toward holding free and fair elections in Mexico came from Wall Street. International investors value long-term stability. By the late 1990s, they did not believe that the PRI rule by fair or foul means could provide such stability; only legitimate rule obtained through fair elections could do so. International brokerage houses, mutual fund companies, bond rating agencies, and significant investors pressed this point upon President Zedillo and his economic cabinet. Zedillo and his economic team were acutely aware of Wall Street's sensitivity to the fairness of the electoral process; these political and economic actors feared a Mexican stock market crash in the wake of an outcome other than the recognition of the people's choice. The fact that the two leading presidential contenders, Francisco Labastida (PRI) and Vicente Fox, had market-friendly views facilitated Wall Street's nonpartisanship.[10] In this fashion, Mexico's prolonged and pronounced international economic engagement and market liberalization, before and after NAFTA's enactment, made an important albeit subtle contribution to Mexico's democratization.

By the late 1990s, there had been less progress with regard to human rights violations, however. In September 1998, the Inter-American Commission on Human Rights published a broad critical assessment of the condition of human rights in Mexico. The commission noted important improvements since it began to focus on Mexican issues ten years earlier. Unlike in the earlier more limited report, this time the commission identified a wide range of violations of Mexico's own constitutional standards and of standards set in international conventions to which Mexico was a party. The commission found insufficient "institutional safeguards against the existence of abuses of authority and violations of human rights"; evidence of "indiscriminate repression of social organizations and leaders," especially in states that had been effectively militarized, and of "enforced disappearances and extrajudicial killings" carried out by the state's security forces; and evidence that "torture and cruel treatment continue to be used by some sectors of the security forces." The commission noted that "overcrowding of the prison population of Mexico is a serious problem," especially because "the Mexican State cannot guarantee prompt and timely trial." The rights of indigenous peoples were especially at risk. During its on-site visit to Mexico, the commission "received genuinely serious and alarming reports and testimony about corruption, abuses, and ill treatment in different police stations in the country."[11] Some U.S. non-governmental organizations, moreover, worried about U.S. training, weapons transfers, and advice to the Mexican military, for fear that the United States would support human rights violations directly or indirectly. There was particular concern with regard to counterinsurgency operations in Chiapas and other southern states.[12]

In the face of this and other international criticisms, the government of President Ernesto Zedillo took a proactive approach. The Mexican government welcomed visits from the Inter-American Commission on Human Rights, the Special Rapporteur from the UN Commission on Human Rights concerned with the practice of torture, and this commission's secretary-general. In each instance, the Mexican government sought to signal its respect for international norms and institutions while continuing to assert its belief in the principles of sovereignty and non-intervention. The Mexican government often indicated a willingness to abide by the recommendations of these international organizations, but the actual implementation of those recommendations was limited indeed. More noteworthy was Mexico's decision in 1998 to accept the jurisdiction of the Inter-American Court for Human Rights, while reserving only the right to expel foreigners from Mexico without trial. The Zedillo administration enacted new procedures to regulate quite closely the actions of international non-governmental human rights organizations and their observers in Mexico. The Zedillo government also successfully persuaded the European Union that Mexico could meet its standards for economic partnership, including respect for democracy and human rights, as part of the negotiations for a free trade agreement.[13] In general, the Zedillo administration's ability to cope with international human rights pressures was more impressive than its capacity to improve human rights conditions in Mexico.

By the start of the twenty-first century, Mexico was no longer even an imperfect dictatorship. Much had changed in its political system, opening the prospects of a more democratic future. Observance of, and protection for, human rights remained weak but probably not weaker than before 1990 when national and international scrutiny and publicity at long last fell on damnable enduring practices. A key change in the 1990s was the internationalization of issues pertaining to Mexico's democracy and human rights. These issues had long escaped international attention, in contrast to the monitoring they had received elsewhere in Latin America. The internationalization of Mexican domestic politics resulted from changes in the international system, especially the collapse of communist and military authoritarian regimes, the spread of the belief that democracy was a right that the international community should enforce in the Americas and consequent changes in U.S. policy, and the pressures to which Mexican foreign economic policy and international economic relations exposed the Mexican government. In November 1999, as we will see below, Mexico signed a free trade agreement with the European Union that went beyond NAFTA in one key respect: this agreement embodied a clause committing all signatories to observe democratic practices. But such internationalization of Mexican domestic political issues occurred above all because the hero of the Mexican political transition, its civil society, reached out beyond the nation's boundaries to bring international actors to counter the weight of those who had long governed Mexico. This partnership between Mexican society and the international system opened a new chapter in U.S.–Mexican relations, and in Mexico's relations with the rest of the world—one marked by both conflict and cooperation, but especially by ongoing substantial change.

The election of Fox and the transformation of the Mexican Congress removed from the U.S.–Mexican agenda the most significant concerns about democratic practice in Mexico. The Fox presidency would build on the policy change begun during the Salinas and Zedillo presidencies, welcoming international advice and assistance to deepen Mexico's democratization down to the levels of states and municipalities and to improve effective protection for the human rights of all Mexicans.

FINANCE, TRADE, AND INVESTMENT

NAFTA is not a panacea, said President Salinas when the U.S. House of Representatives approved it at the end of 1993. Salinas intended to modify the image he had done so much to create during the previous three years—namely, that NAFTA would be the "silver bullet" for all Mexican economic hardships, its ticket to enter the group of developed nations. The first years of NAFTA would prove that NAFTA was not a panacea. It could not break the six-year crisis cycle that the Mexican economy suffered since 1976. At the turn of the millennium, Mexico still faced important economic hardships, considerable poverty, and severe income maldistribution.[14] However, NAFTA fulfilled its main goals of facilitating trade, investment, and economic integration in North America and, in so doing, held out hope for improving the lives of many more of the citizens of its three member countries in the longer term.

Twenty days after President Zedillo's inauguration, on December 20, 1994, a financial crisis erupted in Mexico; it would turn into an economic rout. The financial crisis was precipitated by the combination of Mexican government obstinacy in keeping an unchanged and overvalued exchange rate along with massive, unregulated, and volatile international financial flows.[15] Mexico's overvalued and seemingly stable peso had attracted a very large volume of portfolio investment. Portfolio investment nearly quadrupled from 1990 to 1991; it more than doubled from 1991 to 1993, when it reached $28.9 billion. Foreign funds helped to finance Mexico's burgeoning trade deficits, which amounted to $17.3 billion in 1994. In 1994, however, the Zapatista rebellion, two political assassinations, the uncertainties of presidential transition, and opaque central bank policies discouraged the flow of international funds. Total portfolio investment fell to $8.2 billion in 1994 (see Figure 6.1). When Mexico could not hold any longer the parity of the peso to the dollar, a financial stampede broke; $10.1 billion flew out of the country in 1995. In 1995, Mexico's output fell more than six percent, a sharper one-year drop than during any of the terrible years of the economic depression of the 1980s.[16]

A fuller picture of Mexico's financial volatility is presented in Table 6.1. The volatility of portfolio investment is directly related, of course, to the volatility of the Mexico City stock market. The sharp drop in the Mexican stock market from 1993 to 1995 is one of the key aspects of the 1994–95 financial panic. But the data in Table 6.1 display other patterns as well. Net direct foreign investment and international bond issues remained uninterruptedly positive during the 1990s. Yet, international bond financing showed more volatility than net direct foreign investment. International bond financing was cut nearly in half between 1993 and 1994; it dropped substantially again in 1998, coinciding with another substantial decline in the Mexican stock market and with the Russian financial crash that took place that year. Net direct investment rose from 1993 to 1994—countercyclical to the stock market decline and the drop in international bond financing—and just paused in 1998 as other indicators retreated more sharply. The combined picture summarized in net resource transfers demonstrated very substantial international financial volatility. There were massive net transfers in the early 1990s, a pronounced three-year contraction from 1994 through 1996, a recovery in net transfers in 1997 to 1998 that did not, however, reach the magnitude of the early 1990s, and a retrenchment in 1999 possibly in response to the Brazilian financial panic that year as well as to the start of the Mexican presidential election campaign. This volatility posed a severe challenge to Mexico's polity and economy, but it also illustrated the substantial clout that international financial investors had acquired in Mexico. The Mexican government had sought to dampen such volatility and foster sustained confidence in Mexico, but that goal had yet to be reached as the twentieth century ended.

One small-scale illustration of the vagaries of Mexico's international financial circumstances is the story of The Mexico Fund, Inc., a diversified, closed-end investment management company seeking long-term capital appreciation. It invests in the Mexican stock exchange. Incorporated in Maryland in 1981, the fund is listed on the New York Stock Exchange. Its articles of incorporation and bylaws require that at least 60 percent of the members of its board of directors be citizens and residents of Mexico. In 2000, its board included, among others, a former chairman and CEO of Ford Motor Company, the chairman and CEO of Kimberly-Clark de México, and Jaime Serra Puche, who led Mexico's successful team negotiating NAFTA. At that time, the fund managed about $1.1 billion in assets. Its performance is summarized in Table 6.2. The Mexico Fund's short- to medium-term performance was highly volatile; Mexico may be a good long-term investment, however. Most of the fund's volatility is inherent to investing in the

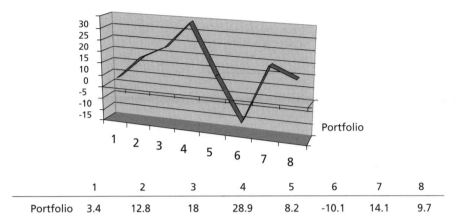

	1	2	3	4	5	6	7	8
Portfolio	3.4	12.8	18	28.9	8.2	-10.1	14.1	9.7

FIGURE 6.1
Foreign Portfolio Investment in Mexico, 1990–1997
(billion dollars)

Note: 1=1990 . . . 8=1997.
Source: *Banco de México*; Mexican Advice on Investment, "Economic Report of Bancomer, September 1997."

Mexican economy, but part of its volatility derived mainly from the relatively small size of the Mexican stock market. One stock alone, Teléfonos de México (Telmex), accounted for over ten percent of the fund's portfolio, and one conglomerate alone (Grupo Carso) through its various companies, including Telmex, accounted for nearly a quarter of the fund's assets.

The 1994–95 financial crisis became an important test for post-NAFTA cooperation between the United States and Mexico. Mexico's financial obligations amounted to approximately $50 billion in 1995. Mexican officials, once again, came to Washington seeking help. On January 11, 1995, President Clinton announced that "the United States is committed to doing what we can do to help Mexico through what I believe is and should be a short-term crisis." The following day, Clinton announced his proposal to request authorization from the U.S. Congress to extend $40 billion to Mexico in loan guarantees. Clinton's decision to help Mexico was noteworthy because it was made at a low point in his presidency. On January 3, 1995, the Republicans took control of both chambers of the U.S. Congress for the first time in 40 years. Republican leaders in congress initially supported the package, but they had miscalculated the extent of support for the president's initiative in the new congress. The so-called freshmen (newly elected) Republican representatives and senators, and a protectionist group of Democrats in the U.S. House of Representatives, opposed the president's proposal. Facing mounting opposition in congress, the administration decided to provide guarantees by using the Exchange Stabilization Fund rather than seeking to enact a law. Many in congress protested that this decision violated the statute creating that fund.[17] In the end, the president's policy prevailed. The Clinton administration's

TABLE 6.1

Mexico's International Financial Volatility

	Net Direct Foreign Investment (billion dollars)	International Bond Issues (billion dollars)	Dollar Index of Mexico City Stock Exchange (6/1997=100)	Net Resource Transfers (billion dollars)
1991	4.7	3.8	88.5	14.8
1992	4.4	6.1	106.2	16.4
1993	4.4	11.3	156.0	18.4
1994	11.0	6.9	91.1	-1.7
1995	9.5	7.6	66.5	-2.1
1996	9.2	17.8	77.3	-9.3
1997	12.8	15.7	114.1	5.9
1998	10.2	8.4	69.5	4.6
1999	11.0	9.7	120.3	-0.5

Source: United Nations Economic Commission for Latin America and the Caribbean, *Preliminary Overview of the Economies of Latin America and the Caribbean,* LC/G.2088-P (New York, December 1999), 96, 97, 98, 100.

support package for Mexico consisted of more than $50 billion. Of that sum, $20 billion came from the United States, $17.8 billion from the International Monetary Fund, $10 billion in short-term swap facilities from a number of central banks channeled through the Bank for International Settlements in Basle, Switzerland, up to $1 billion from Canada, and smaller amounts from other countries in Latin America.[18]

Mexico's economic and political setbacks provided ammunition to the critics of NAFTA. The U.S. organized labor movement presidential candidate Pat Buchanan (from the right wing of the Republican party) and Democrat Richard Gephardt (D-MO), the protectionist-minded minority leader of the U.S. House of Representatives, argued that it had been a mistake to create an economic partnership with Mexico. NAFTA critics emphasized that after NAFTA went into effect, the U.S. trade surplus with Mexico turned into a deficit; moreover, as a consequence of Mexico's economic slowdown, Mexico's imports from the United States continued to shrink, while its exports went on growing. The trade balance turned from $3.5 billion U.S. surplus in 1993 to a $12.4 billion deficit in 1995. In fact, as Table 6.1 shows, Mexico soon regained substantial access to international capital markets. The Mexican economy also recovered quickly; gross domestic product grew between four and seven percent per year each year from 1996 to 1999. And, as we show below, U.S.–Mexican trade boomed.

NAFTA's Impact

NAFTA has been a great success in its primary purpose—namely, to increase trade. During NAFTA's first five years total trade between the two countries grew

TABLE 6.2

The Mexico Fund: Net Asset Value per Share, 1990–2000
(percentages)

1 Year	2 Years	3 Years	5 Years	10 Years
-2.79	17.03	-0.07	59.13	162.11

Source: http//:www.themexicofund.com/indice.html.

TABLE 6.3

Mexico's Trade Balance with the United States, 1993–1998
(million dollars)

	1993	1994	1995	1996	1997	1998	Percentage 1998/1993
Exports	42,851	51,645	66,273	80,574	94,185	102,872	140.0
Oil	4,696	5,286	6,366	8,929	8,624	5,545	18.1
Agriculture	3,572	3,824	5,282	5,081	5,528	6,095	70.6
Manufactured goods	34,583	42,534	54,625	66,564	80,033	91,232	163.8
Imports	45,295	54,790	53,829	67,536	82,002	93,095	105.5
Consumption	5,613	7,367	5,513	6,943	9,292	10,340	84.2
Intermediate	31,987	37,489	40,184	48,916	58,121	64,917	102.9
Capital goods	7,695	9,934	8,132	11,677	14,589	17,838	131.8
Trade Balance	-2,444	-3,145	12,444	13,038	12,183	9,777	——
Trade Total	88,146	106,435	120,102	148,110	176,186	195,967	122.3

Source: Secretaría de Comercia y Fomento Industrial (SECOFI), with supplementary data from the Banco de México.

122 percent, that is, from $88.1 billion in 1993 to $195.9 billion in 1998 (see Table 6.3). Mexican exports to the United States rose 140 percent from 1993 to 1998; they increased over 20 percent per year since NAFTA came into effect, though the 1994–95 peso devaluation accounts for some of that growth rate. Under NAFTA, manufactured exports became the most dynamic Mexican export sector to the United States. From 1993 to 1998, Mexico's exports of manufactured goods to the United States grew 163.8 percent, agricultural exports 70.6 percent, and oil exports 18.1. In 1998, Mexico's three main merchandise exports to the United States were automobiles, color televisions, and cables and plugs, 9.0, 4.7, and 4.3 percent of total exports, respectively (see Table 6.4).

Mexican imports from the United States also grew significantly every year under NAFTA, except for the catastrophic year 1995. Mexican imports from the United States grew 105.5 percent from 1993 to 1998. This growth was broad-based: consumption goods rose 84.2 percent, intermediate goods 102.9 percent,

TABLE 6.4

Leading Mexican Exports to and Imports from the United States
(million dollars)

	Exports			Imports		
Product	1998	Percentage	Product	1998	Percentage
Automobiles	9,320.8	9.0	Automobile parts	3,212.2	3.4
Color televisions	4,813.9	4.7	Integrated circuits	2,751.3	2.9
Cables, plugs, and electric conductors	4,443.2	4.3	Plastics	2,172.1	2.3
Processing machinery, data and units	3,224.0	3.1	Manufactured iron and steel	1,543.1	1.7
Cargo vehicles	3,187.1	3.1	Cathode ray tubes	1,335.9	1.4
Automobile parts	2,495.4	2.4	Automobile engines	1,252.2	1.3
Cotton apparel for men and women	2,100.0	2.0	Automobiles	1,110.9	1.2
Television and radio parts	1,802.8	1.7	Circuit breakers	1,021.6	1.1
Machinery parts	1,793.9	1.7	Printed circuits	702.5	0.7
Motors	1,573.8	1.5	Airplanes and aircraft	631.4	0.7

Source: SECOFI, with data from the Banco de México.

and capital goods 131.8 percent (see Table 6.3). In 1998, Mexico's three main merchandise imports from the United States were auto parts, integrated circuits, and plastic manufactures, 3.4, 2.9, and 2.3 percent of total imports, respectively (see Table 6.4).

NAFTA also fosters investment (see Table 6.1). Net foreign direct investment first peaked in 1994. It slowed down a bit thereafter, but, unlike portfolio investment, net foreign investment remained positive in the 1990s. Foreign direct investors were more likely than portfolio investors to remain in Mexico for the long haul. The U.S. share of total foreign direct investment in Mexico amounted to 60 to 65 percent in 1998.[19] U.S. foreign direct investment in Mexico in 1998 accounted for just three percent of U.S. foreign direct investment worldwide.[20]

A key to NAFTA's success in trade and investment is its impact on production specialization in North America. Economic integration is most valuable when it allows countries to specialize within the same overall industry or economic sector.[21] This permits the development of economies of scale within firms and economic sectors, as is especially evident in the North American automobile industry. In the 1990s, the three U.S. automakers—Chrysler, Ford, and General Motors—invested heavily to upgrade their plants in Mexico to better integrate them to the North American system of production. Mexico specialized in producing light and pick-up trucks and vans.[22] Intra-industry trade, an important measure of specialization, was also evident in the automobile sector: the top U.S. export to Mexico in 1998 was auto parts, and five of the ten principal Mexican exports to the United States were in the automobile sector (see Table 6.4).

Of course, NAFTA increased Mexico's dependence on the U.S. economy. The U.S. share of Mexico's total trade increased from 68 percent in 1993 to 79 percent in 1998. Mexican exports increased their reliance on the U.S. market from 71 percent in 1993 to 82 percent in 1998. North America became Mexico's most dynamic export market. As shown in Table 6.5, the growth rate of Mexican exports to North America outpaced the growth rate of Mexican exports worldwide from 1993 to 1998. Similarly, the growth rate of Mexican imports from North America outpaced the growth rate of Mexican imports from all corners of the world.

There is also a marked economic asymmetry between the United States and Mexico. In 1997, Mexico received 10 percent of total U.S. merchandise exports while the United States purchased 85 percent of total Mexican exports. Nonetheless, the United States also increased its dependence on Mexico. In 1998, Mexico was the second most important U.S. trade partner, ahead of Japan and Germany. From 1994 to 1998, U.S. imports from Mexico grew at 19 percent per year, while U.S. imports from the rest of the world grew at 13 percent per year. The United States increased its reliance generally on the NAFTA region. In 1997, Mexico and Canada represented 32 percent of all U.S. merchandise trade, exceeding trade with Japan and the European Union combined (see Figure 6.2).

Finally, one of the central objectives in the foundation of NAFTA was to provide an effective dispute settlement mechanism that would reach solutions to specific trade disputes and secure the compliance of the adversaries at a minimum of disruption to the bilateral relationship. This was the hope for NAFTA's Chapter Nineteen. It worked. In the 1990s, Chapter Nineteen became an effective mechanism to defend Mexican and Canadian exporters against the arbitrary use of penalties for so-called unfair trade practices (countervailing duties and antidumping duties) by U.S. firms. From 1993 to 1998, NAFTA panels reviewed 43 decisions; 20 reviewed U.S. decisions, 13 considered Canadian decisions, and 10 examined Mexican decisions. NAFTA's review procedures forced officials in the three countries to apply their own trade legislation more carefully and improve the legal reasoning for their final decisions.[23]

In the 1990s, NAFTA's implementation was free neither from frictions nor from decisions that seemed to contradict the text of the agreement. Among the most controversial cases was an anti-dumping petition against Mexican tomatoes and the U.S. delay of Mexican trucks seeking to carry cargo into the border states. The tomato case affected exports worth $450 million. U.S. tomato growers filed a case against fresh tomato imports from Mexico. One study on the case concluded, "none of the proposed measures [restrictions of Mexican exports] actually addresses the fundamental question of how Florida growers can adapt to the evolving reality of globalization by increasing their competitiveness and/or diversifying."[24] The trucking case had a more marked arbitrary character. NAFTA specified that trucks from the United States and Mexico would be permitted to carry cargo to the contiguous states on the other side of the border three years after the signature of the agreement. A few days before the measure was scheduled to go into effect, U.S. officials unilaterally delayed its implementation on the grounds that Mexican trucks were unsafe and Mexican drivers were trained inadequately.[25]

In conclusion, NAFTA succeeded within its own terms. It fostered trade and investment impressively. It made it much easier to resolve complex trade disputes through routine procedures. It facilitated economic integration within North America, promoting efficiencies and economies of scale. NAFTA did not, of course, meet the wildly exaggerated expectations that were employed by some of its proponents to facilitate its approval.

THE SEARCH FOR DIVERSIFICATION

Mexico's search for diversification of its international relations has been a constant in its foreign policy. Diversification is understood as the search for equilibrium faced with the overwhelming presence of the United States. Historically, diversification meant strengthening bilateral linkages with countries other than the United States, reinforcing Mexico's presence in multilateral forums, and establishing bilateral relations with newly independent countries around the world. As noted in chapter four, President Luis Echeverría Alvarez (1970–76) distinguished himself in terms of international activism; during his six-year term, the number of countries with which Mexico had diplomatic relations increased from 67 to 129.[26]

In the 1990s, the search for diversification developed a much stronger commercial focus. The meaning of diversification was also transformed from the search for political balance while facing Washington to bolstering Mexico's economy. The proliferation of free trade agreements highlights the intention of turning Mexico into a hub for domestic and international companies seeking to export their products throughout the Americas.[27] In the 1990s, for example, Mexico signed free trade agreements with Chile, Venezuela, Colombia, Bolivia, Costa Rica, and Nicaragua. In late 1999, Mexico concluded a free trade and cooperation agreement with the European Union; in February 2000, it signed a free trade agreement with Israel. In June 2000, Mexico signed a free trade agreement with Guatemala, El Salvador, and Honduras. Soon after his election as president in July 2000, Vicente Fox announced his interest in signing a free trade agreement with MERCOSUR, the southern South American common market whose members were Argentina, Brazil, Paraguay, and Uruguay.

TABLE 6.5

Mexican Trade by Region, 1993 and 1998
(million dollars)

	Exports		
	1993	1998	Percent
	a	b	b/a
Total	51,832.0	117,442.1	126.6
North America	44,419.5	104,392.4	135.0
Latin American Integration Association (ALADI)	1,601.6	2,992.6	86.9
Central America	649.4	1,671.5	157.4
European Union	2,788.5	3,909.0	40.2
Rest of Europe	151.7	277.4	82.9
Asia*	1,008.6	1,750.8	73.6
Rest of the world	1,212.7	2,448.4	101.9

Note: Balance=Exports minus Imports.
*Japan, China, Taiwan, Hong Kong, South Korea, and Singapore.
Source: SECOFI, with data from Banco de México.

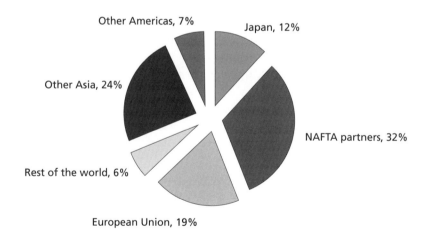

FIGURE 6.2
Composition of U.S. Merchandise Trade, 1997
(percentage)

Source: http://www.secofi-snci.gob.mx/Estadistica/Commx.htm.

TABLE 6.5 continued

	Imports			Balance	
1993	1998	Percent		1993	1998
a	b	b/a			
65,366.5	125,242.4	91.6		-13,534.5	-7,800.3
46,470.0	95,386.9	105.3		-2,050.5	9,005.5
2,165.9	2,560.5	18.2		-564.3	406.1
179.9	237.5	32.0		469.5	1,434.0
7,798.7	11,714.0	50.2		-5010.2	-7,805.0
530.7	648.3	22.2		-379.0	-370.9
6,516.7	10,357.0	58.9		-5,508.1	-8,606.2
1,704.6	4,338.2	154.5		-491.9	-1,889.8

Latin America

In 1991, during the NAFTA negotiations, the Mexican government signed a free trade agreement with Chile, a country with which Mexico had had a very modest commercial exchange but close political connections, particularly during the deposed socialist government of Salvador Allende (1970–73). This agreement had strong political symbolism, signaling that Mexico would continue to diversify its international relations and strengthen its ties with Latin America despite being in the process of negotiating an agreement with the United States and Canada. By the second half of the 1990s, however, the commercial aspect of Mexican foreign policy had become truly significant. Bilateral trade boomed with Chile; trade with the five other Latin American countries with which Mexico had signed free trade agreements increased as well. Between 1991 and 1998, trade with Chile soared by 572 percent to pass $1.2 billion.[28] Similarly, from 1995 to 1999, Mexico boosted its trade with Costa Rica and Nicaragua by 280 percent and 202 percent, respectively (calculated from Figure 6.3). From 1995 to 1999, Mexico also increased markedly its trade with Colombia, Venezuela, and Bolivia (see Figure 6.3). Nonetheless, at the end of the 1990s, all of Latin America accounted for only about two percent of Mexican imports and four percent of Mexican exports.

Mexico's free trade agreements with Latin American countries had a structure similar to NAFTA's. The negotiating team from the Mexican Ministry of Trade and Industrial Promotion (SECOFI) developed a model for free trade agreements inspired by NAFTA and applied it with success to its new trade negotiations.[29] The Zedillo administration also opened free trade negotiations with Panama, Ecuador, Peru, Belize, and Trinidad and Tobago.[30]

Mexico's aggressive strategy of developing free trade agreements with numerous Latin American countries was observed cautiously by U.S. trade officials. Some feared that this strategy would allow Mexico to position itself as the only country with unfettered access to markets throughout the hemisphere; in turn, this could hamper the U.S. effort to create a 34-country free trade area in the Americas. Mexico's campaign developed at a time when the Clinton administration's ability to take the lead in opening markets was hobbled by the loss of "fast-track" negotiating authority.[31]

Europe

President Zedillo's administration considered Mexico's cooperation and free trade agreement with the European Union to be one of its most important foreign policy accomplishments. This agreement differed on two counts from those that Mexico signed with Latin American governments. First, the 15 countries that make up the European Union represent an economic powerhouse comparable only to the United States. Second, the agreement goes beyond trade and investment issues because it contains a clause on cooperation and another on upholding democratic practices within signatory countries; Mexico insisted on the first clause, the European Union on the second.

As noted in chapter four, President Salinas tried unsuccessfully at the outset of his administration to foster trade and investment with Western Europe. His efforts in Europe did achieve an agreement that strengthened cooperation in a variety of areas, such as the environment, technology, and energy efficiency programs but that did not offer preferential trade terms. In the early 1990s, the European Union awarded such conditions only to its neighbors in Eastern Europe. Once NAFTA negotiations concluded at the end of 1992, however, the circumstances had changed. The European Union recognized that its business firms would lose market share in Mexico if a trade agreement were not signed with Mexico. At this point, the European Union approached Mexico, but the Salinas administration rejected the offer for two reasons. The Europeans were not willing to open their markets significantly to Mexico, particularly in the agricultural and automotive sectors, and the Mexican government decided that it preferred to wait until NAFTA showed results.[32]

The uprising in Chiapas and the economic crisis of 1995 convinced President Zedillo of the usefulness of a foreign policy that would help Mexico to recover international credibility, develop new export markets, and identify sources of new investment. Other than the United States, only the European Union could do this.[33] (Japan was mired in a decade-long economic recession; Latin American

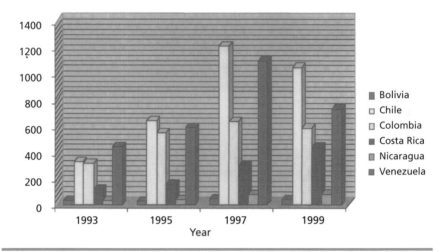

FIGURE 6.3

Mexico's Trade with Its Latin American Free Trade Partners, 1993–1999*
(million dollars)

*Preliminary figure.

Source: http://www.secofi-scni.gob.mx/Estadística/Commx.htm.

countries lacked the resources for what Mexico thought it needed.) The negotiation of the European Union–Mexican agreement was difficult. The Europeans were ready to offer Mexico political support and improve the investment climate, but they were not eager to open some sectors such as agriculture. However, as with the NAFTA signature and its later approval by the U.S. Congress, the Mexican government's political will prevailed; the European Union–Mexican agreement was signed in November 1999.

NAFTA allowed trade between Mexico and the United States to boom, accounting for the new, general, market-friendly direction of Mexican foreign policy and its focus on economic diversification efforts. First, Mexican negotiators succeeded in cutting down barriers to Mexican exports by working with the NAFTA model. Second, NAFTA's internal disciplines sharpened Mexico's export competitiveness toward both the United States and the rest of the world. Third, NAFTA made Mexico's market more appealing for European and Latin American nations because it afforded access to the United States, the largest market in the world.

We have shown in this chapter and in chapter two that the trend in Mexican international economic relations in the 1990s was toward an intensification of its transactions with the United States. If, in the new century, Mexico were to achieve the economic diversification that has hitherto eluded it, then its international economic transactions might resemble Canada's. Economic relations would still heavily focus on the U.S. market, but Mexican firms would have the potential for strong performance in most markets of the world.

DIPLOMATIC PRESENCE OF THE UNITED STATES AND MEXICO IN THE RESPECTIVE COUNTRIES

In any bilateral relationship, the act of relating is decisive and often complex. Interaction can occur on many different levels. In U.S.–Mexican relations, these exchanges are personal, professional, societal, trans-governmental, and political; their frequency, type, and intensity vary widely. In this section, we focus on official government-to-government interactions. They serve as an indicator for the overall relationship, signaling the attempt of any state to advance its own interests abroad. Moreover, official policies, actions, and initiatives can direct and change the business, societal, security, and political aspects of the relationship.

Few issues in U.S.–Mexican relations have been as asymmetrical as the access and political clout of the U.S. embassy in Mexico City and the Mexican embassy in Washington—an acute observation we owe to former Mexican diplomat Andrés Rozental. The U.S. ambassador has direct access to the Mexican president and usually becomes a protagonist in Mexican politics; his "on the record remarks" often make front-page news. In contrast, as dozens of other ambassadors in Washington, the Mexican ambassador competes for White House attention. For example, John D. Negroponte, U.S. ambassador to Mexico (1989–93) during the NAFTA negotiations, met President Salinas once or twice a month; he had a telephone conversation with Salinas's powerful chief of staff, José Cordoba Montoya, almost every day. In contrast, the Mexican ambassadors to Washington in the late 1990s, Jesús Silva Herzog (1995–98) and Jesús Reyes Heroles (1998–2000), met President Clinton only in ceremonies or during presidential visits.[34] Except for Matías Romero, envoy to Washington in the 1860s, who became deeply involved in U.S. politics, the Mexican ambassador has not been a powerful figure in Washington policy-making circles nor has he enjoyed great political access.

Nonetheless, during the 1990s, the Mexican embassy in Washington increased its profile, fielding a large and active delegation similar in size to those of Canada or Japan.[35] At times, the Mexican government hired professional lobbyists to present its case, just as other governments do. The Mexican consular network in the United States also grew in the 1990s; it expanded its role beyond the protection of Mexican migrants in the United States to become involved in cultural promotion, fostering foreign investment and developing linkages with the Mexican community in the United States. These new roles of the embassy and consulates strengthened Mexico's ability to advance its views concerning difficult bilateral issues such as immigration and narcotics.

The Mexican Presence in Washington

On December 5, 1898, the governments of Mexico and the United States agreed to grant to their respective legations the highest-ranking diplomatic categories, transforming them into embassies. President Porfirio Díaz appointed Matías

Romero to become the first ambassador of Mexico to the United States, but Romero died three days before formally presenting his credentials. Romero's appointment recognized his diplomatic talents and adroit knowledge of the power corridors of Washington. Romero had served as President Benito Juárez's envoy during one of the most critical periods for the survival of Mexico as an independent state. His mission was to seek U.S. help to combat the French army that occupied Mexico from 1861 to 1866. President Abraham Lincoln and the U.S. Congress protested the French intervention and provided some help to Juárez but avoided direct military involvement during the U.S. Civil War. Romero went to unusual lengths to secure U.S. help, involving himself in U.S. domestic politics. When he realized that Lincoln refused to give the help he sought, Romero actively joined the "Radical" Republican initiative to contest Lincoln's presidential renomination in 1864. When President Andrew Johnson also refused to help, the influential Mexican supported efforts to impeach Johnson. Romero even attempted to influence assignments to the foreign relations committees of the U.S. House of Representatives and Senate.[36]

Romero was an exception to the more typical quiet Mexican presence in Washington. Mexico's low profile in the U.S. capital was accentuated by the relative stability in bilateral affairs during the Cold War. The tacit bargain—so long as Mexico refrained from supporting communism and did not form close ties with the Soviet Union, the United States would not intervene in domestic Mexican affairs—reinforced the Mexican attitude of non-engagement. "Mexican envoys seldom traveled the twenty blocks from their Hispanic-style mural-adorned embassy on Sixteenth Street to Capitol Hill,"[37] George Grayson has noted.

This diplomatic style did not prevent Mexican diplomats from making their views heard when necessary, however. This is well exemplified by Jorge Espinosa de los Reyes, President Miguel de la Madrid's ambassador to Washington (1982–88). A financier and cautious by temperament, Espinosa de los Reyes rarely ventured beyond the State Department. In 1986, congress enacted the law to require the president every year to certify, subject to congressional review, that countries affected by drug trafficking cooperated fully with the United States in counter-narcotics control, under penalty of economic sanctions (see full discussion in chapter three). In the spring 1988, the U.S. Senate rejected President Ronald Reagan's certification of Mexico. Ambassador Espinosa de los Reyes worked with Speaker of the House Jim Wright (D-TX) to defend Mexican interests, sidelining the bill in the lower chamber.

Mexico's low profile in Washington seemed appropriate for a country with modest international economic engagement; Mexico developed its domestic market through protectionist trade policies. But this approach to the representation of Mexican interests in the United States became insufficient once Mexico opened its economy. During his first visit to Washington as president in October 1989, Salinas opened a new building for the Mexican embassy. Moving the embassy from an old mansion in a shady neighborhood to a modern building on Pennsylvania Avenue, just three blocks away from the White House "epitomized Mexico's diplomatic elan."[38] The new eight-story building was large enough to accommodate the sharp increase of personnel that NAFTA would bring about from 60 in 1989 to 157 in 1995. In 1999, 158 people worked in the embassy[39] (see Table 6.6 and Figure 6.4).

The Mexican embassy in Washington is the largest Mexican representation overseas by far. The typical Mexican embassy is a small operation, fully controlled by the Foreign Ministry, with a career Foreign Service ambassador and career officers. The embassy in Washington, in contrast, has greater independence. The ambassadors to Washington are usually political appointees who generally enjoy a close relationship with the Mexican president; this helps also explain the abundance of non-career officials in the embassy throughout the years (see Tables 6.6 and 6.7). Only two of the last fifteen ambassadors belonged to the Mexican Foreign Service; most had a previous career in the public financial sector. Bernardo Sepúlveda came to Washington in early 1982 having served as general director of international relations at the Ministry of Finance, in a move to prepare him to become foreign affairs minister once de la Madrid became president in December of the same year. Gustavo Petricioli, treasury minister from 1985 to 1988, became very close to his fellow cabinet member, Budget Minister Salinas; when Salinas became president, he appointed Petricioli to Washington. During his time as treasury minister, Petricioli also developed a close relationship with his U.S Treasury counterpart, James Baker, who would become secretary of state under President George Bush (1989–93).

At the end of the 1990s, ten agencies were represented through attachés in the Mexican embassy in Washington (see Figure 6.4). The Ministry of Trade and Industrial Promotion (SECOFI) had by far the largest representation in the embassy (not counting the Foreign Ministry personnel), followed by the defense attachés and the attorney general's office. The SECOFI office had twenty-one people who covered most bilateral trade issues; the representation of the treasury, in contrast, had only four officials who worked just on tax questions. Defense Ministry personnel had mainly a formal role with very little interaction with their U.S. counterparts.[40] Even in the 1990s, when numerous Mexican military officers came to the United States for training, relations with the Pentagon were handled directly by the office of the defense minister in Mexico City.

The establishment of attachés from various agencies participating in U.S.–Mexican affairs became a trend at the U.S. embassy in Mexico City at the end of World War II. Mexico began to mirror this trend in the 1970s with the establishment of agricultural and tourism attachés. In the 1980s, SECOFI and the attorney general's office were added. The NAFTA negotiations encouraged most ministries to establish offices at the embassy in Washington or strengthen the operation of those offices already in existence. The ten attachés shown in Figure

6.4 changed the form, content, and pace of Mexican diplomatic relations with the United States by diminishing the role of the Foreign Affairs Ministry and decentralizing the conduct of bilateral relations. Career foreign service generalists no longer managed many aspects of the bilateral relationship; instead, specialists from each ministry handled them.

The Mexican Consular Network in the United States

The Mexican consulates also expanded and found new roles in U.S.–Mexican relations in the 1990s. By the end of the twentieth century, there were 43 Mexican consulates in the United States. There were 17 consuls-general and 26 career consulates (see Table 6.8). The Mexican Senate confirms all consulates-general just as it confirms ambassadors. Consulates-general supervise the career consulates in their surrounding region and usually have more resources and personnel than the career consulates. For example, the consulates-general in Los Angeles and New York City are the largest Mexican consulates in the United States; they are also the second- and third-largest Mexican diplomatic missions abroad. The location of the consulates is related to the concentration of Mexicans and Mexican Americans in the United States (see Table 6.8). Texas has twelve consulates, California ten, and Arizona four.

In the early 1990s, just as NAFTA negotiations began, the Foreign Affairs Ministry widened the scope of diplomatic activities of the consulates. The ministry instructed the consulates to go beyond their traditional roles protecting the rights of Mexican immigrants in the United States. Almost all consulates-general would open a press office and cultural institute. The Zedillo administration also hired a lobbying firm, Public Strategies Incorporated, based in Austin, Texas, to develop a strategy to strengthen the role of the consular network.

Mexican Lobbying in the United States

For many years, Mexico did not embark on lobbying activities because lobbying was seen as an illegitimate intrusion into the affairs of a host country. The Mexican government disapproved of U.S. government interference in domestic Mexican affairs; it did not wish, therefore, to engage in behavior in the United States that might undermine its principled political opposition to such U.S. activities in Mexico. Mexico deviated from this rule in very few instances before 1991. One example of lobbying took place in 1986 when Mexican trade officials hired Michael Deaver, a former close aide to President Reagan, to help Mexico in its GATT negotiations; Deaver's relationship with SECOFI ended soon after he was accused of a conflict of interest and criminally prosecuted.[41]

The NAFTA negotiations transformed the structure of Mexican representation in the United States and its mode of operation. Mexican trade officials in SECOFI became convinced that lobbying was necessary to negotiate with the United States and ensure ratification of the agreement by the U.S. Congress. In 1991, the

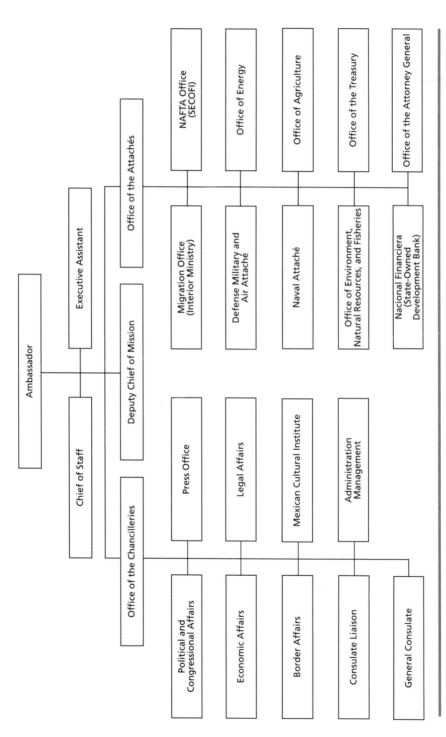

FIGURE 6.4 Structure of the Mexican Embassy

TABLE 6.6

Embassy of Mexico in the United States in 1999

Office	Career officials	Non-careeer officials	Staff	Total
Ambassador	0	2	2	4
Executive Assistant	1	2	2	5
Chief of Staff	0	3	1	4
Deputy Chief of Mission	3	2	7	12
Consulate Liaison	1	0	0	1
Political and Congressional Affairs	4	2	2	8
Special Affairs	0	1	0	1
Border Affairs	0	1	0	1
Economic Affairs	1	3	2	6
Interior Ministry/Intelligence	0	2	0	2
Legal Affairs	2	2	1	5
Press Office	2	3	2	7
Administration Management	0	4	9	13
Mexican Cultural Institute	1	2	7	10
General Consulate	2	10	4	16
Migration Office (Interior Ministry)	1	2	1	4
Defense Military and Air Attaché	0	11	0	11
Naval Attaché	0	3	0	3
Office of the Treasury	0	3	1	4
Office of Energy	0	2	0	2
NAFTA Office (SECOFI)	0	2	19	21
Office of Agriculture	0	3	1	4
Office of Environment, Natural Resources and Fisheries	0	2	0	2
Attorney General	0	5	2	7
Nacional Financiera	0	2	1	3
General Information	0	0	2	2
Total	**18**	**74**	**66**	**158**

Mexican government hired a high-profile team of lobbyists. SECOFI led NAFTA negotiations and coordinated the lobbying team, which consisted of nine firms focused on legal affairs, Democrats and Republicans on Capitol Hill, and the Hispanic community. The Mexican lobbying team worked with other lobbyists hired by both the U.S. and Mexican business organizations created to back NAFTA, namely, USA*NAFTA and COECE (the Mexican business organization for foreign trade). By the end of the NAFTA campaign, the Salinas administration's estimated lobbying expenditures reached $45 million.[42] The high profile of the Mexican lobbying captured U.S. media attention as well as that of several watchdog groups. A

TABLE 6.7

Mexican Ambassadors to the United States

Name	Years	Career	Political Appointees
Francisco Castillo Nájera	1935–1945	X	
Antonio Espinosa de los Monteros	1945–1948	X	
Rafael de la Colina	1948–1953	X	
Manuel Tello	1953–1958	X	
Antonio Carrillo Flores	1959–1964		X
Hugo B. Margaín	1965–1970		X
Emilio O. Rabasa	1970		X
José Juan de Olloqui	1971–1976		X
Hugo B. Margaín	1977–1981		X
Bernardo Sepúlveda Amor	1982		X
Jorge Espinosa de los Reyes	1983–1988		X
Gustavo Petricioli	1989–1993		X
Jorge Montaño	1993–1994	X	
Jesús Silva Herzog	1995–1997		X
Jesús Reyes Heroles	1997–		X
Total		**5**	**10**

reporter from the *Wall Street Journal* claimed that Mexico had "suddenly upstaged Japan as the foreign government with the most visible lobbying muscle in the United States."[43] Similarly, the Center for Public Integrity suggested that Mexico's lobbying campaign might have been the biggest in history.[44]

The Zedillo administration continued to hire lobbying firms. For example, in December 1998, the Mexican embassy hired three lobbying firms to ensure that in the months that would follow, the U.S. government and Congress would certify Mexico as an ally in the drug war. Even though Mexico had been fully certified each year, the embassy's fears were warranted because, in each of the past three years, the U.S. Congress had become increasingly critical of Mexico's cooperation. In the spring 1998, the Clinton administration was forced to make a deal with the senate to ensure that it would not reject Mexico's certification; the administration agreed to submit a biannual report on Mexico's cooperation. The Mexican government's fears heightened in fall 1998 when President Clinton's future seemed uncertain as a result of the Monica Lewinsky scandal. Official Mexico worried that the White House would not be able to mount, as in the previous three years, a serious campaign to prevent congressional rejection of its certification of Mexico's cooperation on drugs.

The three lobbying firms helped the Mexican embassy to develop a strategy to demonstrate to congress Mexico's successful efforts to combat drugs. Ambassador Jesús Reyes Heroles met 20 key legislators, including two meetings with the most

TABLE 6.8

Mexican Consulates in the United States

TOTAL 43

    General Consulates   17
    Career Consulates   26

    TEXAS
        Total   12
            General Consulates   5
            Career Consulates   7

    CALIFORNIA
        Total   10
            General Consulates   4
            Career Consulates   6

    ARIZONA
        Total   4
            General Consulates   1
            Career Consulates   3

      U.S. STATES AND TERRITORIES WITH AT LEAST ONE CONSULATE   18

Source: Embassy of Mexico in the United States.

outspoken critic of Mexico in the senate, Dianne Feinstein (D-CA), who later lessened her criticisms.[45] A new feature of this lobbying campaign was the work with some governors, mainly those of border states. As a result of the effort, the four border governors (California, Arizona, New Mexico, and Texas) urged President Clinton to fully certify Mexico.

Mexico-bashing in the U.S. Congress in spring 1999 was substantially less vociferous than in the three previous years. The legislative measures to reject Mexico's certification did not even make it to the floor of either chamber. These outcomes cannot be attributed solely to the lobbying effort, however. Both domestic and international circumstances helped the Mexican cause. U.S. domestic politics changed again in early 1999; President Clinton emerged strengthened from the impeachment process while his detractors, the conservative Republicans in congress, were weakened by the president's acquittal and by Democratic party gains in the November 1998 congressional elections. A week after being acquitted by the U.S. Senate, President Clinton visited Mexico with a large legislative delegation, which provided an excellent opportunity for President Zedillo to present his case concerning the war against drugs. In addition, congress was distracted by two foreign crises—the alleged Chinese theft of nuclear secrets and the impasse with Yugoslav president Milosevic on Kosovo—as it considered whether to reject the administration's certification of Mexico.

In conclusion, Mexican diplomats adapted well to the increasing complexities of bilateral relations and to the highly fragmented U.S. decision-making policy process toward Mexico. The Mexican delegation in the United States grew, became more specialized, and learned to lobby for its interests. The Mexican government became adept at playing the Washington game and won some matches, ranging from the approval of NAFTA by the U.S. Congress in November 1993 to a smoother drug cooperation certification process in spring 1999. The nation's interests were better served thanks to the change in the government's strategy of diplomatic representation.

THE U.S. PRESENCE IN MEXICO

In the late 1990s, the U.S. embassy in Mexico City employed approximately a thousand people. As is the case with its Mexican counterpart, the U.S. embassy in Mexico was not a typical State Department operation. It was the largest U.S. embassy in the world. There were also 13 consulates throughout the country, most in the northern states. The total U.S. representation in Mexico (personnel in the embassy and in the consulates) came to nearly 1,500 people, which is very similar to the number of people working in the Mexican embassy in Washington and in the 43 consulates. The U.S. embassy has long been located on the main avenue of Mexico City, El Paseo de la Reforma. In the late 1990s, the consular section granted one million visas every year—one-fourth of all U.S. non-immigrant visas granted overseas per year.

U.S. ambassadors to Mexico included both career Foreign Service officers and political appointees (see Table 6.9). Since 1933, there have been eleven career and six political appointees. In the last two decades of the century, only two ambassadors have been career, John D. Negroponte and Jeffrey Davidow. In contrast to Mexican ambassadors to the United States who usually have unlimited access to Los Pinos, U.S. ambassadors to Mexico do not have direct access to the White House. Since the early 1930s, two exceptions to this rule were Josephus Daniels and John A. Gavin.

Daniels communicated directly with President Franklin Roosevelt. Daniels had been Roosevelt's boss at the beginning of the latter's political career. Daniels's close relationship with Roosevelt helped to prevent a bilateral crisis in 1938 when Mexican president Lázaro Cárdenas expropriated all petroleum installations. U.S. secretary of state Cordell Hull and U.S. business leaders advocated a hard line against the Cárdenas administration; Daniels persuaded the president not to react strongly against the Mexican government's nationalistic policies, thus preventing further damage to bilateral affairs.[46]

The other U.S. ambassador with direct access to the White House was John Gavin, a close friend of President Reagan from their days as actors in Hollywood. Few U.S. ambassadors have ever been as controversial, unpopular, and ineffective as this former Hollywood actor. Gavin came very close to causing a crisis in

TABLE 6.9

U.S. Ambassadors to Mexico, 1933–2000

Name	Year	Career	Political Appointee
Josephus Daniels	1933–1941		X
George S. Messersmith	1942–1946	X	
Walter Thurston	1946–1950	X	
William O'Dwyer	1950–1952		X
Francis White	1953–1957	X	
Robert C. Hill	1957–1960		X
Thomas C. Mann	1961–1963	X	
Fulton Freeman	1964–1969	X	
Robert H. McBride	1969–1974	X	
Joseph H. Jova	1974–1977	X	
Patrick H. Lucey	1977–1979		X
Julian Nava	1980–1981		X
John A. Gavin	1981–1986		X
Charles J. Pilliod Jr.	1986–1989		X
John D. Negroponte	1989–1993	X	
James Robert Jones	1993–1997		X
Jeffrey Davidow	1998–	X	
Total		**9**	**8**

U.S.–Mexican relations. He routinely infuriated the Mexican public and government. He also often butted heads with the U.S. secretaries of state and treasury; Secretary of State George Shultz tried unsuccessfully to persuade President Reagan to remove Gavin as ambassador. Despite the friction he caused in U.S.–Mexican relations, Gavin remained ambassador for six years, enjoying President Reagan's full support.[47]

The complicated structure of the U.S. embassy reflects the cumbersome U.S. decision-making process toward Mexico in the late 1990s. Nineteen agencies were represented at the embassy. Some departments, such as the Treasury and Justice Departments, had various bureaus in the embassy. For example, treasury had four bureaus: Customs; Internal Revenue Service; Alcohol, Tobacco, and Firearms; as well as staff concerned with financial issues. The Justice Department had three bureaus: the Drug Enforcement Administration, the Immigration and Naturalization Service, and the Federal Bureau of Investigation. In contrast to the Mexican embassy, almost everyone working under the umbrella of the State Department (at times with the exception of the ambassador) was a career officer, and officials from the other agencies were civil servants.

The embassy's administrative tasks were colossal. An average of 600 U.S. official visitors came to Mexico every week; each required written approval from the embassy. The tasks of the consular offices were also enormous. Consuls should protect and help U.S. citizens traveling and living in Mexico; in the late 1990s, there were 600,000 U.S. citizens living in Mexico. Moreover, half of the worldwide arrests of U.S. citizens abroad took place in Mexico; 50 percent of these arrests occurred in Tijuana, the Mexican city across the border from San Diego, California (that is, 25 percent of all U.S. citizens arrested abroad were arrested in Tijuana).[48] The complexity of the U.S. embassy structure in Mexico as well as its monumental administrative tasks required political talents as well as enormous managerial skills for a U.S. ambassador to be successful in Mexico.[49]

In the 1990s, moreover, U.S. officials became more aware and better attuned to Mexican concerns; these habits of mind and work improved the reception of U.S. government actions by the Mexican government and people. When in 1997, for example, President Clinton met with leaders of Mexico's opposition parties, he was not accused of intervening in Mexican domestic politics. That was a sharp contrast to the reaction in 1983 to Ambassador Gavin's meeting with the leaders of PAN.

The opinions of Mexican officials and the informed public regarding the U.S. presence in Mexico also became less nationalistic. For example, in 1991 a memorandum from Ambassador Negroponte to the U.S. assistant secretary of state Bernard Aronson was leaked to the weekly newsmagazine *Proceso*.[50] The ambassador was quoted as saying that NAFTA approval would be very important to ensure that Mexican foreign policy would become less confrontational toward the United States. Mexican reactions were muted. Had a similar situation occurred ten years earlier, there would have been a huge backlash.

In conclusion, the three U.S. ambassadors to Mexico who served in the 1990s (Negroponte, Jones, and Davidow) continued to have a strong political presence in Mexico but were also aware of Mexican sensitivities and concerns about sovereignty. These U.S. ambassadors and most diplomats who served with them in the 1990s were well prepared on Mexican affairs; they were also quite professional in their approach to Mexico. They served U.S. interests effectively and, in so doing, imparted a positive character to U.S.–Mexican relations.

CONCLUSION

The profound transformation of U.S.–Mexican relations in the 1990s broke taboos and practices. For example, the Mexican government had long sought to insulate its domestic political practices from international scrutiny. U.S. and Mexican business firms had often clashed in the pursuit of their interests and had sought to advance their objectives through the blunt exercise of protectionist political power. And U.S. ambassadors in decades past had attempted to bully the Mexican government while Mexican ambassadors had behaved as nearly invisible representatives from a small country. By the end of the 1990s, important changes had occurred along all of these dimensions.

The United States and Mexico learned to represent their official interests professionally. Their patterns of diplomatic behavior converged and became much more effective than in the past. The NAFTA architecture promoted trade and investment and provided means to resolve the disputes that typically emerge in such intense and multifaceted economic relations. These new styles, strategies, and institutions enabled the two countries to address successfully such dramatic events as the Mexican financial debacle of 1994 to 1995 and manage delicately and subtly the growing international scrutiny over, and engagement in, Mexican domestic political processes and gradual democratization.

Much remained to be done to improve the plight of the Mexican poor, strengthen respect for human rights, and deepen democratization. Yet, Mexican politics and society, not just the Mexican economy, had opened up to the world. The United States, both officially and through the actions of its citizens, had become much more intimately engaged in many aspects of Mexico's society, economy, and polity at long last by the mutual consent of both governments. This bilateral partnership represented an epochal change as the millennium ended.

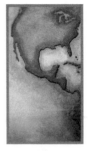

TRANSBORDER
RELATIONS VII

HOW CAN ONE NOT COMPARE THE THREE-METER-HIGH METAL WALL being constructed in Southern California with the fateful Berlin Wall?" So wrote former Costa Rican president and Nobel Prize winner Oscar Arias in 1992. He was reflecting upon the collapse of the Berlin Wall in November 1989—the wall that long stood as the symbol of the East German communist government's totalitarian repression—while gazing upon the new Operation Gatekeeper wall being built along the border south of San Diego, California.[1] The United States rediscovered its 2,000-mile southern border during the 1992 presidential election thanks to Republican candidate Patrick Buchanan, but the Clinton administration actually built the walls that Buchanan advocated along the border. There would no longer be doubt, the U.S. government believed, about where Mexico ended and the United States began.[2]

In this chapter, we examine both the processes of legal and illegal migration from Mexico to the United States as well as the characteristics of the transborder society created between parts of northern Mexico and southwestern United States. We reflect upon those aspects of bilateral relations where the state and the citizen interact most directly and with greatest complexity. Life at the border brought together millions of U.S. and Mexican citizens every day, mostly in lawful and mutually beneficial relationships governed by their personal wishes, interests, and hopes. Yet, life at the border was also deeply affected and shaped by the actions of the U.S. and Mexican governments at their respective federal, state, and local levels. Life across the border, in addition, entailed more than the shipment of goods or the interaction of policies that have filled the pages of this book. It also featured the flow of people, with or without proper documents, mostly from Mexico to the United States in search of a better future for themselves and their children. This movement of people, especially of Mexicans, created mutually beneficial relationships, too, but it also led to severe, sustained, and multilayered conflicts between the two countries and many of their citizens.[3]

We are mindful of these conflicts and good reasons why good people hold views in conflict. Nonetheless, we argue generally that the transborder society and transborder migration can and often do serve the interests of both the United

States and Mexico. We also argue that cooperative relations between the governments at all levels have at times addressed shared border problems effectively. Unfortunately, we also document a number of instances when cooperation broke down or never existed, the main example of which is the construction of walls on the U.S. side of the border.

U.S. BORDER WALLS

The U.S. Operation Gatekeeper wall of corrugated steel landing mats is strong enough to stop trucks that had rammed through earlier barriers; it was built by U.S. army reservists and inaugurated in 1994. The steel fence cuts across miles of scrub while stadium lights illuminate the thick underbrush. The wall is also electronic. An array of gadgets can find hidden compartments where drugs may be stashed, scan license plates to see if a car is stolen, and help law enforcement agents see people concealed in the bushes. In its first four years of operation, undocumented migrant crossings in San Diego (as measured by border apprehensions) fell 46 percent. In 1994 to 1995, U.S. army engineers built a taller 15-foot steel mat fence that is almost five miles long, stretching from one end of Nogales, Arizona, to the other. In January 1996, construction began on a 1.3-mile-long fence in Sunland Park, New Mexico, while another ten-foot-high fence was built to separate the border towns of Jacumba, California, and Jacume, Mexico. The U.S. Illegal Immigration Reform and Immigration Responsibility Act (IIRIRA) of 1996 also authorized the construction of a triple fence along 14 miles south of San Diego.[4]

In the 1990s, the United States committed an increasing level of resources to the southwest border. The number of border patrol agents guarding this border doubled from 3,389 in Fiscal Year 1993 to 8,200 in Fiscal Year 1999; the U.S. budget authorizes further increases to 10,000 agents by 2001. The number of customs agents rose from 2,000 in Fiscal Year 1993 to 2,311 in Fiscal Year 1997.[5] The number of Immigration and Naturalization Service (INS) officers increased from 4,029 in Fiscal Year 1993 to 7,226 in Fiscal Year 1997. More Drug Enforcement Administration and Federal Bureau of Investigation agents were also deployed to this border. The budget for border operations rose accordingly.[6]

To evade capture, illegal aliens or drug traffickers would have to cross through desert or mountainous regions. Either terrain is inhospitable. In the four years after Operation Gatekeeper began, 324 migrants died by drowning or being overcome by heat.[7] Deaths at crossing, alas, are part of the signal sent by these procedures to deter others from attempting it. Tragic and undesired by the U.S. government as these deaths are, their occurrence contributes to a deterrence effect.

The new technology also facilitated legal crossings. For example, frequent commuters at the Otay Mesa crossing on the outskirts of San Diego avoid long lines of up to two hours by using an automated driving lane. Cars in this program are equipped with transponders that emit a sort of radio fingerprint. As the car approaches the border, the license plate number, the names of the authorized occupants, and their photographs appear on a monitor inside the inspector's booth. Inspectors compare these images with the faces inside the cars to see whether there are impostors. Drivers swipe an identity card through a machine, check out, and drive through.[8]

The new measures fortified and hardened the U.S. border with Mexico, but many of its effects were either negligible or counterproductive. Let us focus on San Diego County where the new policies are longest lived and most thorough. Wayne Cornelius's research found that only eight percent of employers noticed any decrease in the number of immigrant workers seeking jobs at their company in the 15 months after Operation Gatekeeper became fully operational; most employers noted no change or even an increase in the number of such job applicants. Moreover, in that same time period, consistently over 80 percent of the migrants interviewed in San Diego made it across the border on their first try.[9]

The tightening of border controls, however, also made it more likely that migrants would depend on professional smugglers, or *coyotes*. The cost of being smuggled increased after Operation Gatekeeper went into effect; the proportion of migrants using *coyote* services also rose. These criminal *coyotes* welcomed the "Berlinization" of the U.S.–Mexican border, therefore. Moreover, these U.S. policies fostered the "psychology of closing the door," even if four-fifths of the migrants in fact succeeded in entering on their first try. This psychology induced migrants to prolong their stay and even settle down permanently in the United States in order to reduce the frequency of crossings and the risk of apprehension.[10] These policies may thus have turned seasonal and temporary migrations into permanent migrations.

THE BORDER REGION

Demography

The border between the United States and Mexico extends almost 3,200 kilometers from the Pacific Ocean to the Gulf of Mexico. The border region is conventionally defined as the area within 100 kilometers of the border. It includes parts of six Mexican states (Baja California, Sonora, Chihuahua, Coahuila, Nuevo León, and Tamaulipas) and four U.S. states (California, Arizona, New Mexico, and Texas).

By the end of the 1990s, over 12 million people lived in this region, approximately half in each country. Almost 90 percent of the population in the border region lived in urban zones, mainly in 14 so-called twin cities formed by the pairing of one Mexican and one U.S. city. About two-thirds of the population of the border region lived in San Diego and Imperial counties in California, the cities of Tijuana, Tecate, and Mexicali in Mexico (all three of which are at the border between California and Baja California Norte), and the Ciudad Juárez–El Paso metropolitan zone. In the first half of the 1990s, the U.S.–Mexican border region grew on each side of the border about three times faster than the growth rate of the respective national populations.

As the twentieth century closed, income levels in the U.S. border region were more than double those on the Mexican side, most markedly so in the San Diego–Tijuana region. Nonetheless, the standard of living on the Mexican side of the border was higher than in Mexico as a whole, while the standard of living on the U.S. side of the border (San Diego excepted) was somewhat lower than for the United States as a whole. For example, in the mid-1990s, per capita income in the U.S. southwest border region was 12 percent below that of the entire country; 30 percent of the border region's children under the age of 18 were living in poverty compared to 23 percent for the United States as a whole. Outside of San Diego–Tijuana, the border region displayed the lowest level of asymmetry in relations between the United States and Mexico.[11]

The Economy: Maquiladoras

The growth of the economy on both sides of the border, but especially on the Mexican side, owed much to the maquiladora industry, which flourished with the support of both the Mexican and the U.S. governments.[12] This industry originated with the end of the Bracero worker programs in 1964. The Mexican government feared skyrocketing unemployment and economic recession in the border region as migrant workers returned. To ward off such a calamity, in 1965, the Mexican government established the Border Industrialization Program to create employment opportunities for these workers; the United States enacted complementary procedures to facilitate this development. Maquiladora plants could import raw materials, components, and capital goods from the United States free of duties into Mexico, then take advantage of low labor costs, assemble the finish goods, and re-export back to the United States while paying import tax only on the value added by all Mexican costs. (In the 1970s and thereafter, maquiladoras also exported some of their output to third countries, that is, countries other than Mexico or the United States.)

In the 1980s, maquiladoras cushioned the impact of Mexico's economic depression on its northern states. The number of maquiladora plants jumped from about 600 in the early 1980s, when the Mexican peso was devalued, to more than 2,000 in the early 1990s before the enactment of the North American Free Trade Agreement (NAFTA) (see Table 7.1). The weaker peso meant that an even lower dollar outlay paid for maquiladora wages. As a result of their strong performance, maquiladoras became one of the most important sources of foreign exchange and employment during Mexico's "lost decade" of the 1980s. In 1992, about half a million Mexicans worked in maquiladora plants; maquiladora gross exports amounted to $19 billion, approximately 40 percent of Mexico's worldwide

TABLE 7.1

Number of Maquiladoras and Jobs, 1974-1998

Year	Number of Maquilas	Number of Jobs
1974	455	75,974
1980	620	119,546
1982	585	127,048
1985	750	211,968
1990	1,938	460,258
1993	2,405	542,000
1995	2,939	644,000
1998	4,234	1,008,000

Source: Paul Ganster, "The United States–Mexico Border Region and Growing Transborder Interdependence," in *NAFTA in Transition*, ed. Stephen Randall and Herman Konrad (Calgary: University of Calgary Press, 1995), 147, for 1974–1992; SECOFI, for 1993–1998.

exports. The early maquiladoras were in the textile sector; in the first half of the 1990s, maquiladoras produced and exported motor vehicle engines, television receivers, and other machinery and equipment.

Maquiladora plants have been controversial because for many years the overwhelming proportion of workers were women who were badly paid by U.S. standards and had low job security. Studies of maquiladora working conditions found that workers often suffered from serious health and safety problems, especially optical nerve disorders and stress-related illnesses.[13] NAFTA dealt with labor standards through the creation of the Commission for Labor Cooperation. This commission, however, serves mainly to highlight poor labor conditions and lacks enforcement powers of its own, thereby limiting its effectiveness to improve labor conditions in the border region.

Yet, already by the mid-1970s, maquiladora workers had incomes and education substantially above those prevailing elsewhere in Mexico; and although Mexican real wages in the maquiladoras declined by 0.7 percent from 1993 to 1997, they declined by 1.6 percent for workers in Mexico as a whole over the same period.[14] More jobs and higher wages turned the Mexican border states into magnets drawing Mexican migrants principally from cities and towns further south.[15] The population on the Mexican side of the border grew faster than the rate of growth of the Mexican population nationwide. U.S. border communities gained as well from the growth of the maquiladoras, primarily through the consumer spending of Mexican workers in U.S. border towns. Thus the population growth on the U.S. side of the border also exceeded the growth rate of the U.S. population nationwide. Migration from other regions within each country, and from Mexico to the United States, was the primary source of the rapid population growth in the combined border region. The maquiladora industry in northern Mexico thus contributed to a certain convergence in the border region between Mexico and the United States. Economic, social, and cultural links grew between the two sides of the border.

NAFTA made the elimination of the maquiladora system only a matter of time. The maquiladora tariff structure would be dismantled under NAFTA and replaced with zero duties on U.S. imports from Mexico, to be phased in over a 10- to 15-year period. This is far better than import duties on value added in Mexico. It allows Mexican and U.S. firms operating in Mexico ready access to the U.S. market with a diverse mix of factors of production, including Mexican raw materials and capital goods, not just low-wage labor. Maquiladora plants had also been limited in what they could ship into the Mexican market itself; these restrictions disappeared in 2001.

These changes will not take away the border region's advantages, however. The plants are in place, the workforce is better educated and more knowledgeable of English, the managers retain the option of living in U.S. cities, and the costs of transportation are lower.[16] The maquiladoras at the border region pioneered the techniques of international production sharing in Mexico. They launched the process, moved up the ladder of production complexity and product mix, and opened channels for Mexican exports to the United States. They were NAFTA's testing grounds. Maquiladoras created jobs for managers and technical personnel, and trained them. They demonstrated the capacities of Mexican workers and rewarded them with substantially higher incomes.[17] This border economy showed that joint economic gains could be reaped despite the existence of the U.S.–Mexican border.

Indeed, building on these continuing advantages, maquiladoras boomed in the years following the implementation of NAFTA. From 1993 to 1998, the number of maquiladoras, and the number of jobs in them, almost doubled, from 2,405 to 4,234, and from 542,000 to 1,008,000, respectively (see Table 7.1). The trade performance of the Mexican border region surpassed that of the rest of the country since the creation of NAFTA. From 1993 to 1998, Mexican exports net of maquiladora exports grew 117 percent while maquiladora exports grew 141 percent (computed from Figure 7.1). From 1994 to 1997, the Mexican border states had a trade surplus of $21.7 million compared to a trade deficit of $39.7 million for Mexico's non-border states.[18]

The Environment

The global ecosystem along the U.S.–Mexican border knows no political border. Events affecting the natural environment north of the Rio Grande/Río Bravo (the same river's respective name in the United States and Mexico) reverberate in the neighboring region south of the same river. The consequences may be positive or negative, but a causal connection is characteristically established. As William Orme noted, "what happens in one side of the border directly affects the other. In the ecology of the borderlands, national sovereignty is an illusion."[19] The intensification of economic transactions along the U.S.–Mexican border since the 1970s had some negative environmental consequences, while the NAFTA negotiating process raised the latter's political salience.

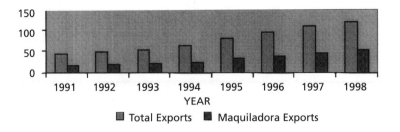

FIGURE 7.1
Mexican Exports, 1991–1998
(million dollars)

Source: http://www.secofi-scni.gob.mx/Estadística/Commx.htm.

Industrial pollution caused by the rapid and unregulated growth of maquiladoras, and the resulting environmental degradation, are among the most serious problems at the border. Maquiladoras long disposed of industrial waste in Mexico without adhering to prevalent international standards or obeying Mexican law; this behavior also imposed environmental costs on the U.S. side of the border through transborder pollution. The lack of agreed upon binational standards, weak institutions, and weak regulatory enforcement exacerbated these problems. As a consequence, border communities fought often over transborder water quality, which is threatened by the dumping of raw sewage, fertilizer, and pesticides from agricultural runoff, and the haphazard disposal of industrial waste.[20]

Border pollution is not just a serious concern but also an example of a long history of gradually deepening cooperation between the United States and Mexico on the most important specifics of this issue.[21] In 1889, the two governments pioneered intergovernmental cooperation across the border by creating the International Boundary Commission. In 1944, they renamed and expanded its mandate, calling it the International Boundary and Water Commission. The immediate reason for this renewed mandate was the problem of access to common water sources from the Colorado and Rio Grande/Río Bravo river basins. Since 1944, the commission focused on broader environmental concerns because of rising salinity in the Colorado River. In August 1983, the United States and Mexico signed the Border Environmental Agreements known as the La Paz (Baja California) Agreements. These agreements improved transborder cooperation to control sewage flows from Tijuana to San Diego, transportation of hazardous wastes across the land border, hazardous waste spills, air pollution from copper smelters in northern Sonora and southern Arizona, and urban air pollution in twin border cities. In addition, the two governments decided to create respective federal offices for environmental cooperation at the border.[22] The La Paz Agreements also helped to mobilize new environmentalist non-governmental organizations in the border region. Before that time, there had been few such non-governmental organizations on the U.S. side of the border and practically none on the Mexican side. The new non-governmental organizations fostered the negotiation of extensions of the La Paz Agreements to cope with practical environmental problems at the border.[23]

Nonetheless, the environmental problems remained severe. On the eve of NAFTA, 25 million tons of raw sewage flowed into the Rio Grande every day at Laredo. Water contamination levels were 1,650 times greater than those considered safe for recreational use. At San Elizario, Texas, where an aquifer shared with Mexico had become contaminated, 90 percent of adults contracted hepatitis "A" by age 35. The NAFTA negotiations jump-started environmental cooperation along the border, especially for water treatment.[24]

NAFTA itself created or led to the creation of three new organizations to address border environmental problems. The Integrated Border Environmental Program and its successor, the Border XXI Program, provide guidelines for binational cooperation along the border. The Border Environmental Cooperation Commission and the North American Development Bank were created to address the lack of an environmental infrastructure (water, sanitary, waste facilities) in the border area. The commission helps in the design of projects; the bank and private investors may finance them.

Border Liaison Mechanisms

Cooperation between the U.S. and Mexican state and local governments at the border had long been limited, especially because of the considerable centralization of authority and power in Mexico in the hands of its national government in Mexico City. Not until 1992 did Mexico and the United States establish border commissions, called Border Liaison Mechanisms (BLMs), to manage routine daily relations across the border, and not until 1995 did these commissions include state and local government officials. By the end of the 1990s, the BLMs included federal and state authorities from both the United States and Mexico, including the Mexican and U.S. consulates in the region. These local border commissions soon proved effective.[25]

Eight BLMs were established along the border during the 1990s, mainly in the major transborder crossing zones. At first, BLMs were designed to cope with incidents at the border related to migration, crime, and judicial cases. The two most developed BLMs are, not surprisingly, those that cope with problems in the Tijuana–San Diego and Ciudad Juárez–El Paso areas.[26] In early 2001, the BLM in Tijuana–San Diego was composed of seven working groups or committees: migration and citizen protection; attention to stolen vehicles; citizen security; water; education and culture; border bridges; and expeditious vehicle crossing. The BLM in Ciudad Juárez–El Paso was composed of three working groups (migration, citizen security, and development of border communities) and four committees (urban development, public health and environment, trade and tourism, and education and culture).[27]

Most BLMs have effectively helped border authorities at different levels to establish a continuous dialogue and create additional special bilateral practices for cooperation. Consider cooperation on the San Diego–Tijuana border. In 1995, joint efforts reduced traffic crossing time from an average of two hours to an average of 20 minutes. Additional steps were taken in the late 1990s to speed up border crossing traffic. In 1998, San Diego and Tijuana institutionalized their cooperation to improve their water supply. In July 1997, the two cities, backed by their respective national governments, established formal means for police cooperation and joint police activities. Cooperation improved the living conditions of communities at the border.

Similarly, the bilateral working group on migration in Ciudad Juárez–El Paso developed a good working relationship. This led to the installation of two offices of the Mexican consulate in El Paso inside two offices of the U.S. government at the border: the regional office of the INS and the INS office at the Abraham Lincoln–Benito Juárez bridge. The presence of Mexican consular officials at the places where the most numerous detentions occurred made it more likely that the human rights of the Mexicans apprehended at such sites would be guaranteed.

BLMs are only minimal efforts to cope with the manifold problems of the U.S.–Mexico border, however. All BLMs are understaffed and funded with minimum budgets. But, as stated by the Mexican consul in El Paso, "even with minimal resources, these mechanisms have shown how necessary it is to improve coordination in the border region in a cross-national fashion and at the three levels of government: federal, state, and local." Thus, early in his administration, President Vicente Fox considered creating a high-level post—a border czar—to better coordinate border issues.[28]

California and Texas: Policies toward Mexico and Mexicans

In the 1990s, the state governments of California and Texas also designed their own quite different policies toward Mexico. Just prior to NAFTA's enactment, Mexico represented one-third of Texan foreign trade but only one-twelfth of California's. When NAFTA went into effect in 1994, 40 percent of Texan exports went to Mexico. Texas was much more likely to cultivate good relations with Mexico because its stakes were so much greater. Moreover, although the proportion of U.S. Latinos was about the same (one-quarter of each) in the populations of Texas and California, three out of four Mexican-origin persons in Texas had been born in the United States whereas only one out of two in California had been born in the United States. In 1990, 92 percent of the Mexican-American residents of Texas who had been born in the United States were either

English-language monolinguals or comfortably fluent in English. At the time of the 1992 U.S. presidential election that highlighted immigration as an issue with electoral potency, California hosted an estimated 1.4 million illegal aliens while Texas had only about 350,000. California was much more affected by immigration from Mexico than Texas. Finally, the more stable Mexican-origin U.S. citizen population in Texas long participated in state and local politics, elected local and state officials, and thus induced politicians (no matter what their ethnic identity) to compete for their votes. That process got under way in California only in the second half of the 1990s.[29]

As a consequence of these and other differences, Texas and California policies toward Mexico differed. Four out of ten California U.S. representatives voted against NAFTA, as did its two U.S. senators, Barbara Boxer and Dianne Feinstein, both Democrats. Each party split its votes, though opposition to NAFTA was stronger among California Democrats. California's Republican governor, Pete Wilson (1990–98), gave lukewarm support to NAFTA before and after its enactment. In contrast, nearly all U.S. representatives from Texas and its two U.S. senators, Phil Gramm and Kay Bailey Hutchinson, both Republicans, voted for NAFTA. Democratic governor Ann Richards and her successor, Republican governor George W. Bush, strongly supported NAFTA before and after its enactment. In the 1990s, Texas signed agreements with Mexico on land management and local police cooperation along the border.[30]

Beginning at the same time as the NAFTA negotiations, Texas state and local governments reached out to their Mexican counterparts, inducing them to behave with greater independence from, though not at odds with, the government in Mexico City. For example, the Texas Park and Wildlife Department signed cooperation agreements with neighboring Mexican states. Texas and Tamaulipas agreed to joint monitoring of air quality in twin cities across the border from the Laredos to Brownsville-Matamoros. At the municipal level, El Paso and Ciudad Juárez came to cooperate over air and water pollution control; the same water source supplies 85 percent of the water consumed by these twin cities.

In the 1990s, on the Mexican side of the Texas border, new conflicts pit not U.S. against Mexican entities but the local versus the national governments in Mexico against each other. This occurred once the voters elected opposition National Action Party (PAN) candidates to office in many state and local governments in northern Mexico while the national government remained in Institutional Revolutionary Party (PRI) hands. For example, Francisco Villareal, PAN mayor of Ciudad Juárez, spent some days in prison for having installed unauthorized tollbooths on the international bridge connecting his city with El Paso.[31]

In contrast, in the 1990s, California's relationship with Mexico was shaped by the political strategy of Republican governor Pete Wilson. In 1993, pummeled by an economic recession that had hit California hard, Wilson was forced to enact unpopular tax and budget measures. This brought his support in the public opinion polls down to 30 percent. He launched his gubernatorial reelection campaign based on mobilizing public sentiment against Mexican immigrants. Wilson promoted anti-immigration policies, most notably endorsing Proposition 187. Proposition 187 compelled hospitals, schools (kindergarten through grade twelve and colleges), welfare agencies, and all their employees to deny their services (except emergency medical services) to illegal immigrants and report the illegals to the police for prosecution. In November 1994, Proposition 187 was approved (the courts blocked implementation of most of its provisions, however); Governor Wilson was reelected.[32] Inter-ethnic tensions in California worsened. As already noted, in response to Proposition 187 and to anti-immigrant legislation enacted by the U.S. government, Mexican-American legal residents, especially in California, sharply increased their applications for naturalization.

In the 1998 state and U.S. Congressional elections, California elected a Democratic governor, a Mexican-American Democratic lieutenant governor, and defeated many Republican officeholders for other posts. During the campaign, California's Democrats actively courted the U.S. Latino vote. Upon assuming office, Democratic governor Gray Davis accorded high priority to his government's relationship with Mexico. Governor Davis visited Mexico early in his administration; President Zedillo returned the visit, the longest ever to California by a Mexican president.

Relations between U.S. and Mexican state and local governments developed with new vigor during the 1990s in response to opportunities opened by the NAFTA negotiations and the agreement itself. All along the border from San Diego–Tijuana to Brownsville–Matamoros, municipal governments intensified their cooperation, as did the state of Texas with its Mexican counterparts. The relationship between California and Mexico was both more intense and conflict-ridden in the 1990s. Although part of the California-Mexican conflict could be explained as a function of Governor Wilson's strategy, fundamental economic, social, and political differences between Texas and California made it more probable that Wilson-like politicians would flourish in California rather than in Texas. Yet, on balance, the new century opened with closer U.S.–Mexican collaboration at the state and local level than the two countries had ever experienced.

Peoples

In 1998, 278 million people (about three-quarter million per day), 86 million cars, and 4 million trucks and rail cars entered the United States from Mexico—all legally.[33] Much of this was commercial traffic headed northward, but a great deal stemmed from the border region's integrated society and economy, notwithstanding the international border. Many Mexicans who crossed the border lawfully had regular daily commuting jobs in the United States. Others were regular shoppers who moved from one "side" of their twin city to the other. Studies by the Chambers of Commerce of San Diego and El Paso indicate that Mexicans spent much more money shopping in these U.S. cities than they did in Tijuana and Ciudad Juárez, the respective Mexican twin cities. Mexicans also spent more on the U.S. side of the border region than did U.S. citizens from the border region on the Mexican side of the border.[34]

The history of the twin cities has a darker side, however. Between 1915 and 1917, California outlawed horse racing, prostitution, dance halls, and professional boxing. San Diego's neighbor, Tijuana, boomed as a result, drawing in tourists from California. Texas went dry in 1918; El Paso's bar owners moved to Ciudad Juárez. As a U.S. consul wrote shortly thereafter, Ciudad Juárez was "the most immoral, degenerate and utterly wicked place" he had known. The U.S. nationwide prohibition of liquor extended these practices across the entire U.S.–Mexican border. San Diego and El Paso have also been important military posts for the U.S. armed forces; sailors and soldiers flocked to the respective Mexican border cities of Tijuana and Ciudad Juárez. The end of Prohibition in the United States curbed some of these activities, but they surged again during World War II and the Korean and Vietnam Wars as U.S. troops were quartered and trained in and around San Diego and El Paso.[35] In the 1980s and 1990s, moreover, the border cities—especially Tijuana and Ciudad Juárez—became major centers for drug-trafficking cartel headquarters and operations. This criminal underworld contributed to continuing high levels of violence in these and other Mexican border cities.

Maligned as the maquiladora industries would be from the 1960s to the 1990s, they provided the principal alternative for Mexican border cities to get out of excessive dependence on "sin" tourism and provide alternatives to jobs in drug-trafficking operations. As Carlos Monsiváis has written eloquently, after 1970, Mexico's northern border region was "morally rehabilitated" thanks to the new maquiladora-led industrial development, from which "it both suffers and benefits," and to a boom in its university system and cultural development. The northern region, averred Monsiváis, was "no longer a way station" en route north but a region with an identity of its own and with its aspirations to full employment within a new North American economy.[36]

Not all of the twin cities of the U.S.–Mexican border region were equally interdependent, however. The most balanced and multifaceted bonds existed between El Paso and Ciudad Juárez, the two Laredos, and Brownsville and Matamoros. There were two contrasts to this pattern of balanced interdependence. On the one hand, citizens of San Diego seemed less likely to think of themselves as living in a border city and had few contacts with Mexicans who lived in Tijuana; their principal contact with "Mexicans" was with those who had moved into San Diego. In the early 1990s, public and private sector policy-makers in Washington, DC, and New York knew their counterparts in Mexico City better than policy-makers in San Diego and Tijuana knew each other. On the other hand, there were the two Nogales. Mexico's Nogales was about six times larger than its Arizona twin. Until fall 1997, when the United States began to erect a wall to split the city, it had been one city anchored on its Mexican side.[37]

The use of both English and Spanish distinguished the border region, but the pattern of bilingualism was not uniform. English was readily heard and employed in Ciudad Juárez's business, tourist, and maquiladora districts but not in its residential districts. Ciudad Juárez had no bilingual or English-language neighborhood where English predominated or where both English and Spanish were used for communication between its residents. The English language was used instrumentally to communicate with English monolingual U.S. citizens. In contrast, its twin city, El Paso, had neighborhoods where Spanish was used as often as English within the community for communication between its residents. In El Paso, one could buy supermarket goods in either language; that was one form of bilingualism. Another form of bilingualism in El Paso was the need to employ both languages to communicate with different people even just within the Mexican-American community: Spanish may be grandmother's language but English that of the ten-year-old. Thus, in the border Mexican city, bilingualism was an individual choice related to a job; in the U.S. border city, bilingualism marked the community of Mexican-origin people who retained Spanish and learned English.[38]

Mexican immigrants to the United States who remained on the U.S. side of the border tended to acquire English quickly and become predominant English-language users even in their households. We already noted that English language use was high among Mexican Americans in Texas; thus, here we focus on California. Studies in southern California showed that English was the language used in three-quarters of the Mexican-American households where the spouses were both born in the United States but of Mexican parents. Between children, English language usage rose to 90 percent in such Mexican-American households; even when both spouses were born in Mexico, children used English to talk among themselves in 60 percent of such households.[39]

Because the volume of Spanish-speaking immigrants is so high, however, Spanish is frequently used and heard in southern California and elsewhere along the border region despite the speed of English-language acquisition. The Spanish-language mass media market at the border is apt evidence of this. Los Angeles is home to one of Mexican Televisa's principal subsidiaries in the United States, broadcasting nationally to the Spanish-language television market but with special attention to southern California. And Los Angeles has been home to La Opinión, founded in 1926 and still the largest-circulation Spanish-language daily newspaper in the United States in continuous publication for three-quarters of a century.[40]

On the U.S. side, bilingualism also featured frequent and intense use of Spanglish, or the mixture of both languages in the same sentence. Predominant Spanish-language users borrowed vocabulary from English while retaining Spanish language syntax. Predominant English-language users borrowed words from Spanish but employed English language syntax. Anglicisms were not peculiar to the U.S.–Mexican border, however; they had become common throughout Mexico both in its metropolitan and rural areas that sent migrants to the United States or received international tourists.

In 1979, Joel Garreau, in *The Nine Nations of North America*, saw a new country emerging, which he named MexAmerica.[41] It is where Dixie's gumbo meets Mexican refried beans, where English and Spanish co-exist and combine, and where local and federal cops and troops sometimes stop Americans of Mexican descent because their image of what an American looks like does not include those shades of brown. This region is hot and dry, dynamic and culturally malleable, at the crossroads of that far-reaching experiment called NAFTA, as well as the longest border between a post-industrial society and a third-world country. But, a decade later, Lester Langley extended the concept of MexAmerica to include cultural, political, and economic trends in Chicago, Pittsburgh, and Mexico City.[42] MexAmerica, in Langley's view, was not a specific geographic region in the U.S. southwest and the Mexican north but a wider conception of life already reaching throughout North America. If so, for good and ill, the U.S.–Mexican border region pioneered in patterns of integration between the United States and Mexico, and it remains the problematic crux of the evolving relationship between their cultures and peoples.

At the physical midpoint of this new North America, coincident with the launching of NAFTA in 1994, the U.S. government built new walls. It seemed to claim to know, in the words of the New England poet Robert Frost, "What I was walling in or walling out," firm in the belief that "Good fences make good neighbors," but perhaps not pausing sufficiently to ponder "to whom I was like to give offence." Indeed, the (nearly) century-old lament from Frost acquired new pertinence at the U.S.–Mexican border just as the millennium closed:

> Something there is that doesn't love a wall,
> That wants it down.[43]

MEXICAN MIGRATION TO THE UNITED STATES

The complexity of Mexican migration to the United States is captured in the following quotation: "there are as many reasons for migration as there are migrants."[44] Nevertheless, economic reasons usually triggered Mexican migration to the United States. The factors that sustain Mexican migration can be summarized into three categories: demand-pull factors in the United States, supply-push factors in Mexico, and a system of networks that bridged the border.[45] The analysis of the three factors shows that the migration of Mexicans to the United States was a dynamic process, which originated largely in the U.S. approval or toleration of recruitment of Mexican workers. Mexican migrants were willing to be recruited because of the earnings gap between Mexico and the United States. In the 1990s, nearly 90 percent of Mexican migrants said they were motivated by job or job opportunities (see Figure 7.2). The cross-border networks of relatives, friends, and labor brokers, in turn, sorted Mexican migrants and where they went in the United States. These networks also helped explain why and how Mexican migrants moved into traditional and nontraditional industries, occupations, and areas of the United States.

Other, 10.67

Job, 34.92

Looking for work, 54.41

FIGURE 7.2
Motivations of Mexican Migrants, 1993–1997
(percentage)

Source: Questionnaire about Migration to the Northern Border, Table 3.1, *Por motivos de cruce a Estados Unidos* (http://www.stps.gob.mx/302a/302_0064.htm).

The dimensions of Mexican migration to the United States are better understood in comparison with other international migration flows. Mexico is the world's major country of emigration; the United States is the world's major country of immigration. In 1996, excluding visitors, the United States received 1,191,000 persons: 916,000 legal immigrants and 275,000 unauthorized migrants (estimates vary on the composition of the unauthorized migrants). Assume that just half (a conservative estimate) of these illegal migrants were Mexican, namely, 137,500. Add 165,000 legal Mexican immigrants during that same year. Then, Mexican immigration to the United States in 1996 amounted to 302,500 persons. This exceeded total immigration in 1996 to Canada (225,000) or to Australia (100,000).[46]

Mexican migration to the United States is more than a century-old phenomenon, although it peaked in the last three decades of the twentieth century. The number of Mexican migrants to the United States who established permanent residence increased almost fivefold in those years (see Figure 7.3). From 1990 to 1996, the Mexican-born population of the United States (that is, the accumulated migration flow) had a net growth of 1.9 million people, or about 315,000 individuals a year. Approximately 510,000 of these were legal immigrants, 630,000 were unauthorized migrants, and 760,000 migrants were legalized after first entering the United States illegally.[47]

The Mexican-origin population in the United States as a percentage of U.S. total population increased from 2.2 percent in 1970, to 6.8 percent in 1996. At the start of the new century, this figure exceeds 7 percent. The proportion of Mexican migrants within the Mexican-born population in the United States declined markedly from 1920 to 1970, but it more than doubled from 1970 to 1996, rising from 16.7 to 37 percent (see Table 7.2).

In 1996, approximately one-third of the total Mexican-born population in the United States was undocumented, that is, between 2.3 and 2.4 million people.

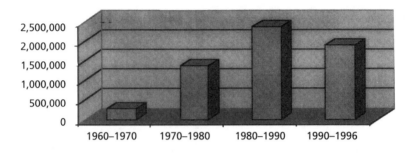

FIGURE 7.3

**Mexican Migrants Who Have Established
Permanent Residence in the United States, 1960–1996**

Source: *Migration between Mexico and the United States: A Report of the Binational Study on
Migration* (Washington, DC: U.S. Commission on Immigration Reform, 1997), 8.

Legal residents numbered between 4.7 and 4.9 million, making the total Mexican-born population in the United States range from 7.0 to 7.3 million.[48] Also in 1996, unauthorized Mexican residents represented 55 percent of the total unauthorized residents in the United States. (El Salvador was the second-highest Latin American country in the number of undocumented residents in the United States, with 7 percent of the total of unauthorized residents.)

The exact number of unauthorized entries of Mexicans into the United States is difficult to ascertain. Traditionally, the number of apprehensions has been used to estimate the number of illegal crossings; apprehensions refer to events, however, not to individuals. The same individual may be apprehended more than once, and many individuals are never apprehended. In 1995, there were 1.3 million apprehensions of Mexicans attempting to enter the United States without documentation.[49] The increased number of Mexicans seeking to enter the United States without documentation, and the enhanced U.S. enforcement efforts implemented in the 1990s, as we noted earlier in this chapter, explain this high total of apprehensions.

The dynamic nature of migration is at the root of the changing characteristics of Mexican migrants. During the Bracero Programs (1946–64), Mexican migration to the United States was principally a circular flow composed of young males from rural areas.[50] The length of their stay varied from six to twelve months. In the 1990s, however, the staying time of migrants lengthened; the likelihood that they would become permanent residents increased.[51] In the closing two decades of the twentieth century, the migratory flow became more complex and heterogeneous. The characteristics of the migrants came to reflect those of the Mexican population at large.[52] The geographic origins of the migration expanded beyond the states and municipalities, mostly in the central and northern parts of the country, that had been its traditional sources. By the late 1990s, more migrants came

TABLE 7.2

Mexican-Born and Mexican-Origin Population in the United States, 1910–1996

Year	Total Mexican-Origin Population* (in thousands)	Percent Mexican-origin in Total U.S. population	Total Mexican-Born Population** (in thousands)	Percent of Mexican-Born in the Total Mexican-Origin Population
1996	18,039**	6.8	6,679	37.0
1990	13,393	5.4	4,298	32.1
1980	8,740	3.9	2,199	25.2
1970	4,532	2.2	759	16.7
1960	1,736	1.0	576	33.2
1950	1,346	0.9	454	33.7
1940	1,077	0.8	377	35.0
1930	1,423	1.2	617	43.4
1920	740	0.7	486	65.7
1910	385	0.4	222	57.7

*Mexican-origin population calculated as a sum of the Mexican-born population and natives of Mexican parentage.

**These figures are based on CPS data that are adjusted for undercount and thus are not comparable to census figures.

Source: Frank D. Bean, Rodolfo Corona, Rodolfo Tuirán, and Karen A. Woodrow-Lafield, "The Quantification of Migration between Mexico and the United States," in *Migration between Mexico and the United States: Binational Study*, vol. 1 (Austin, TX: Morgan Printing, 1998), 5–6.

from urban centers, especially Mexico City. The occupations of migrants also diversified; rural and agricultural workers no longer constituted the majority of Mexicans migrating to the United States. In addition, the schooling levels of migrants rose over time.[53]

The importance of Mexican migration to the United States is likely to grow because the size of the Mexican-origin population in the United States is expected to increase in the twenty-first century thanks to a high birth rate and net immigration.[54] According to projections developed using U.S. Census Bureau data, the Mexican-origin population will more than double its size by 2040 (see Table 7.3). The Mexican-origin population will surpass the projected size of the African-American population by 2050.[55] (Table 7.3 assumes that the Mexican population will continue to represent the same proportion of the Hispanic population in 2040 as in 1990, that is, 59 percent.)

Migration is a major factor in U.S.–Mexican relations, with ramifications for both countries. The perception of migration differs, understandably, between a

TABLE 7.3

Projected Size of the Mexican-Origin Population in the United States, 1995–2040
(thousands)

Year	Hispanic Population	Mexican Population
1995	26,936	16,135
2000	31,366	18,788
2010	41,139	24,642
2020	52,652	31,539
2030	65,570	39,276
2040	80,164	48,018

Source: Frank D. Bean, Rodolfo Corona, Rodolfo Tuirán, and Karen A. Woodrow-Lafield, "The Quantification of Migration between Mexico and the United States," in *Migration between Mexico and the United States: Binational Study*, vol. 1 (Austin, TX: Morgan Printing, 1998), 11.

country that sends migrants and one that receives them. In Mexico, migrants are portrayed in the mass media and political speeches as courageous, hardworking individuals who sacrifice for their families. In addition, they are considered generous toward their families; in 1996, remittances from Mexican workers in the United States accounted for four to five billion dollars.[56] In the United States, particularly in some communities in the border states, Mexican migrants are

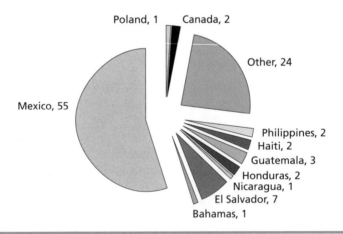

FIGURE 7.4
Countries of Origin for Unauthorized Immigration to the United States, 1996
(percentage)

Source: U.S. Immigration and Naturalization Services, *Illegal Alien Resident Population* (http://www.ins.doj.gov/stats/illegalalien/index), 6.

perceived as people who steal jobs from U.S. citizens of long standing and who overburden the welfare and education systems. Traditionally, the receiving country decides which immigrants it will accept and under what conditions; accordingly, the United States has acted mostly unilaterally on migration matters since the end of the Bracero Agreement in 1964.

U.S. migration policy toward Mexico was permissive from the end of World War II until the mid-1960s. Under the Bracero Programs, 4.5 million Mexicans labored in the United States. From 1965 to the early 1990s, the most significant effort to curb Mexican migration was the enactment of the Immigration Reform and Control Act (IRCA) in 1986. This law had two major provisions: amnesty and sanctions against employers who hired illegal residents. Ironically, only the former was implemented effectively. Thus, the law triggered an increase, not a reduction, in the number of Mexicans in the United States; legal Mexican immigration grew dramatically.[57] In the 1990s, legal immigration from Mexico remained substantial, as the family members of legalized Mexicans obtained permanent resident status. In 1996 alone, about 160,000 Mexicans became legal immigrants, and all but about 5,300 did so under family-based admission categories. This figure represented 17.6 percent of the total number of immigrants admitted legally to the United States that year.[58]

Motivated by an economic recession in the early 1990s, the United States toughened its stance on Mexican migration through legislation and border operations designed to secure the border. In 1994, California approved Proposition 187, denying social services to undocumented immigrants, although, as discussed earlier in this chapter, it remained largely unimplemented. In 1996, the U.S. Congress enacted the IIRIRA, which, combined with welfare reform, created a harder environment for both undocumented and documented immigrants. (Some of the IIRIRA's harsher provisions, such as barring legal immigrants from receiving supplemental security income and food stamps until they become naturalized citizens, were modified soon thereafter, however.) IIRIRA made life more difficult for those remaining in the United States illegally; it also made it more dangerous to cross the border without proper documentation. These efforts induced changes in the routes used in illegal crossings. The new paths were more dangerous and increased accidents. In 1998, the number of people dying while crossing the border reached 189, an all-time high.

The Mexican government's traditional objective has been to avoid abrupt changes in U.S. immigration policy and the flow of migrants, i.e., keeping "the U.S. door open." From the end of the Bracero Programs in 1964 to the late 1980s, Mexico developed a policy of "not having a policy." That is, Mexico was content with the status quo; it purposely left the flow of Mexican immigration into the United States to the forces of supply and demand, and it eschewed official discussions about migration with the U.S. government. In the early 1990s, however, the Mexican government abandoned its policy of non-engagement and began the search for a new understanding. José Angel Gurría, Mexico's foreign affairs minister from 1994 to 1997, sought a formula for Mexico and the United States to "jointly manage" this complicated phenomenon.[59]

Mexico's search for new ground on bilateral migration policy in the 1990s can be explained by two factors. First, Mexican officials perceived that U.S. hostility toward immigration had increased. Second, NAFTA prompted a new attitude among Mexican officials to institutionalize bilateral affairs, that is, to engage the U.S. government, formalize bilateral dialogues, and create mechanisms to manage bilateral affairs.[60] Mexico's search for a new understanding was impeded by the difficulty of reaching basic understandings with its U.S. counterparts and, more important, because the migration issue disappeared from the forefront of bilateral affairs. The U.S. economic boom of the mid- and late 1990s muted the anti-immigration feelings and allowed the Clinton administration and congress to soften some of the harsher provisions of both IIRIRA and the Welfare Reform Act. However, officials in both countries worried that if the U.S. economy were to falter, anti-immigrant efforts could resurface, prompting another episode of anti-immigration activism. This could wed the migration issue to the drug-trafficking issue as two sources of friction between the two countries; together, these issues could severely constrain the spirit of cooperation that developed between the two governments in the post–Cold War era.

Some modest practical collaborative steps were taken, however. In the late 1990s, the U.S. INS and Mexican officials worked together to identify dangerous crossing points along the entire southwest border and developed some specific safety programs with Mexican consuls. For example, the two governments posted warning signs on both the U.S. and Mexican sides of the border in dangerous areas and coordinated public service announcements along the border where migrants are located to warn them about the hazards in crossing the border illegally. The two governments issued news releases to U.S. and Mexican newspapers and placed spots in U.S. and Mexican radio and television. INS border officials worked with Mexican consuls to develop formal agreements on the schedules for returns of migrants to Mexico, with special provisions for children and women, and to share information to identify deceased individuals. In June 2000, following a formal Memorandum of Understanding between the two governments, the INS began to participate in joint training exercises with its Mexican counterparts in order to keep agents on both sides of the border prepared and trained in public safety measures. The INS and the Mexican government agreed also to expand their sharing of information and, where appropriate, equipment.[61]

CONCLUSION

In 1848, the U.S. victory in its war against Mexico and the U.S. seizure of the northern half of Mexico through the Treaty of Guadalupe-Hidalgo moved the U.S.–Mexican border southward. Thus began the modern history of the Mexican-origin population of the United States and the development of a transborder society that would evolve and grow. For the past century and a half, the peoples who live along this border made their respective accommodations to the power and wealth of the United States and to the weakness and poverty of Mexico. In the closing decades of the twentieth century, however, the flow of Mexican migration, and the problems as well as the vibrancy of life at the border region, created new concerns as well as new opportunities in both countries.

The story of U.S.–Mexican relations at and across the physical border during the 1990s focused, above all, on real people whose everyday life is affected by their proximity to the border. These people made millions of moves across the border lawfully every year. They created new sources of transborder wealth and development and new terrible problems of environmental pollution. More than in any other instance of U.S.–Mexican relations, all levels of government in both countries claimed jurisdiction and sought to effect their power on the issues that marked and enlivened the border. Many Mexican migrants to the United States became legal, productive members of their new society, but a significant number of them also broke the laws of the United States when they chose to enter this country without proper documentation.

We argued in this chapter, consistent with the book's argument, that on these issues, too, bilateral cooperation holds much promise. Municipal and state governments serve their citizens better when they choose to cooperate at the border. Some of the best and longest-lasting examples of collaboration between the two national governments were found at the border as well, dealing effectively and peacefully with the sorts of territorial issues that led governments to war in other continents.

On New Year's Eve 2000, the mayors of Laredo and Nuevo Laredo, Betty Flores and Horacio Garza, respectively, walked across the bridge above the Rio Grande/Río Bravo to celebrate the arrival of the new millennium with an international hug and kiss. For them, theirs was one integrated region located in the two countries whose flags fluttered all around them.[62]

These two countries shared the longest border between a very wealthy country and one that still had millions of its citizens living in poverty. On most issues most of the time, this complex relationship at and across the border was managed successfully. U.S. troops have not invaded Mexico for a period of time longer than the lifetimes of most people in both countries; war between them had become unthinkable. Yet, as the new millennium opened, the conflicts that surfaced every day at the U.S.–Mexican border caused pain, suffering, hardship, and, in some cases, death. The challenge to both countries and their governments at every level of their respective federations was to construct the institutions, rules, and practices at the border that would manage these still difficult issues more effectively and with fewer costs. It should be their goal to construct, jointly with Canada, a shared life in North America that better serves the values that they affirm in their own constitutions.

NOTES

I: HISTORY

1. Jesús Velasco Márquez, "Cooperación y conflicto en las relaciones México–Estados Unidos: un enfoque histórico," in *México y Estados Unidos: las rutas de la cooperación*, ed. Olga Pellicer and Rafael Fernández de Castro (Mexico: IMRED-SRE and ITAM, 1999), 216–17.
2. Josefina Zoraida Vázquez and Lorenzo Meyer, *México frente a los Estados Unidos (un ensayo histórico, 1776–1993)* (Mexico: Fondo de Cultura Económica, 1994), 54.
3. Bertha Ulloa, *La revolución intervenida* (Mexico: El Colegio de México, 1969).
4. See Jorge I. Domínguez, ed., *Mexican Political Economy: Challenges at Home and Abroad* (Beverly Hills, CA, 1982), 13–14.
5. Cathryn Thorup has studied this lack of U.S. policy coordination toward Mexico during the Carter and Reagan years. See Cathryn Thorup, *Managing Extreme Interdependence: Alternative Institutional Agreements for U.S. Policy Making toward Mexico, 1976–1988* (Cambridge, MA: Ph.D. dissertation, Harvard University, December 1992).
6. Sidney Weintraub, *A Marriage of Convenience* (New York: Oxford University Press, 1990), 72.
7. Jorge Castañeda (Sr.), "En busca de una posición frente a Estados Unidos," in *Visión del México contemporáneo* (Mexico: El Colegio de México, 1979), 113.
8. The relative vacuum in the literature of U.S.–Mexican relations on cooperation between the two nations is noteworthy.
9. Vázquez and Meyer, *México frente a los Estados Unidos*, 111.
10. Velasco Márquez, "Cooperación y conflicto en las relaciones México–Estados Unidos," 222.
11. Roberta Lajous, *México y el mundo. Historia de sus relaciones exteriores* (Mexico: Senado de la República), vol. IV, 39–84.
12. Vázquez and Meyer, *México frente a los Estados Unidos*, 112–13.
13. Lorenzo Meyer, "México–Estados Unidos: lo especial de una relación," in *México–Estados Unidos, 1984*, ed. Manuel García y Griego and Gustavo Vega (Mexico: El Colegio de México, 1985), 25.
14. Jorge G. Castañeda and Robert A. Pastor, *Límites en la amistad, México y Estados Unidos* (Mexico: Joaquín Mortiz-Planeta, 1989), 136–40.

II: THE CHANGES IN THE INTERNATIONAL SYSTEM: EFFECTS ON THE BILATERAL RELATIONSHIP

1. Thucydides, *The Peloponnesian War*, Book 5, Chapter 17 (Melian Dialogues) (New York: Modern Library, 1951), 331.
2. Mario Ojeda, *Alcances y límites de la política exterior de México* (Mexico: El Colegio de México, 1976), 3, 26, 79.
3. Ibid., 93.
4. Lorenzo Meyer, "La crisis de la élite mexicana y su relación con Estados Unidos: Raíces históricas del Tratado de Libre Comercio," in *México–Estados Unidos, 1990*, ed. Gustavo Vega (Mexico: El Colegio de México, 1992), 73.

5. Kenneth N. Waltz, "The Emerging Structure of International Politics," in *The International System after the Collapse of the East-West Order*, ed. Armand Clesse, Richard Cooper, and Yoshikazu Sakamoto (Dordrecht: Martinus Nijhoff, 1994), 169. For his more general statement, see *Theory of International Politics* (Reading, MA: Addison-Wesley, 1979).

6. See Francisco Gil Villegas, "El estudio de la política exterior en México: Enfoques dominantes, temas principales y una propuesta teórico-metodológica," *Foro internacional* no. 116 (April–June 1989): 670–72; and also his "Opciones de política exterior: México entre el Pacífico y el Atlántico," *Foro internacional* 114 (October–December 1988): 263–88.

7. For the president's own formulation, see pertinent passages from his state of the nation address, September 1, 1979, in *Los Estados Unidos de América en los informes presidenciales de México*, ed. Ricardo Ampudia (Mexico: Fondo de Cultura Económica, 1997), 176.

8. For an early assessment, see Mario Ojeda, "México ante los Estados Unidos en la coyuntura actual," in *Continuidad y cambio en la política exterior de México: 1977*, ed. Centro de Estudios Internacionales (Mexico: El Colegio de México, 1977), 40–41.

9. See Carlos Rico, "El socialismo europeo, la Alianza Atlántica y Centroamérica: ¿Una historia de expectativas frustradas?" *Foro internacional* no. 114 (October–December 1988): 289–318.

10. For the significance of governments, not just market processes, in the process of shaping European integration, see Andrew Moravcsik, *The Choice for Europe: Social Purpose and State Power from Messina to Maastricht* (Ithaca, NY: Cornell University Press, 1998).

11. For a history of these negotiations, see José Antonio Sanahuja, "Trade, Politics, and Democratization: The 1997 Global Agreement between the European Union and Mexico," *Journal of Interamerican Studies and World Affairs* 42, no. 2 (Summer 2000): 35–62.

12. Secretaría de Comercio y Fomento Industrial, Subsecretaría de Relaciones Comerciales Internacionales, "Conclusión de las negociaciones del Tratado de Libre Comercio entre México y la Unión Europea: Comunicado de prensa" (November 24, 1999); Presidencia, "Versión estenográfica del mensaje del Presidente Ernesto Zedillo, con motivo de la conclusión de las negociaciones del Acuerdo Comercial entre México y la Unión Europea" (November 24, 1999); Secretaría de Comercio y Fomento Industrial, Subsecretaría de Negociaciones Comerciales Internacionales, "Comercio México–Unión Europea," http://www.secofi-snci.gob.mx/Negoc. . .Comercio_Mex-UE/comercio_mex-ue.htm.

13. Marvella Colín, "De 2 mill mdd, el déficit comercial de México con la UE," *El Financiero*, July 3, 2000, 48.

14. See the memoirs of former president Carlos Salinas de Gortari, *México: un paso difícil a la modernidad* (Barcelona: Plaza y Janés Editores, 2000), 37–85. See also the account of Mexico's undersecretary of foreign affairs Andrés Rozental, *La política exterior de México en la era de la modernidad* (Mexico: Fondo de Cultura Económica, 1993), 59–62.

15. For succinct accounts, see Robert A. Pastor and Jorge G. Castañeda, *Limits to Friendship: The United States and Mexico* (New York: Knopf, 1988), 159–66, 178–92; Sara Gordon, "La política de Miguel de la Madrid hacia Centroamérica," and Jorge Chabat, "La política exterior de Miguel de la Madrid," both in *México: Auge, crisis y ajuste* (Mexico: Fondo de Cultura Económica, 1992).

16. Carlos Salinas de Gortari, *Segundo informe de gobierno* (Mexico: Presidencia de la República, 1990), 7–8.

17. Ana Covarrubias, "La política mexicana hacia Cuba durante el gobierno de Salinas de Gortari," *Foro internacional* 34, no. 4 (October–December 1994): 652–82.

18. Luis Rubio, "Japan in Mexico: A Changing Pattern," in *Japan and Latin America in the New World Order*, ed. Susan Kaufman Purcell and Robert Immerman (Boulder, CO: Lynne Rienner, 1992), 69–70.

19. The Gallup Poll, 1988.

20. Gabriel Székely, "The Consequences of NAFTA for European and Japanese Trade and Investment in Mexico," in *Mexico and the North American Free Trade Agreement: Who Will Benefit?*, ed. Victor Bulmer-Thomas, Nikki Craske, and Mónica Serrano (London: MacMillan, 1994).

21. Rozental, *La política exterior de México en la era de la modernidad*, 60; Centro de Investigación para el Desarrollo (CIDAC), *Política exterior para un mundo nuevo: México en el nuevo contexto internacional* (Mexico: Editorial Diana, 1992), 111–12.

22. Joseph Grieco, "The Maastricht Treaty, Economic and Monetary Union, and the Neorealist Research Programme," *Review of International Studies* 21, no.1 (January 1995): 34.

23. Robert Keohane, *After Hegemony: Cooperation and Discord in the World Political Economy* (Princeton, NJ: Princeton University Press, 1984), 85–95.

24. Rolando Cordera and Carlos Tello, *La disputa por la nación* (Mexico: Editorial Siglo XXI, 1981).

25. For discussion, see Dale Story, "Trade Politics in the Third World: A Case Study of the Mexican GATT Decision," *International Organization* 36 (Autumn 1982): 767–94.

26. José I. Martínez, "La política de comercio exterior: de la racionalización de la protección a la diversificación comercial," *Relaciones internacionales* (April–June 1994): 80.

27. Bela Belassa, "Trade Policy in Mexico," *World Development* 11, no. 9 (1983): 803. For comparative discussion, including Mexico, see also John S. Odell, "Latin American Industrial Exports and Trade Negotiations with the United States," in *Economic Issues and Political Conflict: US–Latin American Relations*, ed. Jorge I. Domínguez (London: Butterworths, 1982).

28. For an example of the sophisticated defense of their exports by some Mexican producers (in this case, tomato exporters) even in the absence of a bilateral inter-governmental framework, see David Mares, *Penetrating the International Market: Theoretical Considerations and a Mexican Case Study* (New York: Columbia University Press, 1987), 203–25.

29. See B. Timothy Bennett, "Cooperation and Results in U.S.–Mexico Relations," in *The Economics of Interdependence: Mexico and the United States*, ed. William Glade and Cassio Luiselli (La Jolla: Center for U.S.–Mexican Studies, University of California-San Diego, 1989), 169–71. Bennett conducted most of these negotiations on behalf of the United States as U.S. deputy assistant special trade representative.

30. For a discussion of the transformation of Mexican policies on direct foreign investment, see Van R. Whiting, *The Political Economy of Foreign Investment in Mexico* (Baltimore: Johns Hopkins University Press, 1992); Stephen Bland and Jerry Haar, *Making NAFTA Work: U.S. Firms and the New North American Business Environment* (Miami: North-South Center Press, University of Miami, 1998).

31. David Shields, "Energía, primer foco rojo para Vicente Fox," *Reforma*, July 5, 2000, 7A.

32. Among others, see John Williamson, "Mexican Policy toward Foreign Borrowing," in *Coming Together? Mexico–U.S. Relations*, ed. Barry Bosworth, Susan Collins, and Nora Lustig (Washington, DC: Brookings, 1997); Riordan Roett, "Los nuevos vínculos financieros entre México y Estados Unidos," in *Nueva agenda bilateral en la relación México–Estados Unidos*, ed. Mónica Verea Campos, Rafael Fernández de Castro, and Sidney Weintraub (Mexico: Fondo de Cultura Económica, 1998).

33. Stephanie Golob, "`Making Possible What Is Necessary': Pedro Aspe, the Salinas Team, and the Next Mexican `Miracle,'" in *Technopols: Freeing Politics and Markets in Latin America in the 1990s* (University Park: Pennsylvania State University Press, 1997). See also Miguel Angel Centeno, *Democracy within Reason: Technocratic Revolution in Mexico* (University Park: Pennsylvania State University Press, 1994).

34. *The Economist*, December 14, 1991, 19.

35. Peter M. Haas, ed., *Knowledge, Power, and International Policy Coordination* (Columbia, SC: University of South Carolina Press, 1997). For related discussion, see Víctor Godínez, "The Negotiations between the Mexican Government and the U.S. Financial Community: A New Interpretation," in *Bridging the Border: Transforming Mexico–U.S. Relations*, ed. Rodolfo de la Garza and Jesús Velasco (Lanham, MD: Rowman & Littlefield, 1997).

36. Rafael Fernández de Castro, "La institucionalización de la relación intergubernamental: una forma de explicar la cooperación," in *Nueva agenda bilateral en la relación México–Estados Unidos*, ed. Mónica Verea, Rafael Fernández de Castro, and Sidney Weintraub (Mexico: Fondo de Cultura Económica, 1998); Rafael Fernández de Castro and Claudia Ibarguen, "Emerging Cooperation: Case of the NAFTA Commissions," in *A New North*

America: Cooperation and Enhanced Interdependence, ed. Charles Doran and Alvin Drischler (Westport, CT: Praeger, 1996); Sidney Weintraub, "Avances y retos en el comercio y la inversión entre México y Estados Unidos," in *México y Estados Unidos: Las rutas de la cooperación,* ed. Olga Pellicer and Rafael Fernández de Castro (Mexico: Secretaría de Relaciones Exteriores, 1998), 140.

37. Hildy Teegen, "Nuevos actores, negocios: sus alianzas estratégicas," in *Nueva agenda bilateral en la relación México–Estados Unidos,* ed. Mónica Verea Campos, Rafael Fernández de Castro, and Sidney Weintraub (Mexico: Fondo de Cultura Económica, 1998).

38. Carlos Rico, "Migration and U.S.–Mexican Relations, 1966–1986," in *Western Hemisphere Immigration and United States Foreign Policy,* ed. Christopher Mitchell (University Park: Pennsylvania State University Press, 1992).

39. Carlos González Gutiérrez, "México en el Congreso de Estados Unidos: La inmigración," *Foro Internacional,* no. 114 (October–December 1988): 242–45; *Migration between the United States and Mexico: Binational Study* (Washington, DC: U.S. Commission on Immigration Reform, 1998).

40. Rafael Fernández de Castro, "Immigration in U.S.–Mexican Relations," *A Report of the U.S.–Mexican Relations Forum* (Washington, DC: Inter-American Dialogue, 1998).

41. For an elegant original statement of this idea, see Ernst B. Haas, *Beyond the Nation State: Functionalism and International Organization* (Stanford, CA: Stanford University Press, 1964).

42. For a thoughtful assessment of theorizing about regionalism, see Andrew Hurrell, "Explaining the Resurgence of Regionalism in World Politics," *Review of International Studies* 21, no. 4 (October 1995): 331–58.

43. Carlos Fuentes, *The Death of Artemio Cruz,* trans. Sam Hileman (New York: Farrar, Straus, and Giroux, 1964), 112.

III: INTERNATIONAL SECURITY

1. These are the implications for international security policy of the more general assessment of Mexican foreign policy delineated in Mario Ojeda's *Alcances y límites de la política exterior de México* (Mexico: El Colegio de México, 1976).

2. Stephen M. Walt, "Alliance Formation in Southwest Asia: Balancing and Bandwagoning in Cold War Competition," in *Dominoes and Bandwagons: Strategic Beliefs and Great Power Competition in the Eurasian Rimland,* ed. Robert Jervis and Jack Snyder (New York: Oxford University Press, 1991), 55.

3. C. Richard Bath, "Resolving Water Disputes," in *Mexico–United States Relations,* ed. Susan Kaufman Purcell (New York: The Academy of Political Science, 1981), 181–82.

4. Friedrich Katz, *Secret War in Mexico: Europe and the United States in the Mexican Revolution* (Chicago: University of Chicago Press, 1981), 245–48.

5. For general histories of U.S.–Mexican relations, see Josefina Zoraida Vázquez and Lorenzo Meyer, *The United States and Mexico* (Chicago: University of Chicago Press, 1985); Howard F. Cline, *The United States and Mexico* (New York: Atheneum, 1965). For a discussion of U.S. military policy with regard to Mexico during World War I and World War II, see Michael Desch, *When the Third World Matters: Latin America and United States Grand Strategy* (Baltimore: Johns Hopkins University Press, 1993), 19–88.

6. For the evolution of non-military U.S. policy toward Mexico during World War II, see Bryce Wood, *The Making of the Good Neighbor Policy* (New York: Columbia University Press, 1961), 203–59.

7. David R. Mares, "Strategic Interests in the U.S.–Mexican Relationship," in *Strategy and Security in U.S.–Mexican Relations beyond the Cold War,* ed. John Bailey and Sergio Aguayo Quezada (La Jolla: Center for U.S.–Mexican Studies, University of California-San Diego, 1996), 24. For a discussion of security communities, see Karl Deutsch et al., *Political Community and the North Atlantic Area: International Organization in the Light of Historical Experience* (Princeton, NJ: Princeton University Press, 1957). For further application of the concept to U.S.–Mexican relations, see Guadalupe González and Stephan

Haggard, "The United States and Mexico: A Pluralistic Security Community?" in *Security Communities*, ed. Emanuel Adler and Michael Barnett (Cambridge: Cambridge University Press, 1998).

8. John A. Cope, "In Search of Convergence: U.S.–Mexican Military Relations into the Twenty-First Century," in *Strategy and Security in U.S.–Mexican Relations beyond the Cold War*, ed. Bailey and Aguayo.

9. Stephen J. Wager, "Basic Characteristics of the Modern Mexican Military," in *The Modern Mexican Military: A Reassessment*, ed. David Ronfeldt (La Jolla: Center for U.S.–Mexican Studies, University of California-San Diego, 1984), 100–102; Cope, "In Search of Convergence," 194–95.

10. Cole Blasier, *The Giant's Rival: The USSR and Latin America* (Rev. ed., Pittsburgh: Pittsburgh University Press, 1987).

11. Ana Covarrubias, "Cuba and Mexico: A Case for Mutual Nonintervention," *Cuban Studies* 26 (1996): 121–41; Carl Migdail, "Mexico, Cuba, and the United States: Myth versus Reality," in *Cuba's Ties to a Changing World*, ed. Donna Rich Kaplowitz (Boulder, CO: Lynne Rienner, 1993).

12. For a sympathetic characterization of Mexican policy on these issues, see Mexican ambassador Claude Heller, "U.S. and Mexican Policies toward Central America," in *Foreign Policy in U.S.–Mexican Relations*, ed. Rosario Green and Peter H. Smith (La Jolla: Center for U.S.–Mexican Studies, University of California-San Diego, 1989), 172–77, 201–205, quotation from 209. For an articulate elaboration of U.S. policy at this time, see David Ronfeldt, *Geopolitics, Security, and U.S. Strategy in the Caribbean Basin*, R-2997-AF/RC (Santa Monica, CA: Rand Corporation, 1983).

13. Richard Craig, "U.S. Narcotics Policy toward Mexico: Consequences for the Bilateral Relationship," in *The Drug Connection in U.S.–Mexican Relations*, ed. Guadalupe González and Marta Tienda (La Jolla: Center for U.S.–Mexican Studies, University of California-San Diego, 1989), 71–73.

14. Ibid., 74–75; María Celia Toro, *Mexico's "War" on Drugs: Causes and Consequences* (Boulder, CO: Lynne Rienner, 1995), 16–17.

15. Toro, *Mexico's "War" on Drugs*, 17–18, 30–32.

16. Ibid., 64–66. See also Timothy J. Dunn, *The Militarization of the U.S.–Mexico Border, 1978–1992: Low-Intensity Conflict Doctrine Comes Home* (Austin: Center for Mexican-American Studies, University of Texas, 1996).

17. María Celia Toro, "La política mexicana contra el narcotráfico: Un instrumento de política exterior," in *Nueva agenda bilateral en la relación México–Estados Unidos*, ed. Mónica Verea Campos, Rafael Fernández de Castro, and Sidney Weintraub (Mexico: Fondo de Cultura Económica, 1998), 150–55; Peter Reuter and David Ronfeldt, *Quest for Integrity: The Mexican–U.S. Drug Issue in the 1980s* (Santa Monica, CA: The Rand Corporation, 1992), 22–23, 32–34.

18. México, Poder Ejecutivo Federal, *Programa nacional para el control de drogas, 1995–2000* (Mexico: Procuraduría General de la República, 1995). For a thoughtful discussion of the history of the U.S. Drug Enforcement Administration's relations with Mexico, see María Celia Toro, "The Internationalization of Police: The DEA in Mexico," *The Journal of American History* 86, no. 2 (September 1999): 623–40.

19. Donald E. Schulz, "Between a Rock and a Hard Place: The United States, Mexico, and the Challenge of National Security," *Low-Intensity Conflict and Law Enforcement* 6, no. 3 (Winter 1997): 2–5.

20. Tim Golden and Christopher Wren, "U.S. Ignores Mexico's Anti-Drug Failures," *New York Times*, February 14, 1999, 4.

21. Ernesto Zedillo Ponce de León, *The Nation: Progress and Challenges* (Mexico), September 1, 1998, 9.

22. Procuraduría General de la República, *Mexico's Fight against the Scourge of Drugs* (Mexico: Procuraduría General de la República, 1998), 2, 25; International Institute for Strategic Studies, *The Military Balance, 1997–1998* (London: Oxford University Press, 1997),

221–22; Raúl Benítez Manaut, "La fuerzas armadas mexicanas a fin de siglo," *Fuerzas armadas y sociedad* 15, no. 1 (January–March 2000): 16.

23. Schulz, "Between a Rock and a Hard Place," 32.

24. U.S., Department of Defense, "Background Briefing: U.S./Mexico Defense Meeting," Defense*Link*, April 24, 1996, http://www.defenselink.mil:80/news/Apr1996/x042896_x0424mex.html.

25. U.S., Office of National Drug Control Policy, Executive Office of the President, "The National Drug Control Strategy at Work: Fighting Drugs, Protecting Communities, Saving Kids, Producing Results" (Washington, DC, December 12, 1997), 4. See also John Bailey, "Law Enforcement and Intelligence in the Bilateral Security Context: U.S. Bureaucratic Dynamics," in *Strategy and Security in U.S.–Mexican Relations*, ed. Bailey and Aguayo, 171.

26. Robert A. Pastor and Rafael Fernández de Castro, "Congress and Mexico," in *The Controversial Pivot: The U.S. Congress and North America*, ed. Robert A. Pastor and Rafael Fernández de Castro (Washington, DC: Brookings Institution Press, 1998), 38.

27. Procuraduría General de la República, *Mexico's Fight against the Scourge of Drugs*, 51–52.

28. For a remarkably candid assessment of changes in Mexican policy, U.S., Office of National Drug Control Policy, Executive Office of the President, *Report to Congress: United States and Mexico Counterdrug Cooperation*, vol. 1 (Washington, DC, 1997), 3–7, 14, 18, 20. This and the next few paragraphs draw from this source.

29. For a thoughtful discussion of this process, see Miguel Ruíz-Cabañas, "Intereses contradictorios y mecanismos de cooperación; el caso del narcotráfico en las relaciones mexicano-estadounidenses," in *México y Estados Unidos: Las rutas de la cooperación*, ed. Olga Pellicer and Rafael Fernández de Castro (Mexico: Secretaría de Relaciones Exteriores-ITAM, 1998), 124–27.

30. U.S., Department of State, Bureau for International Narcotics and Law Enforcement Affairs, *International Narcotics Control Strategy Report, 1999: Mexico* (Washington, DC: March 2000).

31. Much of this information was obtained through high-level confidential interviews conducted in 2000.

32. Tim Golden, "Study Faults U.S. Military Aid Sent to Mexico's Anti-Drug Effort," *New York Times*, March 19, 1998, A5.

33. U.S., Department of State, Bureau of International Narcotics and Law Enforcement Affairs, *International Narcotics Control Strategy Report, 1999* (Washington, DC: U.S. Department of State, 2000), 8; "Mexican Air Force Buys 73 Cessna Planes for Drug War," *Defense Daily*, December 23, 1999; "Mexico Grounds Copters Donated by U.S.," *New York Times*, April 2, 1998, 10.

34. Ruíz-Cabañas, "Intereses contradictorios y mecanismos de cooperación," 128.

35. High Level Contact Group for Drug Control, "Communiqué" (Washington, DC, October 23–24, 1997), 3.

36. Secretaría de Relaciones Exteriores, "Se reunieron la Canciller Rosario Green y la Secrtaria de Estado Madeleine Albright," November 8, 1999, http://www.sre.gob.mx/comunicados/prensa/dgcs/1999/Nov/B-w02.htm.

37. Ruíz-Cabañas, "Intereses contradictorios y mecanismos de cooperación," 129–31, presents the Mexican perspective well.

38. "Statement of the Attorney General's Office of Mexico on Operation Casablanca" (Washington, DC: Embassy of Mexico to the United States, May 18, 1998); "Statement Made by the Attorney General of Mexico, Jorge Madrazo Cuéllar, Regarding Operation Casablanca" (Washington, DC: Embassy of Mexico to the United States, May 22, 1998); "Government of Mexico Announces Decisions on 'Operation Casablanca'" (Washington, DC: Embassy of Mexico to the United States, February 7, 1999).

39. Quoted in the *New York Times*, May 27, 1998, A3. See also ibid., May 19, 1998, A6, and May 22, 1998, A3.

40. For an excellent discussion of issues at stake and social and political processes in Chiapas, see John Womack Jr., *Rebellion in Chiapas* (New York: The New Press, 1999).

41. Raúl Benítez Manaut, "Mexican National Security at the End of the Century: Challenges and Perspectives," *Latin American Program Working Paper Series* 236 (Washington, DC: Woodrow Wilson International Center for Scholars, 1998), 16. See also his "Dilemas del ejército mexicano a fin de siglo," *Fuerzas armadas y sociedad* 14, no. 1 (January–March 1999): 10–21. For President Salinas's account of his decision-making, see Carlos Salinas de Gortari, *México: un paso difícil a la modernidad* (Barcelona: Plaza y Janés Editores, 2000), 809–831.

42. Stephen J. Wager and Donald E. Schulz, "The Zapatista Revolt and Its Implications for Civil-Military Relations and the Future of Mexico," *Journal of Interamerican Studies and World Affairs* 37, no. 1 (Spring 1995): 1–42. Former president Salinas also presents an informative account. See his *México*, 843–65.

43. International Institute for Strategic Studies, *The Military Balance, 1997–98*, 201, 204, 220–22, 267, 309; International Institute for Strategic Studies, *The Military Balance, 1996–1997* (London: Oxford University Press, 1996), 204, 208, 309; Stockholm International Peace Research Institute, *SIPRI Yearbook 1996: Armaments, Disarmament and International Security* (London: Oxford University Press, 1996), 369, 375.

44. Michael W. Foley, *Southern Mexico: Counterinsurgency and Electoral Politics* (Washington, DC: U.S. Institute of Peace, 1999), 5.

45. Schulz, "Between a Rock and a Hard Place," 22.

46. Wager, "Basic Characteristics of the Modern Mexican Military," 100. For background on the Mexican army, see Stephen Wager, *The Mexican Military Approaches the Twenty-First Century* (Carlisle Barracks, PA: Strategic Studies Institute, U.S. Army War College, 1994); for background on civil-military relations, see Mónica Serrano, "The Armed Branch of the State: Civil-Military Relations in Mexico," *Journal of Latin American Studies* 27, no. 2 (May 1995): 423–48.

47. Secretaría de Defensa Nacional, "Estructura orgánica de la Dirección General de Educación Militar y Rectoría de la U.D.E.F.A.: La educación militar," March 8, 2000, http://www.sedena.gob.mx/educación/art_emil.htm.

48. Secretaría de Defensa Nacional, "Comunicado oficial, 10 November 1999, http://www.sedena.gob.mx/comunica/bp/noviembre/bp101199.html.

49. Foley, "Southern Mexico," 10–11.

50. See also Schulz, "Between a Rock and a Hard Place," 7–10.

51. Stockholm International Peace Research Institute, *SIPRI Yearbook 1996: Armaments, Disarmament and International Security* (London: Oxford University Press, 1996), 369; International Institute for Strategic Studies, *The Military Balance, 1996–97* (London: Oxford University Press, 1996), 204, 208, 309; ibid., *1997–98* (1997), 221–22; Benítez Manaut, "Las fuerzas armadas mexicanas a fin de siglo," 17.

52. Benítez Manaut, "Las fuerzas armadas mexicanas a fin de siglo," 16, 18–20.

53. Cope, "In Search of Convergence," 196–208.

54. "Marine Corps Chief Opposes Pulling Troops from U.S. Border," *Defense Daily* (January 20, 1998): 1.

IV: THE EFFECT OF INTERNATIONAL INSTITUTIONS

1. Olga Pellicer, "México en la OEA," *Foro Internacional* 6, nos. 2–3 (October–December 1965 and January–March 1966), 290.

2. Andrés Rozental, *La política exterior de México en la era de la modernidad* (Mexico: Fondo de Cultura Económica, 1993), 104.

3. Claude Heller, "México en la OEA: tesis y posiciones tradicionales," *Revista mexicana de política exterior*, no. 54 (June 1998), 9.

4. Manuel Tello, "La reforma de la Organización de Naciones Unidas. El caso del Consejo de Seguridad," in *Las Naciones Unidas hoy. Visión de México*, ed. Olga Pellicer (Mexico: Fondo de Cultura Económica, 1994), 98.

5. In the 26-year period, from 1954 to 1980, Brazil was a member of the security council five times (a total of ten years), and Argentina, Colombia, and Panama four times each (a total

of eight years each). See Claude Heller, "México y el Consejo de Seguridad," in *México en las Naciones Unidas* (Mexico: Secretaría de Relaciones Exteriores, 1996), 161.

6. Heller, "México y el Consejo de Seguridad," 24.
7. See Mario Ojeda, *El surgimiento de una política exterior activa* (Mexico: El Colegio de México, 1984).
8. Rafael Velázquez Flores, *Introducción al estudio de la política exterior* (Mexico: Nuestro Tiempo, 1995), 106.
9. George W. Grayson, *The United States and Mexico: Patterns of Influence* (New York: Praeger, 1984), 42.
10. Carlos Rico, *México y el mundo. Historia de sus relaciones exteriores* (Mexico: Senado de la República, vol. 8, 1990), 69–118.
11. This section relies on the article by Ambassador Claude Heller "México y el Consejo de Seguridad," 251.
12. Heller, "México y el Consejo de Seguridad," 252.
13. Heller, "México y el Consejo de Seguridad," 255–56.
14. Rozental, *La política exterior de México en la era de la modernidad*, 105.
15. The law requires the secretary of state to transmit annually to congress a report called *Voting Practices in the United Nations* (previously called *Report to Congress on Voting Practices in the United Nations*). It reports the voting record of each member of the UN in comparison to U.S. votes. The report also includes a listing of votes on several specified issues deemed important by the United States.
16. See Miguel Marín-Bosch, *Votes in the UN General Assembly* (Boston: Kluwer Law International, 1998).
17. Marín-Bosch's system takes into account abstentions and absences.
   He uses the equation: voting coincidence =
   $$\frac{2 \text{ (total identical votes)} + \text{(total abstention/yes + abstention/no)}}{2 \text{ (total resolutions both voted)}}$$
   The results range from a scale of 1–1000, with 1000 representing 100 percent voting coincidence between two countries.
18. Ambassadors Claude Heller and Olga Pellicer make this argument. See Claude Heller, "México en la OEA; tesis y posiciones tradicionales," *Revista mexicana de política exterior*, no. 54 (June 1998): 9–18; and Olga Pellicer, "La OEA a los 50 años: ¿hacia su fortalecimiento?" *Revista mexicana de política exterior*, no. 54 (June 1998): 19–36.
19. Heller, "México en la OEA; tesis y posiciones tradicionales," 10.
20. Pellicer, "México en la OEA," in *Foro Internacional*, 288–89.
21. Personal interview, Ambassador Claude Heller, Washington, DC, June 1999.
22. Pellicer, "La OEA a los 50 años: hacia su fortalecimiento?" 22.
23. Miguel Ruíz-Cabañas, "La OEA y el combate hemisférico contra las drogas," *Revista mexicana de política exterior*, no. 54 (June 1998): 104–105.
24. For a detailed analysis of Mexico's position in the development of CICAD, see Ruíz-Cabañas, "La OEA y el combate hemisférico de drogas," 102–15.
25. See José Alfredo Galván Corona, "La promoción de la democracia en el hemisferio: consensos y límites de la acción de la OEA," *Revista de política exterior*, no. 54 (June 1998): 93–101.
26. Pellicer, "La OEA a los 50 años: ¿hacia su fortalecimiento?" 29.
27. Francisco Suárez Dávila, "La política financiera internacional de México. Relaciones con el Banco Mundial y el FMI," *Comercio Exterior*, 44, no. 40 (October 1994), 854.
28. Carlos Urzúa, "Mexico and the World Bank," in *The World Bank. Its First Half Century* (Washington, DC: Brookings Institution Press, 1998), 49.
29. Urzúa, "Mexico and the World Bank," 107.
30. Urzúa, "Mexico and the World Bank," 64.
31. Suárez Dávila, "La política financiera internacional de México. Relaciones con el Banco Mundial y el FMI," 857.
32. Nora Lustig, *Mexico: The Remaking of an Economy* (Washington, DC: Brookings Institution Press, 1998), 22.

33. Sidney Weintraub, *A Marriage of Convenience* (New York: Oxford University Press, 1990), 136.

34. See Joseph Kraft, *The Mexican Rescue* (New York: Group of Thirty, 1984), and José Angel Gurría, *La política de la deuda externa* (Mexico: Fondo de Cultura Económica, 1995).

35. The price sought by the U.S. officials was $28 per barrel while the international market price was $33. See Nora Lustig, "Los Estados Unidos al rescate de México en crisis," in *La nueva agenda en la relación México-EUA*, ed. Mónica Verea, Rafael Fernández de Castro, and Sidney Weintraub (Mexico D.F.: Fondo de Cultura Económica, 1997), 458.

36. Urzúa, "Mexico and the World Bank," 69.

37. Lustig, *Mexico*, 71.

38. Gurría, *La política de la deuda externa*, 218.

39. Lustig, "Los Estados Unidos al rescate de México en crisis," 484–85.

40. Weintraub, *A Marriage of Convenience*, 72.

41. Jorge Miranda, "An Economic Analysis of Mexico's Use of Trade Remedy Laws from 1987 to 1995," in *Trading Punches: Trade Remedy Law and Disputes under NAFTA*, ed. Beatriz Leycegui, William B. P. Robson, and Dahlia Stein (Washington, DC: The National Policy Association, 1995), 140.

42. See Richard Gardner, *Silver Dollar Diplomacy, Sterling-Dollar Diplomacy in Current Perspective* (New York: Columbia University Press, 1980); Charles Kindleberger, *The World Depression, 1929–1939* (Berkeley: University of California Press, 1973).

43. *Economic Report of the President* (Washington, DC: U.S. Government Printing Office, 1980), 24.

44. William R. Cline, *Trade Policy in the 1980s* (Washington, DC: Institute for International Economics, 1983), 91.

45. Cline, *Trade Policy in the 1980s*, 98.

46. See Gary C. Hufbauer, *The Free Trade Debate* (New York: Twentieth Century Fund, 1989), 146.

47. I. M. Destler, *American Trade Politics* (Washington, DC: Institute of International Economics, 1995), 154.

48. The steel VER lasted from 1985 to 1989. See Rafael Fernández de Castro and Judith Mariscal, "La industria siderúrgica de norteamérica ante el TLC," in *México y el acuerdo trilateral de libre comercio*, ed. Eduardo Andere and Georgina Kessel (Mexico: ITAM-McGraw-Hill, 1992), 146–49.

49. See Herminio Blanco, *Las negociaciones comerciales de México con el mundo* (Mexico: Fondo de Cultura Económica, 1994), 24–25.

50. Lustig, *Mexico*, 117.

51. B. Timothy Bennett, "Recent U.S.–Mexico Trade Relations: Positive Results and Increased Cooperation," in *Mexico and the United States Managing the Relationship*, ed. Riordan Roett (Boulder, CO: Westview Press, 1989), 90.

52. Sidney Weintraub, "The North American Free Trade Agreement," in *Economic Integration Worldwide*, ed. Ali M. El-Agraa (New York: San Martin's Press, 1997), 204.

53. See Patrick Low, *Trading Free* (New York: Twentieth Century Fund Press, 1993); Destler, *American Trade Politics*; and Weintraub, "The North American Free Trade Agreement."

54. Low, *Trading Free*, 31.

55. Hufbauer, *The Free Trade Debate*, 135.

56. Low, *Trading Free*, 182–83.

57. Destler, *American Trade Politics*, 51–52.

58. The United States had signed a previous FTA accord with Israel in 1987. The relevance of this accord was more political than commercial; there was modest trade between the two nations.

59. Weintraub, "The North American Free Trade Agreement," 205.

60. Michael Hart, *Trade: Why Bother?* (Ottawa: Center for Trade and Policy Law, 1992), 94.

61. Destler, *American Trade Politics*, 135.

62. This was argued for the first time by Jorge Hernández Campos in "Cerrazón Europea," *Uno Más Uno*, August 17, 1990. See also the memoirs of Carlos Salinas de Gortari, *México: un paso difícil a la modernidad* (Barcelona: Plaza y Janés Editores, 2000) 39–85.

63. Weintraub, "The North American Free Trade Agreement," 210.

64. Ronald Wonnacott, *The Economics of Overlapping Free Trade Areas and the Mexican Challenge* (Toronto and Washington, DC: Canadian-American Committee), 91.

65. See NAFTA, chapter four, "Rules of Origin."

66. Sidney Weintraub, "The North American Free Trade Agreement as Negotiated," in *Assessing NAFTA: A Trinational Analysis*, ed. Steve Globernman and Michael Walker (Vancouver, British Columbia: The Fraser Institute, 1992), 3.

67. Each panel is required to apply the standard of judicial review and the law applicable in the country where actions were taken to provoke the other country to adopt the anti-dumping and countervailing duty measures. Thus, each country is judged in terms of whether it applies its own rules fairly, correctly, and consistently. See Guillermo Aguilar Alvarez, Jonathan T. Fried, Charles E. Roh Jr., Christianne M. Laizner, and David W. Oliver, "NAFTA Chapter 19: Binational Panel Review of Anti-Dumping and Countervailing Duty Determinations," in *Trading Punches: Trade Remedy Law and Disputes under NAFTA*, 24–42.

68. Article 27 of the Mexican Constitution, Section I, incorporates the principles embodied in the Calvo Doctrine.

69. Peter Truell, "U.S. and Mexico Agree to Seek Free-Trade Pact," *Wall Street Journal*, March 27, 1990, A3.

70. Carlos Arriola, *Tratado de Libre Comercio de América del Norte: Documentos básicos* (Mexico: Miguel Angel Porrúa, 1994), vi.

71. Sidney Weintraub, *NAFTA, What Comes Next?* (Washington, DC: The Center for Strategic International Studies, 1994), 28.

72. Annex 2001.2 provides a comprehensive list (nine committees, three subcommittees, one council, six working groups, and one subgroup).

73. Remarks by Governor Bill Clinton, North Carolina State University, Raleigh, NC, October 4, 1992.

74. Lance Compa, "International Labor Rights and NAFTA's Labor Side Agreement," *LASA Forum* 30, no. 2 (Summer 1999): 14–17.

V: THE DOMESTIC CONTEXT FOR
FOREIGN POLICY DECISION-MAKING

1. A prominent scholar of the presidency, Richard Neustadt, has argued that the separateness of institutions and sharing of authority make persuasion the president's real power. See Richard E. Neustadt, *Presidential Power and the Modern Presidents* (New York: The Free Press, 1990), 29–49.

2. Secretary of State Madeleine Albright sent a letter to Treasury Secretary Robert Rubin asking him to "keep the Department of State informed about all actions developed in Mexico." Dolia Estévez, "Albright pide cuentas al Secretario Rubin," *El Financiero*, May 23, 1998, 1.

3. The Mexican Senate elected for the period 1997–2000 had 128 members, of whom 77 were from the PRI (60 percent), 33 from PAN (26 percent), 16 from the PRD (13 percent), and one each from the workers' party (PT) and the green or environmentalist party (PVEM). See Roderic Ai Camp, *Politics in Mexico: The Decline of Authoritarianism*, 3d. ed. (New York: Oxford University Press, 1999), 166.

4. The Mexican diplomatic service was created in 1948.

5. There have been very few studies of Mexican foreign policy decision-making; the reason, according to Chabat, is its centralization in the president's hands. Jorge Chabat, "La toma de decisiones en la política exterior mexicana," in *La política exterior México–Estados Unidos*, ed. Rosario Green and Peter H. Smith (Mexico: Fondo de Cultura Económica, 1989), 87.

6. Robert A. Pastor and Jorge G. Castañeda, *The Limits of Friendship: The United States and Mexico* (New York: Alfred A. Knopf, 1988), 79–80.

7. George W. Grayson, "Lobbying by Mexico and Canada," in *The Controversial Pivot: The*

U.S. Congress and North America, ed. Robert A. Pastor and Rafael Fernández de Castro (Washington, DC: Brookings Institution Press, 1998), 70–96.

8. Interview with Jesús Reyes Heroles, Mexican ambassador to the United States, Washington, DC, March 30, 1999.

9. For a seminal article, see Bayless Manning, "The Congress, the Executive, and Intermestic Affairs: Three Proposals," *Foreign Affairs*, 55 (January 1977): 309.

10. Hildy Teegen, "Nuevos actores: negocios, sus alianzas estratégicas," in *Nueva Agenda Bilateral en la relación México–Estados Unidos*, ed. Mónica Verea, Rafael Fernández de Castro, and Sidney Weintraub (Mexico: Fondo de Cultura Económica, 1998), 402–404.

11. Blanca Torres, "La cooperación bilateral para la protección del medio ambiente," in *Nueva agenda de la relación bilateral México-EUA*, ed. Mónica Verea, Rafael Fernández de Castro, and Sidney Weintraub (Mexico: Fondo de Cultura Económica, 1998), 228–29.

12. Mary R. Kelly, Dick Kamp, Michael Gregory, and Jan Gilbreath Rich, "U.S.–Mexico Free Trade Negotiations and the Environment: Exploring the Issues," *The Columbia Journal of World Business* (Summer 1991): 49.

13. Torres, "La cooperación bilateral para la protección del medio ambiente," 222–23.

14. Thomas A. Constantine, "Remarks before the Senate Caucus on International Narcotics Control," U.S. Congress, February 24, 1999, 3.

15. Ibid., 1–2.

16. The *Washington Post* reported that 57 federal departments and agencies were fighting to participate in an ever-growing budget for combating drugs. See Glenn Frankel, "U.S. War on Drugs Yields Few Victories; Federal Agencies Duplicate Efforts," *Washington Post*, June 8, 1997, 1.

17. Roderic Ai Camp, "Militarizing Mexico," *Policy Papers on the Americas: CSIS Americas Program* 10, no. 1 (1999): 14.

18. Peter M. Haas, "Introduction: Epistemic Communities and International Policy Coordination," *International Organization* 46, no. 1 (1992): 1–36.

19. This section draws on Robert A. Pastor and Rafael Fernández de Castro, "Congress and Mexico," in *The Controversial Pivot: The U.S. Congress and North America*, ed. Robert A. Pastor and Rafael Fernández de Castro (Washington, DC: Brookings Institution Press, 1998), 29–49.

20. The Omnibus Trade Act of 1974 created the "fast track" procedure. Its goal is to provide for an expeditious process to give certainty to foreign countries negotiating trade agreements with the United States. Congress imposes on itself time limits for debate and it must approve or reject the treaty without amending it. See I. M. Destler, *American Trade Politics* (Washington, DC: Institute for International Economics, 1992), 142–45.

21. Robert D. Putnam, "Diplomacy and Domestic Politics: The Logic of Two-Level Games," *International Organization* 42, no. 2 (1988): 427–60.

22. See Jorge I. Domínguez, "Ampliando horizontes: aproximaciones teóricas en el estudio de las relaciones México–Estados Unidos," in *Nueva agenda de la relación bilateral México-EUA*, ed. Mónica Verea, Rafael Fernández de Castro, and Sidney Weintraub (Mexico: Fondo de Cultura Económica, 1998), 25–56.

23. See Rafael Fernández de Castro, *Cooperation in U.S.–Mexican Relations: An Emerging Process of Institutionalization* (Washington, DC: Ph.D. dissertation, Georgetown University, 1996), 101–105.

24. Fernández de Castro, *Cooperation in U.S.–Mexican Relations*, 106–109.

25. The United States versus Verdugo Urquídez and the United States versus Alvarez Machaín.

26. *Excélsior*, June 16, 1992, 1.

27. Press Release, Secretaría de Relaciones Exteriores (Mexico: December 18, 1992).

28. Pastor and Castañeda, *Limits to Friendship*, 110–11.

29. For an analysis of the performance of Carter's special coordinator for Mexican affairs, see Cathryn L. Thorup, "Capacidad de influencia estadounidense en México," in *La política exterior y la agenda México–Estados Unidos*, ed. Rosario Green and Peter H. Smith (Mexico: Fondo de Cultura Económica, 1989), 145–86.

30. Fernández de Castro, *Cooperation in U.S.–Mexican Relations*, 77.
31. See Daniel C. Esty, *Greening the GATT* (Washington, DC: Institute for International Economics, 1994).
32. Interview with Mack McClarty, Washington, DC, March 4, 1999.
33. Antonio Ocaranza, "Medios de comunicación y política en Estados Unidos," in *¿Qué son los Estados Unidos?*, ed. Rafael Fernández de Castro and Claudia Franco Hijuelos (Mexico: McGraw-Hill, 1996), 285.
34. Sergio Aguayo, *Myths and [Mis] Perceptions: Changing U.S. Elite Visions of Mexico* (La Jolla: Center for U.S.–Mexican Studies, University of California-San Diego, 1998), 232–62.
35. John Bailey, "Mexico in the U.S. Media, 1979–88: Implications for the Bilateral Relation," in *Images of Mexico in the United States*, ed. John Coatsworth and Carlos Rico (La Jolla: Center for U.S.–Mexican Relations, University of California-San Diego, 1989). See also Roberta Lajous de Solana and Jesús Velasco Márquez, "Visión de México en la prensa de Estados Unidos: 1984," in *México–Estados Unidos, 1984*, ed. Manuel García y Griego and Gustavo Vega (Mexico: El Colegio de México, 1985).
36. Delal Baer, "Misreading Mexico," *Foreign Policy* (Fall 1998): 138–50.
37. Ibid., 138.
38. Enrique Sánchez Ruiz, "Los medios de difusión masiva y la centralización en México," *Mexican Studies* 4, no. 1 (Winter 1988): 25–54.
39. Stephen D. Morris, "Exploring Mexican Images of the United States," *Mexican Studies* 16, no. 1 (Winter 2000), 136.
40. Sergio Aguayo, "México en la transición y Estados Unidos: ¿Un problema de percepciones o de seguridad nacional?" in *México y Estados Unidos: El manejo de la relación*, ed. Riordan Roett (Mexico: Siglo XXI, 1989), 204.
41. Dolia Estévez, "Media and U.S.–Mexican Relations," paper presented at the annual conference for journalists covering international affairs, ITAM, Mexico City, October 8, 1999.
42. Personal interview with Dolia Estévez, Washington, DC, July 24, 2000.
43. Pablo Arredondo Ramírez and María de Lourdes Zermeño Torres, "La política informativa de Televisa en los Estados Unidos: El caso de '24 Horas,'" *Mexican Studies* 2, no. 1 (Winter 1986): 83–105.
44. For example, we have found that Mexican elites in particular have been surprised when we have reported these findings.
45. John Rielly, ed., *American Public Opinion and U.S. Foreign Policy* (Chicago: Chicago Council on Foreign Relations). The sample sizes of the elite samples are as follows: *1979*, N=366; *1983*, N=341; *1987*, N=343; *1991*, N=377; *1995*, N=366; *1999*, N=379. In each case, these are U.S. men and women 18 years of age and older. The questions pertinent to our analysis were asked for the first time in 1978; the approach and actual wording of many questions remained consistent across the surveys. The Gallup Organization conducted the poll in each case. Surveys were carried out during the last quarter of the year in 1978, 1982, 1986, 1990, 1994, and 1998.
46. *New York Times*, "Mexico Survey, 1986," Inter-University Consortium for Political and Social Research, ICPSR 8666. National probability sample, N=1576, living in communities of 2,500 or more people.
47. The Gallup Organization, "The Gallup Poll, 1988." For description of this and other surveys, see Jorge I. Domínguez and James A. McCann, *Democratizing Mexico: Public Opinion and Electoral Choices* (Baltimore: Johns Hopkins University Press, 1996), Appendixes 1 and 2.
48. Miguel Basáñez, Marta Lagos, and Tatiana Beltrán, *Reporte 1995: Encuesta Latino Barómetro* (August 1996), Table 47A. N=1204.
49. Neil Nevitte and Miguel Basáñez, "Trinational Perceptions," in *The Controversial Pivot: The U.S. Congress and North America*, ed. Robert Pastor and Rafael Fernández de Castro (Washington, DC: Brookings Institution Press, 1998), 159.
50. *New York Times*, "Mexico Survey, 1986."
51. Nevitte and Basáñez, "Trinational Perceptions," 167. See also Charles Davis, "Mass Sup-

port for Regional Economic Integration: The Case of NAFTA and the Mexican Public," *Mexican Studies* 14, no. 1 (1998): 105–30.

52. Basáñez, Lagos, and Beltrán, *Reporte 1995: Encuesta Latino Barómetro*, Table 57. Gallup Organization, "The Gallup Poll, 1988."

53. Times Mirror Center for the People and the Press, *Eight Nation, People and The Press Survey: Mixed Message about Press Freedom on Both Sides of Atlantic* (Washington, DC: Times Mirror Center for the People and the Press, 1994).

54. "Neighbors . . . and Friends," *Wall Street Journal Americas* (1998).

55. Idem.

56. Carlos González Gutiérrez, "Decentralized Diplomacy: The Role of Consular Offices in Mexico's Relations with Its Diaspora," and Rodolfo de la Garza, "Foreign Policy Comes Home: The Domestic Consequences of the Program for Mexican Communities Living in Foreign Countries," both in *Bridging the Border: Transforming Mexico–U.S. Relations*, ed. Rodolfo de la Garza and Jesús Velasco (Lanham, MD: Rowman & Littlefield, 1997).

57. For these two paragraphs, we draw mainly from the Latino National Political Survey. See Rodolfo de la Garza, Louis DeSipio, F. Chris Garcia, John Garcia, and Angelo Falcon, *Latino Voices: Mexican, Puerto Rican, and Cuban Perspectives on American Politics* (Boulder, CO: Westview Press, 1992), 100–106, 178. See also Rodolfo de la Garza and Louis DeSipio, "Interests and Passions: Mexican-American Attitudes toward Mexico, Immigration from Mexico, and Other Issues Shaping U.S.–Mexican Relations," *International Migration Review* 32, no. 2 (Summer 1998): 401–22.

58. Thomas J. Espenshade and Maryann Belanger, "U.S. Public Perceptions and Reactions to Mexican Migration," in *At the Crossroads: Mexican Migration and U.S. Policy*, ed. Frank Bean, Rodolfo de la Garza, Bryan Roberts, and Sidney Weintraub (Lanham, MD: Rowman & Littlefield, 1997), 240–42, 250–52.

59. Rodolfo de la Garza, Miguel Baraona, Manuel Orozco, Harry Pachon, and Adrian Pantoja, *Family Ties and Ethnic Lobbies: Latino Relations with Latin America* (Claremont, CA: The Tomás Rivera Policy Institute, 1998), 23.

60. Quoted in Domínguez and McCann, *Democratizing Mexico*, 81–83.

61. Ibid., chap. 4.

62. Cuauhtémoc Cárdenas, "Encuentros euroamericanos para el redescrubrimiento de los pueblos de las Américas," *Ideas políticas* 1 (May–June 1992): 225.

63. Cuauhtémoc Cárdenas, "The False Hopes of Economic Reform," in *Political and Economic Liberalization in Mexico*, ed. Riordan Roett (Boulder, CO: Lynne Rienner, 1993), 152–53.

64. Cuauhtémoc Cárdenas, *Democratic Transition and Economic Strategy: My Proposal for Mexico* (Los Angeles: World Affairs Council, April 27, 1994), 4–5. For a more elaborate, thoughtful critique of NAFTA along these lines, see Adolfo Aguilar Zinser, "Is There an Alternative? The Political Constraints on NAFTA," in *Mexico and the North American Free Trade Agreement: Who Will Benefit?*, ed. Victor Bulmer-Thomas, Nikki Craske, and Mónica Serrano (London: MacMillan, 1994).

65. For a general description of the NAFTA debate in Mexico, see Guy Poitras and Raymond Robinson, "The Politics of NAFTA in Mexico," *Journal of Interamerican Studies and World Affairs* 36, no. 1 (Spring 1994): 1–35.

66. Quotation from Ginger Thompson, "Victor in Mexico Plans to Overhaul Law Enforcement," *New York Times*, July 5, 2000, A1. See also Agustín Gutiérrez Canet, "Nueva política exterior," *Siempre*, July 8, 2000, 15.

67. Computed from George W. Grayson, *The North American Free Trade Agreement: Regional Community and the New World Order* (Lanham, MD: University Press of America, 1995), 68–71.

68. The Democrats who voted for NAFTA were more likely to lose reelection bids in 1994. For statistically significant results, see Gary C. Jacobson, "The 1994 House Elections in Perspective," *Political Science Quarterly* 111, no. 2 (Summer 1996): 219.

69. For a discussion of the politics of NAFTA, see Grayson, *The North American Free Trade Agreement*, 68–71, 219–20.

70. Thomas Schelling, *The Strategy of Conflict* (Cambridge: Harvard University Press, 1960), 19. See also Putnam, "Diplomacy and Domestic Politics: The Logic of Two-Level Games."
71. See the reflections of the former Mexican ambassador to the United States Jorge Montaño, "El Congreso de los Estados Unidos y su política hacia México," in *Nueva agenda bilateral en la relación México–Estados Unidos*, ed. Mónica Verea Campos, Rafael Fernández de Castro, and Sidney Weintraub (México: Fondo de Cultura Económica, 1998), 391–94.
72. Computed from Margaret Taylor and T. Alexander Aleinikoff, *Deportation of Criminal Aliens: A Geopolitical Perspective* (Washington, DC: Inter-American Dialogue, 1998), 4.

VI: CONTENT AND CONDUCT OF FOREIGN POLICY

1. Quote from Jorge Chabat, "Mexico's Foreign Policy in 1990: Electoral Sovereignty and Integration with the United States," *Journal of Interamerican Studies and World Affairs* 33, no. 4 (Winter 1991), 12.
2. For analysis, see Wayne A. Cornelius, *Mexican Politics in Transition: The Breakdown of a One-Party-Dominant Regime*, Monograph Series no. 41 (La Jolla: Center for U.S.–Mexican Studies, University of California-San Diego, 1996).
3. Chabat, "Mexico's Foreign Policy in 1990," 10–14.
4. M. Delal Baer and Sidney Weintraub, "The Pressures for Political Reform in Mexico," in *The NAFTA Debate: Grappling with Unconventional Trade Issues*, ed. M. Delal Baer and Sidney Weintraub (Boulder, CO: Lynne Rienner, 1994), 176–78.
5. Andrés Rozental, *La política exterior de México en la era de la modernidad* (Mexico: Fondo de Cultura Económica, 1993), 124–31. See also Carlos González Gutiérrez, "Decentralized Diplomacy: The Role of Consular Offices in Mexico's Relations with Its Diaspora," and Rodolfo de la Garza, "Foreign Policy Comes Home: Consequences of the Program for Mexican Communities Living in Foreign Countries," both in *Bridging the Border: Transforming Mexico–U.S. Relations*, ed. Rodolfo de la Garza and Jesús Velasco (Lanham, MD: Rowman & Littlefield, 1997).
6. Rosario Green, "Las ONG y la defensa de los derechos humanos de los trabajadores migratorios mexicanos," in *Nueva agenda bilateral en la relación México–Estados Unidos*, ed. Mónica Verea Campos, Rafael Fernández de Castro, and Sidney Weintraub (Mexico: Fondo de Cultura Económica, 1998).
7. For example, see investigations carried out by the American Friends Service Committee of human rights violations by U.S. enforcement agencies along the U.S.–Mexican border. See Michael Huspek, Roberto Martinez, and Leticia Jimenez, "Violations of Human and Civil Rights on the U.S.–Mexico Border, 1995–1997," *Social Justice* 25, no. 2 (Summer 1998): 110–30.
8. On the 1994 electoral reforms, see Juan Molinar Horcasitas, "Renegociación de las reglas del juego: El Estado y los partidos políticos," in *La reconstrucción del Estado: México después de Salinas*, ed. Mónica Serrano and Victor Bulmer-Thomas (Mexico: Fondo de Cultura Económica, 1998). One of us, Domínguez, is a personal witness to the prohibition of exit polling by the Mexican Ministry of Government in 1988.
9. Susan Kaufman Purcell, "The New U.S.–Mexico Relationship," in *Mexico under Zedillo*, ed. Susan Kaufman Purcell and Luis Rubio (Boulder, CO: Lynne Rienner, 1998), 120–25.
10. Confidential interviews, June 2000, with a Mexican minister with extensive responsibility over aspects of economic policy, and with senior Wall Street investment advisers responsible for analysis of Mexico's financial condition.
11. Organization of American States, Inter-American Commission on Human Rights, *Report on the Situation of Human Rights in Mexico*, OEA/Ser.L/V/II.100 (Washington, DC: General Secretariat, 1998), especially 158–60.
12. See, for example, Michael Foley, "Southern Mexico: Counterinsurgency and Electoral Politics," in *Special Report* (Washington, DC: U.S. Institute of Peace, 1999), 4–5, 13.
13. For a fine account of these issues, see Ana Covarrubias Velasco, "El problema de los derechos humanos y los cambios en la política exterior," *Foro internacional*, no. 158 (October–December 1999): 429–52. See also José Antonio Sanahuja, "Trade, Politics, and

Democratization: The 1997 Global Agreement between the European Union and Mexico," *Journal of Interamerican Studies and World Affairs* 42, no. 2 (Summer 2000): 49–56.

14. Nora Lustig argues that the distance between the haves and the have-nots widened from the 1980s to the 1990s. See Nora Lustig, *Mexico: The Remaking of an Economy* (Washington, DC: Brookings Institution, 1998), 201–10.

15. Ignacio Trigueros, "El Tratado de Libre Comercio de América del Norte y la situación macroeconómica de México," in ¿*Socios naturales? Cinco años de Tratado de Libre Comercio de América del Norte*, ed. Beatriz Leycegui and Rafael Fernández de Castro (Mexico: Miguel Angel Porrúa-ITAM, 2000), 103–105.

16. Lustig, *Mexico*, 154.

17. Robert A. Pastor and Rafael Fernández de Castro, "Congress and Mexico," in *The Controversial Pivot: The U.S. Congress and North America*, ed. Robert A. Pastor and Rafael Fernández de Castro (Washington, DC: Brookings Institution Press, 1998), 43–44.

18. Sidney Weintraub, *NAFTA at Three: A Progress Report* (Washington, DC: The Center for Strategic and International Studies, 1997), 61.

19. Consejo Mexicano de Inversión, *Informe anual* (1998): 23.

20. Council of the Americas and the U.S. Council of the Mexico–U.S. Business Committee, *NAFTA at Five Years*, 12.

21. Weintraub, *NAFTA at Three*, 17.

22. Isabel Stúder, "El sector automotriz," in ¿*Socios naturales? Cinco años del Tratado de Libre Comercio de América del Norte*, ed. Beatriz Leycegui and Rafael Fernández de Castro (Mexico: Miguel Angel Porrúa-ITAM, 2000), 283–84.

23. Beatriz Leycegui, "Acordar para disentir: La solución de controversias en el TLCAN," in ¿*Socios naturales? Cinco años de Tratado de Libre Comercio de América del Norte*, ed. Beatriz Leycegui and Rafael Fernández de Castro (Mexico: Miguel Angel Porrúa-ITAM, 2000), 29.

24. Armand Pechard-Sverdrup, *The U.S.–Mexico Fresh Winter Tomato Trade Dispute: The Broader Implications* (Washington, DC: Center for Strategic and International Studies, 1996).

25. Weintraub, *NAFTA at Three*, 51.

26. Mario Ojeda, *México: el surgimiento de una política exterior activa* (Mexico: Secretaría de Educación Pública, 1986), 64.

27. Personal interview with Luis de la Calle, Undersecretary for International Negotiations, Ministry of Trade and Industrial Promotion (SECOFI), Mexico City, 1999.

28. Esther Schrader, "Mexico Learns Lesson in Pursuit of Trade Pacts," *Los Angeles Times*, September 14, 1999, 3.

29. Personal interview with Luis de la Calle, undersecretary for international negotiations, Ministry of Trade and Industrial Promotion (Secofi), Mexico City, 1999.

30. http://www.secofi-snci.bob.mx/tratados/tratados.htm.

31. Schrader, "Mexico Learns Lessons in Pursuit of Trade Pacts," 3.

32. Personal interview with Andrés Rozental, undersecretary of foreign affairs (1988–1994), Mexico City, 1999.

33. Stephan Sberro, "Las relaciones entre México y la Unión Europea: ¿el fin del desencuentro?" in *La Unión Europea y México: una nueva relación política y económica* (Madrid: Instituto de Relaciones Europeo-Latinoamericanas, 1997), 82–83.

34. Dolia Estévez, "Embajadores/asimetrías," *El Financiero*, May 17, 1999, 1.

35. The Canadian and Japanese embassies in Washington have 210 and 130 officials, respectively.

36. For analysis of Matías Romero's lobbying, see Thomas D. Schoonover, trans. and ed., *Mexican Lobby: Matias Romero in Washington, 1861–1867* (Lexington: University of Kentucky Press, 1986).

37. George W. Grayson, "Lobbying by Mexico and Canada," in *The Controversial Pivot*, ed. Robert A. Pastor and Rafael Fernández de Castro (Washington, DC: Brookings Institution Press, 1998), 78.

38. George W. Grayson, *The North American Free Trade Agreement: Regional Community and the New World Order* (Boston: University Press of America, 1995), 156.

39. Information gathered at the Office of Personnel, Mexican Embassy, in Washington, DC.

40. Estévez, "Embajadores/asimetrías," 1.

41. For analysis of the few instances of lobbying prior to NAFTA, see Rafael Fernández de Castro, "Jugando el juego de Washington con profesionales," in ¿Qué son los Estados Unidos? ed. Rafael Fernández de Castro and Claudia Franco (Mexico: McGraw Hill, 1996), 143–51; Claudia Franco, "El cabildeo mexicano en Washington," in Foro Internacional 28, no. 3 (January–March 1988): 460–61; and Todd Eisentadt, "Nuevo estilo diplomático: Cabildeo y relaciones públicas (1986–1991)," in Foro Internacional 32, no. 5 (October–December 1992), 676.

42. The Trading Game (Washington, DC: Center for Public Integrity, 1993), 28. In his memoirs, ex-president Salinas reports the sum as $35 million. See Carlos Salinas de Gortari, México: un paso difícil a la modernidad (Barcelona: Plaza y Janés Editores, 2000), 94.

43. Wall Street Journal, April 25, 1991, A16.

44. The Trading Game, 30.

45. Personal interview with Jesús Reyes Heroles, ambassador of Mexico to the United States, Washington, DC, May 1999.

46. Lorenzo Meyer, México y los Estados Unidos en el conflicto petrolero, 1917–1942 (Mexico: El Colegio de México, 1968), 330–45.

47. See Alan Riding, Distant Neighbors: A Portrait of the Mexicans (New York: Vintage Books, 1986), 472–73.

48. Telephone interview with John Hamilton, press section, U.S. Embassy in Mexico, May 1999.

49. Personal interview, John D. Negroponte, Washington, DC, May 1999.

50. Carlos Puig, "Conclusión de Negroponte: Con el Tratado de Libre Comercio, México quedaría a disposición de Washington," Proceso, no. 758 (May 1991): 6–11.

VII: TRANSBORDER RELATIONS

1. Oscar Arias Sánchez, "El muro de California," Excélsior (Mexico: June 2, 1992), quoted in Miguel León Portilla, "California: Land of Frontiers," in Common Border, Uncommon Paths: Race, Culture, and National Identity in U.S.–Mexican Relations, ed. Jaime E. Rodríguez O. and Kathryn Vincent (Wilmington, DE: Scholarly Resources, 1997), 25–26.

2. For a thoughtful study of these issues, see Peter Andreas, Border Games: Policing the U.S.–Mexico Divide (Ithaca, NY: Cornell University Press, 2000).

3. For a thoughtful history of the region, see David E. Lorey, The U.S.–Mexican Border in the Twentieth Century (Wilmington, DE: Scholarly Resources, 1999).

4. Elise Ackerman, "Finally, an Effective Fence," U.S. News and World Report (October 19, 1998): 27–28; Verne Kopytoff, "A Silicon Wall Rises on the Border," New York Times, January 14, 1999, E1; Peter Andreas, "The U.S. Immigration Control Offensive: Constructing an Image of Order on the Southwest Border," in Crossings: Mexican Immigration in Interdisciplinary Perspectives, ed. Marcelo Suárez-Orozco (Cambridge, MA: David Rockefeller Center for Latin American Studies, Harvard University, 1998), 345–46.

5. For a discussion of customs at the border, see Lawrence S. Graham and José Luis Méndez, "Los regímenes aduanales en la frontera México–Estados Unidos: Efectos nacionales y transnacionales," Foro internacional, no. 158 (October–December 1999): 545–87. On the border patrol, see Andreas, Border Games, 90.

6. U.S., Office of National Drug Control Policy, "The National Drug Control Strategy at Work: Fighting Drugs, Protecting Communities, Saving Kids, Producing Results" (Washington, DC: Executive Office of the Presidency, December 12, 1997), 3–4.

7. Ackerman, "Finally, an Effective Fence."

8. Kopytoff, "A Silicon Wall Rises on the Border," E1, E5.

9. Wayne A. Cornelius, "The Structural Embeddedness of Demand for Mexican Immigrant Labor: New Evidence from California," in Crossings: Mexican Immigration in Interdisciplinary Perspectives, ed. Marcelo Suárez-Orozco (Cambridge, MA: David Rockefeller Center for Latin American Studies, 1998), 129–30.

10. Cornelius, "The Structural Embeddedness of Demand for Mexican Immigrant Labor," 131–32; Andreas, "The U.S. Immigration Control Offensive," 348–51.
11. For evidence supporting this short section, see Juan Carlos Belausteguigoitia and Luis F. Guadarrama, "United States–Mexico Relations: Environmental Issues," in *Coming Together?: Mexico–U.S. Relations*, ed. Barry Bosworth, Susan Collins, and Nora Lustig (Washington, DC: Brookings Institution Press, 1997), 95–96. See also "Profile of the Southwest Border Region," http://www.treas.gov/sw_border/profile/html.
12. See analysis in Clark W. Reynolds and Robert McCleery, "Border Economics and National Integration," in *Una frontera, dos naciones* (Mexico: Asociación Nacional de Universidades e Institutos de Enseñanza Superior, 1988).
13. Judith Ann Warner, "The Sociological Impact of the Maquiladoras," in *The Maquiladora Industry: Economic Solution or Problem?*, ed. Khosrow Fatemi (New York: Praeger, 1990).
14. Alejandro Dávila Flores, "Impactos económicos del TLCAN en la frontera norte de México (1994–1997)," in *¿Socios Naturales? Cinco años del Tratado de Libre Comercio de América del Norte*, ed. Beatriz Leycegui and Rafael Fernández de Castro (Mexico: ITAM-Miguel Angel Porrúa, 2000), 195, Table 4.
15. Wolfgang König, "Efectos de la actividad maquiladora fronteriza en la sociedad mexicana," and Mónica Gambrill, "Composición y conciencia de la fuerza de trabajo en las maquiladoras; resultados de una encuesta y algunas hipótesis interpretativas," in *La frontera del norte: Integración y desarrollo*, ed. Roque González Salazar (Mexico: El Colegio de México, 1981).
16. Sidney Weintraub, *NAFTA: What Comes Next?* (Washington, DC: Center for Strategic and International Studies, 1994), 47–49.
17. Paul Ganster, "The United States–Mexico Border Region and Growing Transborder Interdependence," in *NAFTA in Transition*, ed. Stephen Randall and Herman Konrad (Calgary: University of Calgary Press, 1995), 146.
18. Dávila Flores, "Impactos económicos del TLCAN en la frontera norte de México," 203–204.
19. William A. Orme, *Continental Shift, Free Trade, and the New North America* (Washington, DC: The Washington Post Company, 1993), 116.
20. Ganster, "The United States–Mexico Border Region and Growing Transborder Interdependence," 165.
21. For background, see Roberto A. Sánchez R., "Las relaciones binacionales como un marco conceptual en el análisis de los problemas ambientales transfronterizos entre México y Estados Unidos," and Stephen Mumme and Joseph Malven, "Managing the Border Environment: Advances, Issues, and Options," both in *Una frontera, dos naciones* (Mexico: Asociación Nacional de Universidades e Institutos de Enseñanza Superior, 1988).
22. Belausteguigoitia and Guadarrama, "United States–Mexico Relations," 92.
23. Blanca Torres, "Las ONG ambientalistas en las relaciones México–Estados Unidos," *Foro internacional*, no. 158 (October–December 1999): 457.
24. Robert A. Pastor, *Integration with Mexico: Options for U.S. Policy* (New York: The Twentieth Century Fund, 1993), 53–61.
25. This section draws generally from Luis Herrera Lasso, "La cooperación fronteriza México–Estados Unidos: El caso de la región Tijuana–San Diego," in *México y Estados Unidos: Las rutas de la cooperación*, ed. Olga Pellicer and Rafael Fernández de Castro (Mexico: Secretaría de Relaciones Exteriores-ITAM, 1998).
26. The leadership of two recent Mexican consuls-general in San Diego and El Paso, Luis Herrera Lasso (1995–99) and Armando Ortiz Rocha (1993–2000), respectively, has been key in the development of the Border Liaison Mechanisms.
27. Luis Herrera Lasso, Magali Muria, and Gabriela Lemus, *Diagnóstico sobre la administración de la frontera México-Estados Unidos en los albores del siglo XXI* (Mexico: ITAM-Miguel Angel Porrúa, forthcoming), 14.
28. "Delinea futuro gobierno su política exterior," *Reforma*, August 2, 2000, 1.
29. Katrina Burgess and Carlos González Gutiérrez, "Socio renuente: California en las relaciones México–Estados Unidos," in *Nueva agenda bilateral en la relación México–Estados*

Unidos, ed. Mónica Verea Campos, Rafael Fernández de Castro, and Sidney Weintraub (Mexico: Fondo de Cultura Económica, 1998), 294–96; Jan Gilbreath, "La relación México-Texas: Redefinición del regionalismo," in ibid., 313, 331.

30. Burgess and González Gutiérrez, "Socio renuente," 279–83, 294; Gilbreath, "La relación México-Texas," 317–18, 320.

31. Gilbreath, "La relación México-Texas," 303, 305, 309.

32. Burgess and González Gutiérrez, "Socio renuente," 284–90. See also Manuel García y Griego and Mónica Verea Campos, "La crisis fiscal de California y la nueva ofensiva verbal en contra de los indocumentados," in *California: Problemas económicos, políticos, y sociales,* ed. Rosa Cusminsky (Mexico: Universidad Nacional Autónoma de México, 1995).

33. U.S., Office of National Drug Control Policy, *National Drug Control Strategy* (Washington, DC: Executive Office of the President, 1999), 69.

34. Ramón Eduardo Ruiz, *On the Rim of Mexico: Encounters of the Rich and Poor* (Boulder, CO: Westview Press, 1998), 14–15.

35. Ruiz, *On the Rim of Mexico,* 42–48.

36. Carlos Monsiváis, "Cultural Relations between the United States and Mexico," in *Common Border, Uncommon Paths: Race, Culture, and National Identity in U.S.–Mexican Relations,* ed. Jaime E. Rodríguez O. and Kathryn Vincent (Wilmington, DE: Scholarly Resources, 1997), 117.

37. Cathryn L. Thorup, "Redefining Governance in North America: The Impact of Cross-Border Networks and Coalitions on Mexican Immigration into the United States," DRU-219-FF (Santa Monica, CA: Rand Corporation, 1993). See also Ruiz, *On the Rim of Mexico,* 31, 41.

38. Guadalupe Valdés, "Consideraciones teórico-metodológicas para el estudio del bilingüismo inglés-español en el lado mexicano de la frontera," *Mexican Studies* 6, no. 1 (Winter 1990): 54–56.

39. Adalberto Aguirre Jr., "Language Use and Media Orientations in Bilingual Mexican-Origin Households in Southern California," *Mexican Studies* 4, no. 1 (Winter 1988): 115–30.

40. Mario García, "La Frontera: The Border as Symbol and Reality in Mexican-American Thought," *Mexican Studies* 1, no. 2 (Summer 1985): 195–225.

41. Joel Garreau, *The Nine Nations of North America* (Boston: Houghton Mifflin, 1981).

42. Lester D. Langley, *MexAmerica: Two Countries, One Future* (New York: Crown, 1988). See also the discussion in Norma Klahn, "Writing the Border: The Languages and Limits of Representation," in *Common Borders, Uncommon Paths,* ed. Jaime E. Rodríguez O. and Kathryn Vincent (Wilmington, DE: Scholarly Resources, 1997), 134–35.

43. Robert Frost, "Mending Wall," in *Frost, Robert. 1920. Three Volumes, &c.* http://www.columbia.edu/acis/bartleby/frost/44.html.

44. Agustín Escobar Latapí, Philip Martin, Katharine Donato, and Gustavo López Verdusco, "Factors That Influence Migration," in *Migration between Mexico and the United States: Binational Study,* vol. 1 (Austin, TX: Morgan Printing, 1998), 175.

45. Rodolfo Tuirán, "La migración mexicana a Estados Unidos; tendencias recientes y desafíos futuros," in *México y Estados Unidos; Las Rutas de la Cooperación,* ed. Olga Pellicer and Rafael Fernández de Castro (Mexico: SRE-ITAM, 1998), 166–70.

46. Escobar Latapatí, Martin, Donato, and López Verdusco, "Factors That Influence Migration," 175.

47. *A Report of the Binational Study on Migration* (Washington, DC, and Mexico: Commission on Immigration Reform and Secretaría de Relaciones Exteriores, 1997), iii.

48. *A Report of the Binational Study on Migration,* ii.

49. Frank D. Bean, Rodolfo Corona, Rodolfo Tuirán, and Karen A. Woodrow-Lafield, "The Quantification of Migration between Mexico and the United States," in *Migration between Mexico and the United States: Binational Study,* vol. 1, 11.

50. From 1946 to 1964, Mexico and the United States negotiated five migration agreements, which came to be known as the Bracero Program. Under these agreements, 4.5 million Mexicans came to the United States to work. For analysis, see Manuel García y Griego, *The Importation of Mexican Contract Laborers to the United States, 1942–1964:*

Antecedents, Operation, and Legacy (La Jolla: Center for U.S.–Mexican Studies, University of California-San Diego, 1981).

51. Tuirán, "La migración mexicana a Estados Unidos; tendencias recientes y desafíos futuros," 162.

52. Jorge A. Bustamante, Guillermina Jasso, J. Edward Taylor, and Paz Trigueros Legarreta, "Characteristics of Migrants: Mexicans in the United States," in *Migration between Mexico and the United States: Binational Study*, vol. 1, 92.

53. Tuirán, "La migración mexicana a Estados Unidos," 163–65.

54. Alene H. Gelbard and Marion Carter, "Mexican Immigration and the U.S. Population," in *At the Crossroads: Mexican Migration and U.S. Policy*, ed. Frank D. Bean, Rodolfo O. de la Garza, Bryan R. Roberts, and Sidney Weintraub (Lanham, MD: Rowman & Littlefield, 1997), 136–37.

55. Bean, Corona, Tuirán, and Woodrow-Lafield, "The Quantification of Migration between Mexico and the United States," 11.

56. Escobar Latapatí, Martin, Donato, and López Verdusco, "Factors That Influence Migration," 207.

57. See Frank Bean, Edmonston Barry, and Jeffrey Passel, ed., *Undocumented Migrations to the United States; IRCA and the Experience of the 1980s* (Washington, DC: The Urban Institute Press, 1990). Starting in 1987, about 1.7 million long-term unauthorized migrants and 1.3 million unauthorized Special Agricultural Workers applied for legalization, making use of the legalization provisions in IRCA; see *A Report of the Binational Study on Migration*, 1.

58. Bustamante, Jasso, Taylor, and Trigueros Legarreta, "Characteristics of Migrants," 10.

59. José Angel Gurría, Mexico's foreign affairs minister, made this remark at a meeting with the Mexican researchers participating in the Mexico–United States Binational Migration Study, Mexico City, May 1996. One of us, Fernández de Castro, attended this meeting.

60. See Rafael Fernández de Castro, "The Mexican Government's Positions on Migration: From Non-Engagement to an Active Search for a New Understanding. Is It Worth It?" in *Immigration in U.S.–Mexican Relations* (Washington, DC: Inter-American Dialogue, 1998), 27–32.

61. U.S., Department of Justice, Immigration and Naturalization Service, "Fact Sheet: INS Border Safety Initiative" (June 26, 2000) and "News Release: INS Intensifies Life-Saving Measures along the Southwest Border" (June 26, 2000).

62. Jim Yardley, "An International Hug at Mexico–U.S. Border," *New York Times*, January 2, 2000, 12.

INDEX